D1443051

From Me to We

"A compelling, timely and masterfully written volume with a global reach…a must-read for firms large and small. Ernst and Haar have penned a thought-provoking, practical opus that takes 'shared value' to the next level."

—Alvaro Fernandez Garza, CEO, *Alfa SAB de CV*

"The concept of M2W involves rethinking the business corporation. Ernst and Haar offer an illuminating analysis of how to build the foundation of socially-conscious enterprises following the principles of stakeholder involvement, fairness, and sustainability. It will open your eyes to a new conception of what the firm can do for society."

—Mauro F. Guillén, Dean, *Cambridge Judge Business School*

"An inspiring read about the role of businesses, governments, academe, and NGOs in the creation of an ecosystem where everyone is accountable and everyone wins. Ernst and Haar enhance the concept of shared value to a Me to We approach for real, private sector-led social change."

—Catalina Garcia, *Global Director of Corporate Affairs, AB InBev*

Ricardo Ernst • Jerry Haar

From Me to We

How Shared Value Can Turn Companies Into Engines of Change

palgrave
macmillan

Ricardo Ernst
McDonough Sch of Business
Georgetown University
Washington, DC, USA

Jerry Haar
Florida International University
Miami, FL, USA

ISBN 978-3-030-87423-0   ISBN 978-3-030-87424-7   (eBook)
https://doi.org/10.1007/978-3-030-87424-7

This Palgrave Macmillan imprint is published by the registered company Springer Nature Switzerland AG.
The registered company address is: Gewerbestrasse 11, 6330 Cham, Switzerland

This book is dedicated to our families whose love, understanding, support—and patience above all—make all our collaborative undertakings possible.

Foreword

As the Executive Chairman of Arcos Dorados (ARCO NYSE) with operations in twenty countries and territories in Latin America, I am acutely aware of the social and environmental challenges that we face, not just in the Americas but worldwide. The intersection of government and the private sector is getting more challenging and more complex, and the solution of these daunting issues is leading companies to take a more proactive leadership role. I have known the authors for quite some time through their active involvement in the Latin American Program of the Woodrow Wilson International Center for Scholars, and I have often shared and discussed with them how in our firm we engage our 90,000 employees and why it is so important that we take care of all our stakeholders—consumers, employees, suppliers, and shareholders.

Shared value creation (SVC) is only a decade old, and the challenge from Dr. Ernst and Dr. Haar is to up the ante by going from merely "shared" values to "owned" benefits and accountability—a challenging task. How can we achieve that goal? We go to a "Me To We" approach to issues that better include those at the bottom of the pyramid.

While I find the proposition to be difficult and intellectually challenging, it is nevertheless very compelling. For any venture or system to work well it must be in equilibrium, and that state is by definition not a stable state—it is constantly adjusting and evolving in minute twists and turns in order to remain balanced. Shareholder priorities give way to employees' needs, that give way to farmers, who give way to environmentalists, who give way to societal health, and back to the customer who started it all.

In the context of business, whether a multinational like Arcos Dorados or small- and medium-sized enterprises across a variety of industries, it is not only about me, the shareholder. It is about us, the collective we! And the process needs to be done in a balanced and democratic way, but recognizably not every stakeholder has the same number of votes. The customer, I would argue, is the most important constituent of them all. The trick is to cobble it all together and, importantly, get the commitment of all stakeholders, the collective "we."

This timely and thought-provoking book explores this circular chain and makes a very important contribution to the business literature, as it places ownership and accountability at the core of the new challenge for firms. What we are witnessing is the adoption of a shared value approach that is accelerating among firms worldwide, and this engaging volume begs more questions than it answers.

Montevideo, Uruguay   Woods Staton

Preface

"What is the role of the corporation in society?" That is a query that is easy to answer, and there have been tomes on the topic, both scholarly and non-scholarly. On the other hand, posing the question "What *should be* the role of the corporation in society?" there are a great many books and articles as well; however, the answers to that question are numerous and varied.

Debate over the role of the corporation in today's world expanded and intensified following the global financial crisis of 2007–2008. This crisis sparked what is known as the Great Recession, a global recession, which, until the coronavirus pandemic, was the most severe recession since the Great Depression. According to the US Financial Crisis Inquiry Commission, the causes of the crisis were primarily due to widespread failures in financial regulation, including the Federal Reserve's failure to stem the tide of toxic mortgages; severe breakdowns in corporate governance including too many financial firms acting recklessly and taking on too much risk; and a toxic mix of excessive borrowing and risk by households and Wall Street that put the financial system on a collision course with crisis.

As with the corruption scandals that bankrupted Enron, Arthur Anderson, and Adelphia Communications previously, the federal government stepped in. The Sarbanes-Oxley Act of 2002 set new or expanded requirements for all US public company boards, management, and public accounting firms. A number of provisions of the Act also apply to privately held companies, such as the willful destruction of evidence to impede a federal investigation. In the case of the Great Recession's bank lending calamity, Congress responded with the Dodd-Frank Wall Street Reform and Consumer Protection Act, targeting the sectors of the financial system that were believed to have caused the 2008 financial crisis, including banks, mortgage lenders, and credit rating agencies.

But we digress. While governments the world over play a role in how corporations function in society, it is the shareholders of the firm and the stakeholders of the entire value chain (internal and external) through their relationship that are reshaping capitalism in the twenty-first century. More companies are now building and rebuilding business models around social good, which sets them apart from the competition and augments their success. Profit maximization should not be the *be all and end all*. Newer generations see the need to broaden the main objective of companies and include a much greater set of players. With the help of NGOs, governments, and other stakeholders, business has the power of scale to create real change on monumental social problems. It has the potential to achieve a true win-win situation. Traditionally, companies have wanted to boost market share, resulting in an increase in potential revenues (and therefore profits). This scenario is essentially a zero-sum game since the size of the "pie" remains fixed. The new challenge is to enlarge the size of the "pie." We argue that broadening the focus to stakeholders provides an opportunity for expanding the "pie." For a larger "pie" will definitely create the conditions for a more mutually beneficial and sustainable outcome.

As academics and consultants, we have researched and observed firsthand how the evolving role of business in society is transforming the economic and social landscape in a globalizing world. Within this evolving environment we have been impressed by how free market capitalism is becoming more inclusive and more compassionate, anchored in more than the bottom line. Throughout this evolution we find numerous cases and examples of how the nexus between the firm and society is imbibed with sense of "shared value." Germany is a classic example of a sociopolitical and economic system of a market economy that adheres to a stakeholder model for companies.[1]

Among the written works that center on shared value is the seminal article penned a decade ago by Michael E. Porter and Mark Kamen in *Harvard Business Review*. In their piece they elucidate that shared value is a management strategy in which companies find business opportunities in social and environmental problems.[2] Illustrative is a consumer goods firm that lowers its

---

[1] Benedikt von Liel, *Creating Shared Value as Future Factor Competition*, Munich: Springer, 2016.

[2] While philanthropy and corporate social responsibility (CSR) focus efforts on "giving back" or minimizing the harm business has on society, shared value focuses on company leaders on maximizing the competitive value of solving social problems in new customers and markets, cost savings, talent retention, and more.

cost of packaging (saving money) while decreasing its environmental footprint at the same time.

For Porter and Kramer, shared value is manifested in three ways: reconceiving products and markets, redefining productivity, and strengthening local clusters. We broaden this "trio" by enlarging it to a "quintet"—adding the indispensable features of *ownership* and *accountability*. In upgrading and broadening the concept of shared value, we refer to it as the shorthand "Me to We."

Given the growing convergence of shareholder-stakeholder relations in shaping the business ecosystem, Me to We (M2W) will gain ever more influence and impact. For as the approach is bottom-up as well as top-down—closing the loop—it creates a win-win for all with a clear sense of shared responsibility. In fact, many assert that the concept of Me to We could reshape capitalism and its relationship to society. It could also drive the next wave of innovation and productivity growth in the global economy as it opens managers' eyes to immense human needs that must be met, large new markets to be served, and the internal costs of social deficits—as well as the competitive advantages available from addressing them. Attaining it will require managers to develop new skills and knowledge and governments to learn how to regulate in ways that enable a Me to We approach rather than work against it.

The organization of the book is structured to sequentially examine the emerging phenomenon of stakeholder value—the Me to We concept—shareholder-stakeholder comparisons, the role of government in the stakeholder environment, and operational issues such as implementation, communication, and leadership in their relationship to stakeholder value. Additionally, we examine Me to We value in the larger context of globalization, competitiveness, and governability—themes that mirror the title of our previous Palgrave book.

The authors are most grateful to doctoral students Siddharth Upadhyay and Maria Lapeira for their invaluable research assistance, AB InBev for their support, and Marcus Ballenger and his colleagues at Palgrave Macmillan for their guidance and support throughout this book project.

Washington, DC   Ricardo Ernst
Miami, FL   Jerry Haar

Contents

List of Figures

1

Introduction

Business managers can more effectively contribute to the solution of the many complex social problems of our time. There is no higher responsibility, there is no higher duty of professional management.
—Frank Abrams, *Harvard Business Review*, 1951.

In our previous book, *Globalization, Competitiveness and Governability,* we talked about the three major forces that affect the businesses of the twenty-first century. We showed how one action in any of these dimensions causes a chain reaction with the other two, making them inseparable, and hence should be at the core of business decisions. Consequently, if we take into account the larger picture of global forces in modern business strategies, we cannot commit the unforgivable sin of ignoring the inner forces that drive the business.

The ecosystem of stakeholders that keeps businesses operational is what makes firms thrive in any market. By stakeholder we mean any unit that contributes to the business, from consumers, to shareholders, to supply chain members, or to the citizens that dwell in the environment where the business operates (Fig. 1.1 shows an example of a business ecosystem). In simple terms, a business ecosystem is the network of organizations—including suppliers, distributors, customers, competitors, and government agencies—that participate in the achievement of a common goal. This could be providing a particular product or service and often requires a balance between cooperation and competition among the aforementioned players. All these stakeholders form an ecosystem that is essential for the very survival of a business as well as its growth.

© The Author(s), under exclusive license to Springer Nature Switzerland AG 2022
R. Ernst, J. Haar, *From Me to We*, https://doi.org/10.1007/978-3-030-87424-7_1

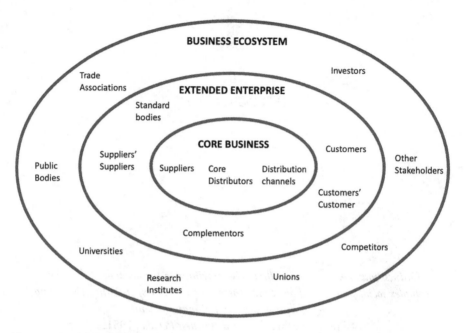

Fig. 1.1 Business ecosystem (Adapted from Moore (1993; tinyurl.co,/cygzy6o))

Amazon, for example, is a company that understands the value of its ecosystem. It has consistently reported a tremendous increase in revenue each year, and even in 2020 the firm grew by 37%. However, in 2019, independent sellers that Amazon had labeled as "ecosystem partners" were doing much better in sales than Amazon itself. Instead of seeing this as a threat, Jeff Bezos saw in it an opportunity. He realized that by cultivating these third-party sellers as "complementors" in Amazon's ecosystem, the company would gain the volume it required to leverage the investments needed for innovations in retailing. This relationship also allows Amazon to experiment with its retail strategy while increasing the amount of information it collects from its clients—a core value of Amazon's business strategy. Now the company is completely in charge of its selling platform and has created the environmentally conscious brand we recognize today. This shows that modern businesses have now recognized the value that each entity in their operating environment brings and have also understood that, in order for their business to evolve, these stakeholders need to evolve as well.

Businesses began giving back to the stakeholders through corporate social responsibility (CSR) initiatives, which then matured into the shared value concept proposed by Michael Porter and Mark Kramer (2011). They define shared value as: "Policies and operating practices that enhance the competitiveness of a company while simultaneously advancing the economic and social conditions in the communities in which it operates. Shared Value Creation (SVC) focuses on identifying and expanding the connections between societal and economic progress." However, despite addressing broader participants in the business ecosystem, SVC does not fully encompass all the stakeholders. Often, the bottom of the pyramid (BOP) players, that is, units that contribute to the earliest stages of value creation, are left out.

For example, in a value creation chain of a fruit juice company such as Tropicana or Minute Maid, the first unit of contribution is from the farmers who pick the fruit. In the top-to-bottom approach, the concerns or ambitions of the farmer are not clearly understood by the top management of individual ownership. Consequently, with the lack of ownership at the bottom level also comes a lack of accountability to the farmer, as it is impossible for the firm to control this particular unit of contribution beyond what the unit can account for itself. We argue that organizations need to think beyond the SVC model of "sharing" the benefits across the ecosystem by introducing "ownership" and "accountability" as the required variables that will complement the coordination with a bottom-up approach (resulting in a full "shared" responsibility).

This brings us to our proposal of stakeholder value or what we will call the Me to We (M2W) principle. For centuries, businesses have been asking the guiding question for any ideas or strategy, "What's in it for *me*?" However, because every stakeholder is important and contributes to business growth, businesses should now ask, "What's in it for *us*?" Figure 1.2 illustrates this idea.

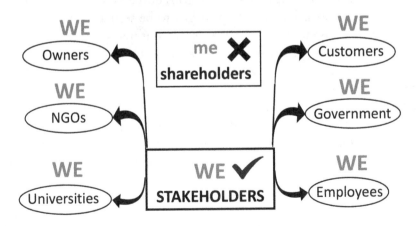

Fig. 1.2 From shareholders to stakeholders

Stakeholder Value—The "ME to We" Shift

In the neoclassical theory of the firm, corporations have been seen as entities that take inputs, mainly labor and capital, and use these to create gains. However, as the understanding of firms has evolved, cynicism about the intentions of companies and the methods they incorporate to achieve and maintain their competitive advantage has increased. Eventually, an industrial organization theory of the firm called Bain-type industrial organization (IO) became popular, which proposed firms as output restrainers. This view argues that firms use monopoly power or collusion with other firms to restrain productive output (Conner, 1991).[1] In simple terms, the goal of the firm is to control the "product" in a way that can maximize profit as much as possible. This means that any profits are basically the higher price minus the cost due to monopoly.

Even today, we see scandals that shake people's faith in corporations. Take the example of one of the largest corporate scandals of the past decade: in 2015 Volkswagen cars were found to be violating U.S. Environmental Protection Agency (EPA) regulations by emitting high levels of nitrogen oxide, a highly poisonous gas. This resulted in Volkswagen being forced to recall some 482,000 diesel passenger cars that had been sold in the United States. Moreover, it was discovered that these car models were equipped with illegal software that made detection of these gases difficult, thereby allowing these vehicles to pass emission tests. Later, an additional 11 million vehicles were also found to be equipped with this software, and VW had to pay a fine of over $25 billion. Incidents such as these lead people to think of organizations as evil entities that operate only in terms of their own self-interest.

Because of scandals like this, firms began to be seen as malicious entities that seek to increase profits at the expense of consumers or employees. Over the years, the guiding principle for most businesses has been profit maximization because it is directly associated with shareholder value. When asked about the number one objective of any company, the most widely heard response is "to make money" and to take care of the shareholders. According to a poll for the Confederation of British Industry (CBI), "Consumers believe businesses put profits before staff wellbeing and customer service."[2] These practices were prominent in the 1990s as investors were more interested in stock prices than

---

[1] Conner, K. R. (1991). A historical comparison of resource-based theory and five schools of thought within industrial organization economics: do we have a new theory of the firm? *Journal of management*, *17*(1), 121–154.

[2] https://www.theguardian.com/money/2015/feb/24/consumers-believe-businesses-put-profit-before-staff-and-customers.

in good corporate governance. This behavior has led to calls for government intervention and enactment of anti-trust public policies.

In light of accounting scandals and the consequent impact of corporate collapses on the stock market, the US government responded with the Sarbanes Oxley Act (SOX) of 2002 to restore public trust in the accuracy of financial statements by making corporate executives directly accountable. While the idea of what firms actually are has evolved over time, questions about the morality of firms still linger in today's society. To quote Michael Porter: "Business must reconnect company success with social progress."

Thus, the moral compass of the corporations is at a significant inflection point, and through "stakeholder value" or M2W, we intend to suggest the right direction for corporations to advance the interests of both shareholders and stakeholders. Of course, the initial natural reaction to new ideas, including this one, will be resistance, just as every time we face a change in paradigms as individuals or as a society. In most situations, the switching costs of that change are high until clear demonstrable benefits result. Eventually a "new normal" is accepted.

We seek to upgrade, enlarge, and enrich the concept of the "shared value" model. We wish to also introduce the term "stakeholder value" and the concept of Me to We (M2W), with the two terms being interchangeable. We recognize the fact that today's consumers and workers are both much more aware than they were in the past. They not only ask about the cost or quality of the products or services being offered to them, but also need to know the moral costs involved. Everything—from acquisition, production, brand judgment, recognition, company culture, and treatment of partners and employees—is under constant moral scrutiny. Additionally, corporations recognize the importance of intrinsic value that they can gain when operating the right way and constantly seek best practices that will give them good moral standing.

We argue that M2W is the new normal for businesses in the twenty-first century, with an implied switching cost that is minimized by the proven benefits. A prime example is the immense shift that was needed in consumer behavior when the transition from retail to online shopping took place. The advantages of online shopping progressively became the norm and a de facto sales platform for most businesses, just as M2W is the de facto focus for a sustainable society. As we have pointed out earlier, the shift toward corporations giving back to society has become inevitable at this point.

For instance, Toms Shoes, Inc., a shoe company, introduced a buy-one-give-one model in 2006. In their model, if an individual buys a pair of shoes from Toms, the company will give away one pair to the needy. When the business model was introduced it was called the "worst charity ever" by many business economics scholars, and the model's sustainability was called into doubt because it could eventually destroy the local industries where the "free" shoes were going. However, Toms' willingness to share with the entire ecosystem was much appreciated, and by 2014 the company was valued at $625 million. Their business model has been so successful that Toms' customers can now choose which cause their donations will go to (such as women's rights or ending gun violence). Such an expansion has also helped the company to explore wider markets in developed countries where the range of social issues was not limited by poverty, as it is in many developing countries. Using this approach helped Toms expand its business to customers who believe in different causes compared with the few options that they initially started with. This system is an example of winning customer faith by contributing to social change with a sustainable model in which the feedback for the strategy comes from bottom to top, not from top to bottom.

Another example of M2W at work is Starbucks surviving the resistance to changing beliefs of the shareholder and stakeholder values that resulted in long-term returns. When Howard Schultz, its emeritus chairman, was asked about focusing on profitability, he emphasized the company's original mission to embrace stakeholders, which did not jeopardize profits but rather grew them. As indicated by Schultz, "Starbucks's initiatives included providing part-time baristas with health care and tuition-free college education; volunteering in neighborhoods; talking openly about racism; and helping impoverished youth find first jobs. The ethos fueling such efforts—that companies have a responsibility to enhance the societies in which they flourish—was integral to Starbucks's ability to employ great people and attract customers, which in turn drove a 21,826 percent return to shareholders between 1992 and 2018, the year I stepped down as executive chairman.[3]"

Milton Friedman argued that generating profit and giving it to the shareholders was a means of doing good for society with the expectation that the shareholders could use this largesse, or at least some of it, for the benefit of something or someone other than themselves. However, due to the shifting view of what business should be in the modern world, the idea of shareholder capitalism has faded away as businesses have recognized the value of involving all stakeholders, with each of them gaining something valuable.

To quote a recent NYT article: "*the Friedman doctrine has been widely eroded, as a growing consensus of business leaders, investors, policymakers and leading members of the academic community have embraced stakeholder capitalism as the key to sustainable, broad-based, long-term American prosperity. This is*

---

[3] https://www.wsj.com/articles/starbucks-to-subsidize-workers-online-degrees-1402876800.

illustrated by the World Economic Forum's adoption in 2016 of The New Paradigm and, in 2020, the Davos Manifesto embracing stakeholder and E.S.G. (environment, social and governance) principles. Stakeholder governance is the bedrock of American capitalism now and in the future.[4"]

Our contention is that today the business focus has changed from purely a shareholder mentality to recognizing the importance of *directly* expanding the beneficiaries of real and potential benefits to explicitly include the entire set of players involved in any business (or social) transaction. This universal set of players is labeled as *the stakeholders* and includes all the entities across the operating cycle and value chain of businesses. It comprises, but is not limited to, the buyers, sellers, government, environmental organizations, consumers, educational institutes, NGOs, and the community at the bottom of the pyramid.

All current and past concepts such as corporate social responsibility, shared value, growing the pie, and reimagining capitalism[5] have essentially tried to explain the meaning of this change by inclusion of all the stakeholders instead of just the conventional ones. At the core of this change is the recognition of every individual unit involved in the economic cycle of businesses and an enlarged view of the "self." Therefore, we propose thinking in terms of M2W.

Before proceeding with a discussion of M2W, we need to mention ESG (environmental, social, and governance)—a subject that will be addressed more completely in Chap. 9. Environmental, social, and governance (ESG) factors and related metrics cover a broad spectrum of issues that are generally not a part of financial analysis even though they have financial relevance. This could include a firm's responses to climate change, management of their supply chains, and the treatment of their workers.[6] ESG was first found in the UN and Swiss Government Report *Who Cares Wins* and has since led to two other UN-supported initiatives: Principles for Responsible Investment and Sustainable Stock Exchanges Initiative, with the former comprising over 1600 members and $70 trillion under management.[7] ESG investing and ESG as a performance assessment tool can best be understood as a proxy for how markets and societies are changing and how valuation criteria operate in tandem with those changes. Recognizably, ESG has been associated with shared value as a way of incorporating metrics that go beyond purely financial performance.

---

[4] "Greed is Good. Except When it is Bad," *The New York Times*, September 13, 2020.
[5] Rebecca Henderson, *Reimagining Capitalism in a World on Fire*, PublicAffairs, 2020; Alex Edmans, Grow the Pie: How Great Companies Deliver Both Purpose and Profit, Cambridge University Press, 2020.
[6] George Kell, "The Remarkable Rise of ESG," *Forbes*, July 11, 2018.
[7] Ibid.

And while there are limitations that will be discussed later in the book, the benefits of ESG nonetheless are much greater than its limitations.

M2W in Practice

Instead of a top-down approach in which the corporation bestows value to the recipients in a mutually beneficial arrangement (and often social as well), we take the M2W approach in which shared value is embraced simultaneously from the bottom-up as well and encompasses two critically important features absent in the initial shared value paradigm: ownership and accountability. In essence, we move the goalpost from a donor-recipient model to one of shared obligation of mutual responsibility. It is embraced by the recipients at the same time that it is generated by the top-down. When companies start the process, the bottom is a recipient and follows the guidelines. The bottom would not be able to start the process by itself. What we advocate for is a mutual process (top-bottom and bottom-up) with clear delineation of ownership and accountability, with each stakeholder embracing their respective responsibility. This is the essence of shared responsibility.

Many businesses use a bottom-up approach for training employees or for contributor partners in the form of apprenticeships. While apprenticeships are most common in fields regulated by licenses, companies like Walmart, Sears, Roche, Siemens, Virgin Media, Schneider Electric, and Volkswagen have used this model of training. In terms of accountability and ownership, apprentices are responsible for mastering a technical body of trade skills, attending any required courses the employer specifies, adhering to health and safety standards, and following company processes. Apprenticeships foster a sense of ownership in apprentices since they work in partnership with regular employees of the firm and are considered "members of the team."

M2W and Trade Associations

Trade association protocols are other examples of incorporating bottom-up shared value creation in which one entity establishes protocols that embody ownership by, and accountability of, members to meet standards of responsible corporate behavior, especially as it regards women and children in developing countries. In 2018, a total of 123 apparel and footwear companies signed the American Apparel & Footwear Association and the Fair Labor Association (AAFA/FLA) Commitment to Responsible Recruitment, reflecting the industry's commitment to the fair treatment of workers in the global apparel, footwear, and travel goods supply chain. The Commitment is a proactive industry effort to address potential forced labor risks for migrant workers in the global supply chain. Each signatory commits to work with its partners to create conditions where workers are paid for their job, they retain control of their travel documents and have full freedom of movement. They are also informed of the basic terms of their employment before joining the workforce. The signing companies also agree to work to "seriously and effectively" implement these practices, to incorporate the Commitment into their social compliance standards by December 31, 2019, and to periodically report the company's actions through sustainability and/or modern slavery legal disclosures.

Nike had been accused of using sweatshops since the 1970s to produce its sneakers and activewear, but it was only in 1991, when activist Jeff Ballinger published a report detailing the low wages and poor working conditions in Nike's Indonesian factories, that the sportswear brand came under fire. The FLA counts some of the world's leading brands among its affiliates— organizations that have committed to ensuring fair labor practices and safe and humane working conditions throughout their supply chains. Companies that have signed on to FLA's Code of Conduct and established systems to identify and remedy ethical violations are making significant strides toward that goal. Firms such as Hanes, New Balance, Nike, and Patagonia are all active members of the association and are working with FLA to develop and improve social compliance systems that flag issues and lead to sustainable solutions when workers are at risk. FLA membership is on a voluntary basis, but the members must meet strict labor standards for as long as they are affiliated. The organization holds participating companies accountable for monitoring 100% of their supply chains for compliance with FLA standards, and FLA conducts independent assessments of a random sample of each company's supplier factories.

M2W and Fair Trade

The theory of M2W in general and the importance of stakeholder value have been discussed extensively; however, what about its practical implementation? Fair trade is one way of "testing" the true implementation of the M2W idea on a larger scale. When observing the behavior within the entire "ecosystem" and all the players of the value chain, the actual "sharing" can be tested and validated if it goes beyond just the shareholders. Thus, fair trade is an example of enforcing through social pressure what can be accomplished with a stakeholder mentality.

In simple terms, fair trade is the concept that every player should get a fair price in return for their contribution. For instance, farmers' markets in India are very popular where the farmers directly take their produce to the so-called merchants, who distribute it to the wholesalers, who then sell the product to distributors and retailers. However, due to this long chain of distribution, the first individual—the farmer—gets the lowest price and barely any profit for the work, while the profit margin increases along the way to the final consumer. Despite growth, this is one of the core factors for income inequality. The individuals at the bottom of the pyramid get the minimum value for their contribution, while the maximum benefit is reaped by the stakeholders at the top.

This is where the importance of M2W strategy is highlighted through fair trade. In this system, products are priced at a premium compared to other products, but the profits directly benefit the first unit of the value chain. One may ask why a consumer would be interested in paying a premium price. The answer can be found in psychological research on prosocial motivation, which refers to an individual's desire to benefit other people or groups (Batson, 1987)[8] and is a driver of prosocial behavior among human beings. We must accept the fact that price is no longer a primary differentiator in a competitive environment. Consumer motivation to buy a certain product or service is more complex than ever before.

Since 2015, Ben & Jerry's, one of the most popular American ice cream brands, has had most of their ingredients obtained through fair trade practices. The company got the ingredients such as sugar, cocoa, vanilla, coffee, and bananas that are used in the flavors of both ice cream and frozen yogurt certified by Fairtrade International. This organization is committed to justice for the people who grow and produce the ingredients we consume in the form of fair price payment for their work, as a symbol for ethical sourcing. Ben & Jerry's commitment toward ethical outsourcing has resulted in great benefits for farmers around the world.

Thus, cocoa imported from cooperatives in Ghana and the Ivory Coast, vanilla from a network of independent small farmers in Uganda, and coffee from cooperatives in Mexico are products that are Fairtrade certified, which helps these farmers get their fair share. In return, the farmers take accountability and ownership of their own product and commit to using

---

[8] Batson, C. D. (1987). Prosocial motivation: Is it ever truly altruistic? In *Advances in experimental social psychology* (Vol. 20, pp. 65–122). Academic Press.

environmentally sound farming practices, implementing fair working standards, and using their earnings to reinvest in their own communities. Thus, fair trade can be used to create shared responsibility at the bottom of the value creation chain.

Another level of the value chain that M2W seeks to emphasize is the relationship between the corporation and its SME partners. M2W is about value creation at all levels of the pyramid, and not just the bottom; therefore, the idea of fair trade must be vertical across all levels instead of being horizontal. We will elaborate on this concept more in the book and explain how fair trade can be seen as an example of successful implementation of the M2W strategy.

M2W and Clusters

Another important part of the M2W model is clusters. These are the geographic concentration of interconnected businesses, suppliers, and associated institutions in a particular field. Clusters are established to increase the productivity with which companies can compete, both nationally and globally. Silicon Valley, Route 128, India's Bangalore software cluster, and the textile cluster in Catalonia are some of the better-known clusters. And while we commonly think of cluster development as top-down, in reality it can be bottom-up and also symbiotic. As an example, the clustering of producers of rattan furniture in West Java resulted in a whole village being absorbed and created many small-scale satellite industries in nearby locations. In the United States, the existence of Stanford and the University of California at Berkeley on the West Coast and Harvard and MIT on the East Coast were the "bottom" that attracted the information technology, defense, and pharmaceutical industries to relocate to those locales.

The industrial base in Mexico is illustrative as well. Mexico has numerous clusters, electronics being among the most prominent. The country is the sixth-largest producer of electronics worldwide and third largest of computers. Guadalajara, in the State of Jalisco, is known as "The Silicon Valley of Mexico." The region's constellation of public and private universities focusing on STEM education and vocational-technical institutes provides a vital source of human capital for OEMs such as Samsung, LG, Toshiba, Foxconn, Flextronics, and Hewlett-Packard. In 2019, foreign investment injected $312 million into the electronics industry, creating 5000 jobs. Jabil alone invested $20 million to manufacture GoPro cameras. Parallel to investment projects in the cluster, Ciudad Creativa Digital (CCD) is underway. This project will create a hub for the digital media industry within Mexico. Its goal is to create a world-class hub of digital media development. CCD will span the creative industries, from TV, cinema, and advertising to video games, digital animation, interactive multimedia, and e-learning. In the M2W model, we include the value that businesses gain from their operating clusters in terms of innovation, information, and partnerships.

While assets of human and physical infrastructure—the "bottom"—catalyze companies to move into a geographical space, coordinating bodies play a vital role as well. In the case of Mexico, the Mexican Chamber of Electronics, Telecommunications and Information Technologies (CANIETI) has been an advocate for these industries in the country for more than 70 years, promoting their growth and development within a global setting through high-quality services. CANIETI is a self-governing, public interest institution, with legal status and capital of its own, different from that of its members. As regards the State of Jalisco and its electronics cluster, its iCluster Jalisco Network serves as a mechanism for linking and coordinating the efforts of people and triple helix organizations interested, involved, and committed to the clustering processes and their impact on the competitiveness and innovation of the Jalisco economy.

Sustainability of the M2W Approach

With most past approaches, which we have discussed, the key issue has been sustainability. Corporate social responsibility (CSR) was seen by many as a charity. The shared value creation (SVC) model, while being quite popular, has been criticized as difficult to sustain in the long-term, and in which thinking in stakeholder terms has been equated with an increase in cost and consequent decrease in profitability. While there are examples of the SVC model being sustainably implemented, the approach for putting it into practice has been mostly top-down. By proposing a bottom-up approach with M2W, we close this loop and provide a better approach that creates long-term sustainability. It is widely believed that the more businesses shift away from pure maximization of profits, the more they can minimize shareholder value. M2W could create unavoidable conflicts with the shareholders who provide the investment and expect a return.

For example, Nespresso, a subsidiary of Nestlé, produces coffee capsules that can be used only in machines that they manufacture. The intention behind using the capsules was to help farmers get fair value for their coffee and to sustainably create a shared value for the company and society. At first glance, it seems like an ideal example of shared value. However, if we look at the entire value chain, we can see that this shared value plan does not truly achieve its goals. The capsules for the coffee were made from a blend of aluminum, plastic, and organic material that cannot be disposed of without harming the environment.

When Nespresso Spain became aware of this recycling issue, they attempted to collect the used capsules from stores and municipal waste centers, and, through a deconstruction process, they created residuals to be reused for fertilizing rice fields. While this process helped to create rice for the poor, the process as a whole was extremely resource-intensive at all stages of the value chain, from mining of the metal and the farming of coffee beans to the deconstruction and disposal of the capsules. As the company wished to make it fair for the farmers, the expenses of sustaining these resources came out of the consumer's pocket.

If Nestlé had adopted a bottom-up rather than a top-down approach to creating shared value, they would have realized the issues in the internal parts of its value chain and their impact on the environment and consumer society. Moreover, they could have implemented a different design for these capsules, which would have saved Nespresso millions of dollars and the embarrassment of creating an environmentally irresponsible product. With the flow of information traveling from society to top management and the impact on the environment taken into account, they would have truly accounted for all stakeholders.

Sustainability must function on a financially independent basis—meaning that it must generate enough revenues to be self-supported. Any "business proposition" cannot rely on sources beyond those implicit to the nature of the business. Hence, the skepticism is related to sustainability of all the "giving to others" models.

So how does M2W bring the magic where other approaches may not? First, the M2W idea, when properly executed and managed, is indeed capable of accomplishing both shareholder and stakeholder value creation. There are examples of stakeholder focus that actually provide more profit than the traditional, exclusive focus on shareholder value. This has also been the main contribution of shared value creation: to demonstrate how to properly execute and manage the "new" shift which results in higher levels of profitability for the entire ecosystem while providing value to all stakeholders. Moreover, measurement of the benefits is clearly a challenge that goes beyond purely financial rewards. Klaus Schwab, founder and executive chairman of the World Economic Forum, states: "For stakeholder capitalism to become a reality, we must be able to measure companies' performance on environmental, social and governance metrics."[9]

Through M2W, we bring in the "the collective" and the "individual units" that form the foundation of the value creation process. While shared value implies a larger set of direct and indirect beneficiaries, it still maintains a top-down approach. Companies evaluate and execute a different set of strategies with a larger scope, including more stakeholders. This does provide sustainability in terms of profits, but still does not address sustainability at the business unit level. By implementing the M2W bottom-up approach, we close the loop left open by the shared value concept. Bottom-up considerations are required and provide a more comprehensive approach that will make the process equally sustainable but with a higher degree of involvement and responsibility from the smallest units and individuals as responsible stakeholders. We propose to enlarge the current approach by requiring two additional elements to the shared value concept—*ownership* and *accountability*—which will be further elaborated in the chapter.

All stakeholders in the system need to have a sense of responsibility (ownership) and a set of metrics (accountability) by which their involvement is measured. Just being the recipient of a shared value benefit is limiting. M2W involves a close loop of shared responsibility obtained through collective engagement. Stakeholder value implies and requires shared responsibility to be complete as illustrated in Fig. 1.3.

Additionally, we believe that this inflection point in the approach to be taken by corporations has brought with it the realization that satisfaction is measured by more than just financial reward. It is also a way for corporations to reconcile their wrongdoing (real or perceived) at the expense of consumers and society, thereby addressing their own corporate "guilt." There is an increased moral reward that is at the core of the process, however difficult it may be to measure. As long as the implementation is sustainable, the moral reward can compensate for a reduction in potentially larger financial benefits. The M2W goes beyond companies to include also the entire behavior of individuals within society.

[9] World Economic Forum, "Measuring Stakeholder Capitalism: World's Largest Companies Support Developing Core Set of Universal ESG Disclosures," News Release, January 22, 2020.

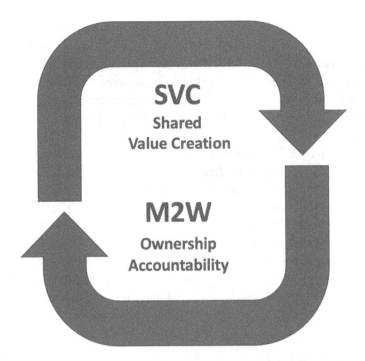

Fig. 1.3 The full circle of shared responsibility in stakeholder value

Sharing Responsibility Through M2W

According to Kramer and Pfitzer, (2016), shared value[10] is a result of "policies and practices that contribute to competitive advantage while strengthening the communities in which a company operates." They propose three ways by which companies can create shared value: (1) by reconceiving products and markets; (2) by redefining productivity in the value chain; and (3) by strengthening local clusters.[11] However, such acts are only possible in robust market systems, as ripples of changes in a clustered system are bound to affect all key players. Therefore, we argue that these three ways are not enough to create value for the collective and therefore there is the need to add ownership and accountability as part of the process.

While businesses are realizing the value of aligning investment goals with societal interests, there is an implicit understanding that communities and

---

[10] Mark R. Kramer and Marc W. Pfitzer, "The Ecosystem of Shared Value," *Harvard Business Review*, October 2016.

https://hbr.org/2016/10/the-ecosystem-of-shared-value

[11] Source: https://www.ncbi.nlm.nih.gov/books/NBK395631/.

societies are not only philanthropic groups but also customers. This is where the importance of reaching to the bottom of the pyramid comes in, which in most cases also contributes to the very first levels of value creation. In the ecosystem of value creation, individuals who collectively form the society should be the primary drivers of the value creation, and not the shareholders themselves. This is why we think that including a bottom-up approach of value creation is better than simply the top-down model suggested by Porter and Kramer. Figure 1.4 illustrates how ownership and accountability affect units at each level of the value chain.

As a result, new market research should no longer be limited to customer desires or the product or service needs but also the needs of individuals, communities that form the collective, and the cluster of partners or small businesses that contribute to the value creation for all stakeholders. Only after taking into account these considerations can the internal needs, such as the strategy toward capital and a company's direction, be designed. Additionally, the idea of ownership and accountability is not limited to external

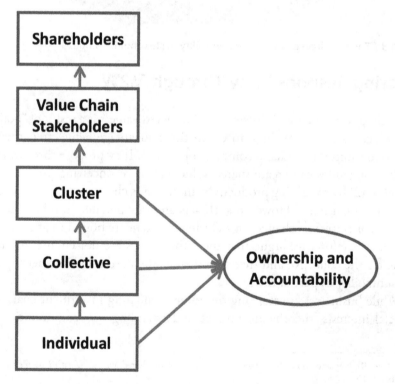

Fig. 1.4 The bottom-up approach including individual ownership and accountability

contributors; it also addresses ownership and accountability of operational staff at each management level.

We can explain the model illustrated in Fig. 1.4 with a competitive example. The "individual," such as a farmer himself who grows the product, is the first contributor to the value chain. The "collective" is the group of farmers who combine to create enough yield for the input to the corporation. The "cluster" comprises all the process contributors who together help refine the raw materials into the processed feed as needed. The "value chain stakeholders" are the managers and supervisors who oversee these processes. Finally, the "shareholders" in this system are the investors.

This, as we have explained, eliminates the burden of explaining to the investors how participation of society is necessary for the benefit of the company because now it is easier to see that the society is driving the business and not the other way around. Hence, the symbiotic relationship among all stakeholders becomes self-explanatory. This will further encourage the investors to ask "How does everyone involved with our business benefit?" rather than asking, "How are we benefitting from everyone involved?" This is the only way that a healthy, long-term, and a sustainable relationship is established within the business ecosystem. And that is the core of the M2W approach.

M2W: Globalization, Competitiveness, and Governability

As we mentioned earlier, with the idea of M2W, we ultimately propose a strategy that businesses can use to navigate through the three disruptive forces of the twenty-first-century business landscape we introduced in our previous book. Globalization, competitiveness, and governability are disrupting business in the twenty-first century, resulting in an impact on the economic and business environment far greater than the effects of any of these three individually. Both globalization and competitiveness are essentially governed by market forces that force the introduction of significant changes aimed at increasing efficiency so that a better use may be made of the advantages of globalization (i.e., the traditional "invisible" hand). Responsibility for bringing about these changes lies not only with the private sector but also with the government (i.e., the "visible" hand). So, how does M2W relate to these three forces?

Globalization

Globalization has played a role in "normalizing" the set of expectations around the world. The bar for performance of corporations is much higher. The idea is that the world overall is doing better than before. In *The New York Times* op-ed, David Brooks suggested that "globalized capitalism" has been the reason for wages increasing for workers around the globe. While this change is significant, the problem of inequality is getting worse, globally. In fact, inequality within countries is increasing, while inequality among countries is *decreasing* (refer to Fig. 1.5). P.N. Cohen presents an interesting quantification of the global inequality within and between countries, and elaborates on the debate on how to measure inequality.[12] This is why businesses need to ask, "How do we all benefit?" when operating globally and fulfill the need of involving the bottom of the pyramid through M2W.

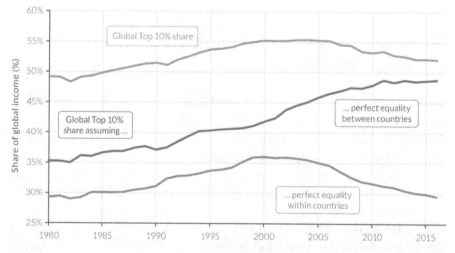

Fig. 1.5 Share of global income over the years. (Source: WID. World (2017). See wir2018.wid.world/methodology.html for date series and notes. In 2010, 53% of the world's income was received by the top 10%. Assuming perfect equality in average income between countries, the top 10% would have received 48% of global income)

---

[12] https://familyinequality.wordpress.com/2014/05/23/global-inequality/.

Competitiveness

The idea of M2W complements the competitiveness landscape. Naturally, there are some industries better suited for taking advantage of "We" value creation, especially through competitive supply chains. As we mentioned in our previous book, the idea of competitiveness has evolved from "my company against your company" to "my supply chain against your supply chain." M2W ensures benefits for every contributor within the entire cycle of value creation, including supply chains. Therefore, it can be used as a credible conveyor/provider of competitiveness. Similar to Porter's claim that capitalism is evolving toward the creation of shared value rooted in a more socially conscious approach to business with a higher level of economic profit, the same could be said about competitiveness. M2W offers a higher degree of competitiveness by enlarging the ecosystem and including all members of the supply chain, thereby increasing the size of the pie by creating synergies. Businesses can compete by asking, "Am I creating more value for all stakeholders compared to others?" If the answer to this question is yes, then we can safely say that the business has established a sustainable long-term hold on the market.

As we discussed earlier in the chapter, Amazon's strategy is to partner with independent retailers and turn them from competitors into contributors, giving them accountability and ownership as individual units while at the same time making them part of the Amazon business ecosystem. This ensures that a win-win situation is created, starting from the bottom to top. Therefore, when the businesses of the individual retailers grow, the business of Amazon grows as well. Growth becomes not only exponential, but also sustainable.

Governability

As the visible hand in the current system, government can either help or hinder business strategies, and that is true in the M2W model as well. The right implementation of M2W as a catalyst (or not) seeks the cooperation between all players in the ecosystem. The government is "there" most of the time since being "external" and not directly involved in the actual "business" of companies provides the incentives for a better redistribution of "benefits" for all. In the coming chapters, we will discuss many instances in which the government participates as the provider of policies and regulation for the rules of the game and as an active partner in situations such as public-private partnerships. When we say that businesses should go about presenting their strategy as "this is what you get" to every stakeholder, we cannot leave the government out as it is the central stakeholder for businesses in any given country. The government not only seeks to get a piece of the pie through the social development of its citizens but can also decide how the pie is distributed though compliance and regulation. The government is the only "stakeholder" with the capability of enforcing M2W through the right implementation or development of public policies.

Challenges to M2W

We close this chapter by discussing challenges in implementing the M2W model. Admittedly, while the road to successful implementation of such a model is not without its obstacles, we do emphasize that the benefits are worth the pursuit. There are many points for reflection:

- How rewarding is moral satisfaction vis-à-vis financial satisfaction? Is it possible to quantify moral reward?
- Are the results of this strategy measurable? If yes, what are the metrics? How does one properly implement a bottom-up approach?
- What are the leadership requirements for the strategy to be able to span across organization (in terms of culture) and geographies, that is, what are the internal or within-organization requirements for its scalability?
- Are certain environments more suitable for stakeholder value implementation?
- What is the role of the government?

The answer to each of these questions is tied to each other, and we intend to answer all of them throughout the book.

Conclusion

The growing symbiosis between shareholders and stakeholders is shaping a business ecosystem in which Me To We (M2W) will gain ever more influence and impact. Within this domain, shared value expands beyond a top-bottom approach and requires embracing the bottom-up toward true and genuine shared responsibilities. By embracing M2W, the essential sense of shared responsibility by all is accomplished, most assuredly with the addition of accountability and ownership that we advocate, closing the loop for a true win-win for all.

The following chapters begin by addressing the "quintet" of shared values (reconceiving products and markets; redefining productivity in the value chain; strengthening local clusters, ownership, and accountability). Assessing the dynamics between shareholders and stakeholders, evaluating the role of government within the business ecosystem, and examining how competitiveness, globalization, fair trade, and consumers at the bottom of the pyramid shape the shared value environment are all keys to understanding this system. The final chapters analyze the linkages between the multinational firm and small and medium size businesses as well as the challenges of implementing M2W in the firm.

2

The Quintet of M2W

Proponents of shared value have focused on three ways of achieving economic and societal value: by reconceiving products and markets, by redefining productivity in the value chain, and by building supportive industry clusters. We propose two other ways: *by embracing a broader meaning of competitiveness (i.e., ownership)*, and *by elevating the role of governability (i.e., accountability)*. By including these strategies, companies can truly achieve shared value on a broader scope, which is what we call the "Stakeholder Value" or the Me to We (M2W) principle. Figure 2.1 summarizes the quintet of M2W.

As introduced in our previous book, globalization, competitiveness, and governability should be part of the entire business process and therefore should also be included in the concept of shared value. In doing so, companies can create societal and economic value by embracing the entire "ecosystem," which encompasses the entire supply chain. This will further solidify the new dynamics of competition, which entails supply chains rather than companies competing against one other. For example, Bosch and Denso, two auto parts companies, compete based on their supply chains in terms of speed, quality, price, and reliability while both are part of car manufacturers' supply chains. A sugar manufacturer can be part of both the Coca-Cola and Pepsi-Cola supply chains. Since neither is fully vertically integrated, Coca-Cola and Pepsi-Cola compete on the basis of all the participants of their respective supply chains.

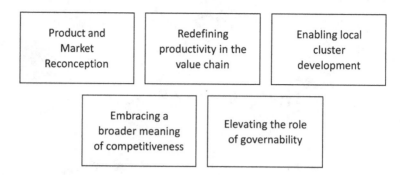

Fig. 2.1 The quintet of M2W

The Essence of the Quintet of M2W

Porter and Kramer have identified three distinct ways to put shared value into action, as explained in the following sections.

Reconceiving Product and Markets

Reconceiving product and markets involves thinking about creating products and services that meet societal needs and unserved customers, many of which have been largely ignored by firms.[1] These unmet needs may include health, nutrition, financial security, and less environmental damage. A growing demand for products that meet societal needs has been growing rapidly, especially in developed economies. For example, the health and wellness trend has caused consumers to refocus on the nutritional value of food products and their overall contribution to a healthy life. These concerns are forcing companies in the food industry to reformulate their products so that, aside from having great taste, they can meet nutritional needs. For example, Kellogg's has continued to look for innovative ways to enhance the nutrition profile of their products and has made substantial efforts over the past few years to reduce the sugar, sodium, and fats in their products.[2] Environmentally conscious consumers are also purchasing products that are more eco-friendly, whether it be in terms of packaging, energy consumption, or waste production, forcing companies to rethink their entire supply chains to meet these concerns.

In order for companies to meet these societal needs and serve overlooked customers, companies must ask themselves several questions about the

[1] Porter, M. E., and M. R. Kramer. "Creating Shared Value. Harvard Business Review, January" (2011).
[2] Retrieved from: https://www.kelloggcompany.com/en_US/our-nutrition-journey.html.

product and service offerings in relation to their customer base. For example, one of the most basic questions that many companies seem to have forgotten about is whether their products fit customers' needs—whether their products and services are *good* for their customers. If the answer is no, this opens up a multitude of avenues for innovation and rethinking product and service portfolios.

It is also important for companies to consider previously unmet demands from customers, such as those in developing countries and disadvantaged communities. Despite societal needs being more pressing in these markets, companies have often ignored many as they consider them unviable. However, developing economies present an opportunity to reach out to the millions of new consumers. For example, most individuals at the base of the pyramid have little to no access to financial services, sanitation services, water, and basic healthcare.[3] Similar opportunities exist in nontraditional or poor urban areas in developed countries that have often been overlooked despite their purchasing power. By looking into these markets, companies can create shared value by tailoring products and services to meet the needs of disadvantaged and lower-income communities.

By asking simple questions about the needs met by their products, their customer base, and the location of the customers, companies can unlock opportunities for innovation and expansion, all the while meeting societal needs. This requires an ongoing exploration, since these opportunities change with the evolution of new technologies, growth and development of economies, and shifts in societal priorities. This kind of strategy triggers innovation by raising awareness of the need to redesign products and rethink supply chains, allowing companies to compete more effectively in existing markets and position themselves in new ones.

Redefining Productivity in the Value Chain

The second way to create shared value, as proposed by Porter and Kramer, focuses on redefining productivity in the value chain. Companies' supply chains have been receiving significant attention given their effect on societal issues while simultaneously being affected by these issues. These problems can potentially increase costs in the firm's value chain, such that poor production and distribution practices and inefficient use of inputs can decrease efficiency

---

[3] Retrieved from: http://documents1.worldbank.org/curated/en/779321468175731439/pdf/391270 Next040billion.pdf

and increase costs. This creates an incentive for companies to find congruence between societal progress and productivity in the value chain.

To achieve this redefinition of productivity in the supply chain, companies must evaluate their value chain from an efficiency perspective without falling into the trap of short-term reductions that are unsustainable in the long term. This requires transforming in multiple areas including procurement, resource use, distribution practices, and energy.[4] For example, Walmart has made substantial efforts in multiple areas of their value chain, working with suppliers to expand efforts to improve the sustainability of its private brand product packaging with an emphasis, making it easier for customers to recycle, as well as increasing fleet efficiency by delivering more products while driving fewer miles.[5] Companies must take a good look at the value chain and focus on aspects such as accessing and utilizing resources, energy, inputs, logistics, and employees in a way that is economically viable, environmentally sustainable, and generates well-being to stakeholders.

Companies must also be willing to engage in investments that can help obtain both cost reductions and environmental sustainability through a more efficient use of resources and decreased waste. This includes implementing strategies to reduce energy usage, increasing the use of renewable sources, decreasing water consumption, minimizing packaging, and reducing waste to ensure a more sustainable production process. Another way to achieve this is by prioritizing local sourcing. This can contribute to improving the well-being of local economies where companies operate.

The main purpose of redefining productivity in the supply chain is for companies to focus on distinct activities taking place in the supply chain with the purpose of lessening their environmental and sustainable impact. To do so, companies must optimize the distinct activities taking place in their supply chain (e.g., acquisition and inventory management, packaging, assembly, warehousing, internal and external transportation). Therefore, it is necessary to work closely with all other organizations involved in the production and distribution of goods to ensure that their objectives and practices align. By doing this, companies can ultimately obtain improvements in their productivity and reduce costs while significantly advancing their environmental practices, human rights practices, and working conditions, thus achieving shared value. Productivity in the value chain is illustrated in Fig. 2.2 from Porter and Kramer's seminal article.

---

[4] Ibid.

[5] Retrieved from: https://corporate.walmart.com/global-responsibility/environment-sustainability/truck-fleet.

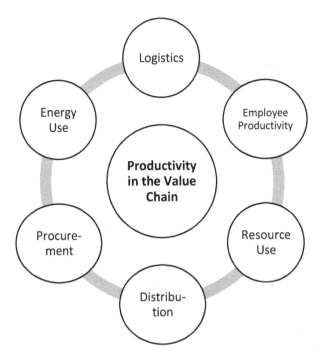

Fig. 2.2 Productivity in the value chain

Building Supportive Industry Clusters

In addition to the aforementioned strategies, firms can achieve shared value creation through cluster development. Clusters are predominant in all successful regional economies. They include firms, infrastructure, suppliers, distributors, service providers, and institutions that can play an essential role in driving innovation, productivity, and competitiveness. The key entities in a cluster are government agencies, which provide the necessary infrastructure investment; universities, which provide a steady supply of highly skilled people and new knowledge that lends itself to commercialization and experiments that feed the constant hunger for new knowledge; non-governmental organizations (NGOs), which is a category that overlaps significantly with the nonprofit sector; and businesses (business associations), which provide the cluster with its economic engine.

Clusters have gained attention because a significant part of companies' success depends on the local businesses supporting it. They are often referred to as a geographic concentration of firms and can largely influence companies' opportunities for innovation and value creation. Unfortunately, companies have seldom explored clusters from a shared value perspective and have instead focused solely on how clusters can drive their economic growth. However, clusters present an opportunity for firms to recognize and take advantage of organizations in geographic proximity as a means to drive economic and societal development.

Companies immersed in clusters have the opportunity to raise awareness among some cluster participants about working and production practices as ways to meet societal needs while simultaneously creating economic value. One way to achieve this is by setting ethical codes of conduct and environmental standards among its participants. In doing so, organizations involved can ensure that they are generating prosperity and well-being among local communities and employees. This is indeed a long-term strategy that requires investing in the promotion and training of cluster members and local stakeholders; this helps to improve the efficiency and competitiveness of the cluster while also helping achieve the sustainability goals and boost prosperity among local communities, generating a win-win situation.[6]

In a shared value perspective, clusters provide firms with opportunities to develop social capital with other organizations, including universities and research centers. This allows for potential collaboration on projects that can create economic and societal value. Additionally, inter-cluster relationships have the potential to develop shared value initiatives and can facilitate the improvement of societal issues and foster employee well-being, community development, and sustainability. However, clusters are not without their enduring challenges, as illustrated in Fig. 2.3.

In addition to these three ideas developed by Porter and Kramer, we present two additional requirements to enlarge the scope of what firms must do to achieve shared value creation. The first of these requires companies to *embrace a broader meaning of competitiveness*, which entails the redefinition of *ownership* throughout the entire value chain with clear definition of responsibility and expectations. The second is *elevating the role of governability*, which requires assigning specific metrics of *accountability*.

Embracing a Broader Meaning of Competitiveness

As explained in our previous book, competitiveness is the required response to take full advantage of the available benefits from globalization, which are fundamentally objective and do not subsidize inefficiencies. For example, Americans do not buy an American car simply because it is American. The car

---

[6] Pezzi, A., & Amores, X. (2020, July 13). Shared value through clusters. Retrieved July 21, 2020, from https://www.clustercollaboration.eu/news/shared-value-through-clusters.

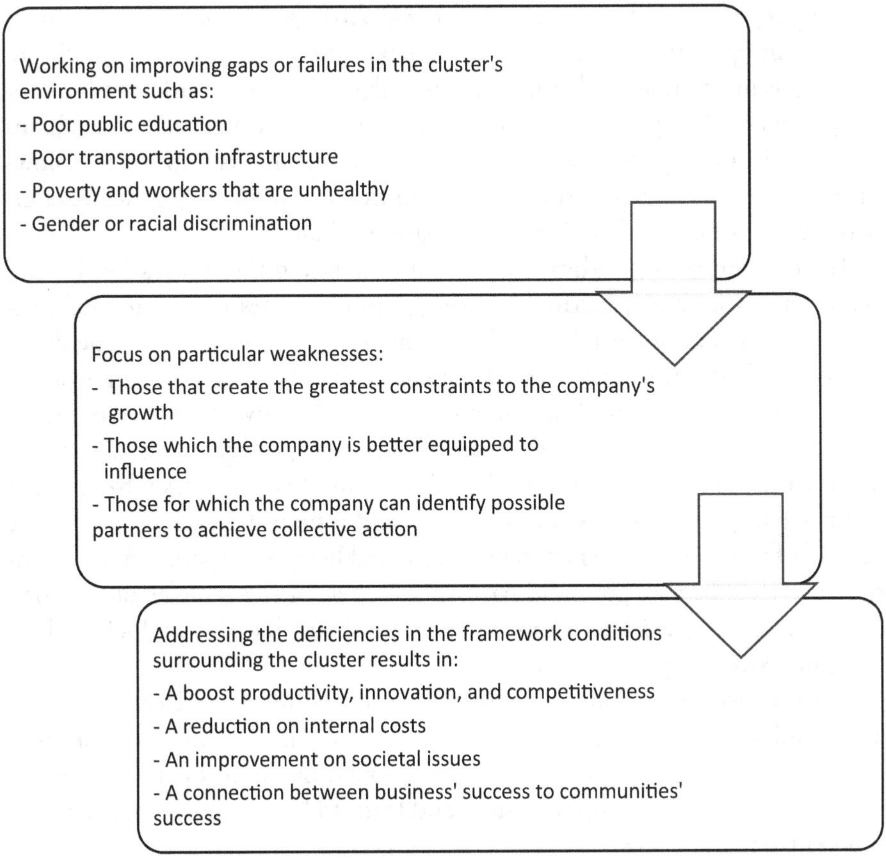

Working on improving gaps or failures in the cluster's environment such as:

- Poor public education

- Poor transportation infrastructure

- Poverty and workers that are unhealthy

- Gender or racial discrimination

Focus on particular weaknesses:

- Those that create the greatest constraints to the company's growth

- Those which the company is better equipped to influence

- Those for which the company can identify possible partners to achieve collective action

Addressing the deficiencies in the framework conditions surrounding the cluster results in:

- A boost productivity, innovation, and competitiveness

- A reduction on internal costs

- An improvement on societal issues

- A connection between business' success to communities' success

Fig. 2.3 Cluster challenges. (Source: Based on Porter, M. E., and M. R. Kramer. ": Creating Shared Value. Harvard Business Review, January." (2011))

must also be deemed superior in terms of value, which encompasses price, design, quality, service, and reliability.

Therefore, all the members in the supply chain need to embrace ownership with a sense of responsibility for the overall well-being of the actors in the chain, which makes it sustainable. For the entire supply chain to succeed and benefit from the explicit benefits of shared value, all members must embrace the expanded concept of ownership.

The dynamics of competition have evolved, moving beyond competition between firms into a new battlefield in which the focus is no longer seen as *my company against yours* but rather as *my supply chain against yours.* Supply chains provide an opportunity for firms to move beyond a shareholder mentality to a shared value mentality, shifting the focus from the optimization of individual players to the optimization of the entire ecosystem. Because value chains are conduits linking all players in a business, embracing its importance allows firms to create synergies in the entire chain that can ultimately generate competitiveness for each of the firms in the supply chain.[7]

The concept of ownership involves understanding the motivation behind certain activities and ensuring that the output matches their intended purpose. Ownership means taking full responsibility for what needs to be done, and it entails learning and questioning rather than blindly following instructions.[8] It is worth mentioning that in this approach to ownership, responsibility plays a crucial role because it drives actors to perform their duties and achieve measurable outcomes. In the value chain, this translates into different actors having a strong sense of ownership and responsibility, being proactive instead of waiting for others to take action, and being transparent in decision-making. The ultimate goal is to have all members of the value chain empowered to make strategic decisions and achieve their objectives, which will, in turn, improve competitiveness.

In order to attain competitiveness, companies must set clear goals and avoid ambiguity. Involved actors must have as much relevant information as possible to ensure more effective decision-making. Additionally, all parties involved must build a support system and learn to fully delegate ownership of different activities.

Embracing competitiveness as a redefinition of ownership throughout the value chain also requires autonomy. However, it is important to understand that this does not imply that leadership is no longer needed. Autonomous organizations will still need guidance and support from other actors of the supply chain in order to achieve desired objectives. Everyone needs to know what they need to do, how to do their job, who they should coordinate and align activities with, and who to ask for support and guidance. Two firms that embody these ideas are Zappos and Patagonia. The former is an online shoe and clothing retailer based in Las Vegas, Nevada. The latter is an American clothing company that markets and sells outdoor clothing and is based in Ventura, California. Both are employee-centric enterprises that foster an inclusive, participatory, and human environment for workers at all levels.

---

[7] Tozan, Hakan, and Alper Ertürk, eds. Applications of Contemporary Management Approaches in Supply Chains, 2015.

[8] Ownership &, Accountability. (2020, February 21). Retrieved August 05, 2020, from https://businessagility.institute/learn/ownership-accountability/.

The aforementioned practices will lead to improved performance and unify strategies and objectives. However, it is very common to achieve results in the short run while failing to sustain success in the long run. When given more responsibility, ownership may increase in the beginning, but over time there is a tendency to relax rules and decrease the focus on achieving desired goals. Avoiding this requires frequent communication and discipline to support the message of ownership, ensure expectations are met, and that responsibilities are clear. Trust is necessary, and so are empowerment and support, to ensure that ownership expectations are met over the long term. In essence the culture must be one of commitment, rigor, and community throughout the value chain.

Increasingly, ownership requires taking initiative. Actors take action regardless of where it emanates from, whether it is their responsibility or not.[9] In other words, ownership makes companies and individuals care about the outcomes because they are stakeholders, creating a sense of obligation to act on strategies that impact and improve results. Taking ownership fosters ideas and strategies to improve performance. As a result, companies become more analytical and observe things that are outside the scope of their jobs or roles, and when something needs to be done, they either do it, help someone else do it, or bring it to the attention of the appropriate individual or organization. This causes actors to focus on these issues that are not even part of their job. Companies that exemplify these principles are Hilton, Cisco, and Stryker.[10] Taking ownership requires ensuring all actions that are taken contribute to the achievement of social and economic goals, creating shared value. Ownership is reflected in an organization's willingness to help tackle societal issues as well, even if it is not technically its job. This allows for all companies in the value chain to be connected with the success of their organization and society as well, not just their own objectives.

Improving ownership and maximizing competitiveness require explaining to others why certain decisions are made. This explanation takes significant time but is critical to create a *culture of ownership and responsibility*. By doing so, all actors are kept in the know, and all participants have a voice and a process through which relevant information is shared and discussed. This affords all involved members the opportunity to participate and will increase their willingness to accept more responsibility because they can understand the motivation behind decisions and expected outcomes.

---

[9] Tanner, W. (2017, June 22). Here's how you get employees to take ownership over their work. Retrieved August 05, 2020, from https://medium.com/@warrentanner/heres-how-you-get-employees-to-take-ownership-over-their-work-ebe1f7ebf508.

[10] *100 Best Companies to Work For*, https://fortune.com/best-companies/.

According to McKinsey's Ramiro Prudencio: "Businesses should see the current environment—one of low trust and increasing expectations—not as a source of frustration, but an opportunity to build lasting and sustainable advantage. By serving a wider set of stakeholders, such as employees, customers, value-chain partners, and local communities, in addition to shareholders, companies and brands will foster loyalty and resilience essential to long-term growth."[11]

Creating ownership among value chain participants requires a culture that fosters engagement and a sense of inclusivity in the process of achieving greater organizational outcomes. When organizations (and individuals) feel included, they understand why things are being done rather than just being told how things are done. A culture of inclusivity in which everyone understands why decisions are being made allows for involvement and ownership in all areas and results in improved performance.[12] Case studies also validate the notion that effective organizational change leads to a more engaged workforce.[13] In 2014, Microsoft CEO Satya Nadella undertook a major restructuring of the tech giant to eliminate its destructive internal competition. Microsoft products and platforms no longer exist as separate groups. Instead, all employees focus on a limited set of common goals—and on bringing them all together. Right at the beginning, Nadella shared a new sense of mission with his employees: "To empower every person and every organization on the planet to achieve more."

Google and British Airways have also instituted organizational changes that proved to be effective and more inclusive for their workforces; the latter brought about a major revamp of its customer service system, processes, and activities since the airline had suffered from a reputation of terrible customer service.

When organizations and actors feel ownership for the work they do, they work with others to overcome unanticipated challenges and obstacles and are willing to challenge decisions if they believe these will improve the quality of their work and their results. Ownership for their work shifts the focus to outcomes and pushes organizations to do whatever it takes to achieve these results in collaboration with other organizations. This approach provides these actors

---

[11] Correspondence from Ramiro Prudencio, Partner, Global Director of Communications, McKinsey & Company, Inc. June 22, 2021. Also see https://www.mckinsey.com/business-functions/strategy-and-corporate-finance/our-insights/the-case-for-stakeholder-capitalism.

[12] Ownership and Accountability: The Key to More Effective Results. (2020, May 04). Retrieved August 05, 2020, from https://cmoe.com/blog/ownership-accountability/.

[13] Lori Li, "Organizational Change Done Right: Examples from the Giants of the Industry," TINYpulse, blog post, June 16, 202.

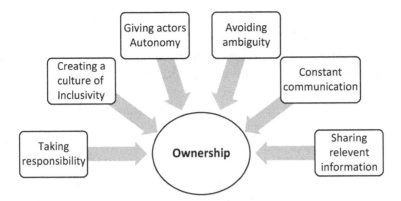

Fig. 2.4 Creating ownership. (Source: Authors)

with the agency and autonomy to do so. Additionally, ownership drives responsibility for their own decisions and outcomes, contributing to the overall strategy.

In sum, a broader meaning of competitiveness requires an ownership-oriented value chain where organizations are committed to results, understand the details and relevant information necessary for decision-making, are willing to take responsibility for their actions and outcomes, are disciplined, and are focused toward achieving improved results for the business and society. A high-performance value chain involves organizations that are committed to communicating effectively, presenting relevant information and using it to make better decisions to achieve the desired results. A greater focus on ownership and responsibility throughout the value chain creates engagement, fosters productivity, and results in greater competitiveness. Figure 2.4 summarizes the elements of creating ownership.

Elevating the Role of Governability

The concept of governability was introduced in our previous book, and in this case, it is required in the form of specific metrics to objectively determine *accountability*. We equate elevating the role of governability with an explicit sense of accountability. It is important to completely eliminate the notion of "entitlements" by any of the members in the supply chain. The notion of metrics should go beyond being vertically and functionally focused into metrics that are horizontal and assess accountability across functions. More than belonging to a particular supply chain, members need to be accountable for their contribution and participation. The only way of determining their specific share is through the right metrics.

Accountability requires follow-through, responsibility for results, and acknowledging that one's actions have an effect on another's ability to accomplish their objectives and goals. It entails consequences, providing answers to external actors, and, in general, it is about the fulfillment of duties and responsibilities. Therefore, when one fails to achieve what one was supposed to achieve, accountability requires accepting responsibility for the failure. After accepting responsibility, there must be a consequence and a change in actions. If this does not occur, then the same failure will happen and objectives will not be met. For example, former Citi executive Robert Rubin stepped down from his position following the Great Recession of 2008, admitting he had not foreseen the credit crisis and market deterioration, which caused roughly 88 percent of Citigroup's share price to evaporate over a two-year period. Healthy business cultures encourage accountability, which should motivate individuals and actors to be proactive in their actions and avoid waiting for someone else to do something in order to achieve established objectives.[14]

There is growing acceptance of "failure-tolerant" leaders. As Richard Farson and Ralph Keyes observed in a *Harvard Business Review* article some time ago: "A business can't develop a breakthrough product or process if it's not willing to encourage risk taking and learn from subsequent mistakes."[15] Capital Zone, Monsanto, and GE have a history of conveying to their employees that constructive mistakes are not only acceptable but also worthwhile. As the late Jack Welch of GE exclaimed: "We reward failure."[16]

To achieve accountability in the organization and across the supply chain, organizations and actors need authority to make relevant decisions. Giving authority within and across organizations takes time and requires making relevant information widely available in order to reduce the likelihood of uninformed decisions. It also requires a change in the way success is measured, shifting from *output* metrics to *outcome* metrics.

Traditionally, delivering results on time and within a budget was considered a success, but not anymore. Today, key performance indicators must align with outcomes. This means that instead of measuring *what* is achieved by a business, or the tangible and intangible products (i.e., products manufactured, transaction processed), the focus should be on *why* the company tries

---

[14] Granger, B. (2019, May 20). What does accountability mean, really? Retrieved August 05, 2020, from https://medium.com/@getsupporti/what-does-accountability-mean-really-bb3c7f867a53.

[15] Richard Farson and Ralph Keyes, The Failure-Tolerant Leader, Harvard Business Review, September 2002. 80(8):64–71.

[16] Ibid.

to achieve this (i.e., environmental sustainability, employee satisfaction, and profitability). Outcomes focus on the benefits delivered by a project, requiring a change of paradigm in which the focus is placed on the higher-level goals, or shared value goals which we hope businesses will contribute to.[17]

Although accountability is necessary to achieve shared value goals, firms must be aware of the anxiety that it can create. Organizations across the supply chain must clearly understand what they are held accountable for and why doing so is important. Accountability fosters growth and increases motivation rather than creating anxiety. Accountability puts in motion a culture in which organizations and individuals make commitments that are visible to others and acknowledge the visibility of consequences as well.

This culture shift must start from the leadership team, which must lead by example. This is paramount. Mary Barra at GM and Reed Hastings at Netflix are often cited as the personification of good leadership. Other organizations noted for engaged leadership are Starbucks, FedEx, Nordstrom, Foot Locker, and Marriott.[18]

Accountability must consistently be required of everyone, and organizations must avoid holding only select members accountable. Also, accountability cannot be delegated. It must be accepted for a person or an organization to take responsibility for certain outcomes. One of the best ways to achieve acceptance of that obligation is to set them up for success, giving them the tools and information necessary for success. Because no one is willing to take accountability for something that will most likely fail, individuals and organizations must believe and remain confident in their chances for success in order for them to accept responsibility for their actions. Asking them about whether they believe they have everything needed to succeed is essential in the process of accepting accountability.[19]

Executing accountability requires a few principles: making results visible to all so that all stakeholders can clearly see their contribution to higher-order objectives, provide timely feedback based on data to ensure timely corrections, and using data to identify areas of improvement that need corrective actions and feedback. Execution is often the biggest challenge because leadership tends to spend too little time reviewing relevant data and actively taking

[17] Ownership & Accountability. (2020, February 21). Retrieved August 05, 2020, from https://businessagility.institute/learn/ownership-accountability/.

[18] *Fifty Most Engaged Companies*, https://www.forbes.com/insights/50-most-engaged-companies/#19c8aa9c2dfa.

[19] Tredgold, G. (2017, September 14). 7 Truths About Accountability That You Need to Know. Retrieved August 05, 2020, from https://www.inc.com/gordon-tredgold/7-truths-about-accountability-that-you-need-to-kno.html.

corrective measures to improve performance of those being held accountable. Successful accountability requires monthly reviews to address whether organizations are on the path to achieving their objectives and taking appropriate action before it is too late to have an impact.

Finally, accountability requires constant work because just telling others they are accountable and leaving them to it is highly unlikely to work. True accountability requires regular review sessions to check up on how everyone is doing and providing them with feedback. These checkups have multiple purposes: reminding others that they will be held accountable, providing them with the support they need if they are not in the right path toward achieving their outcomes, and offering encouragement and reinforcement for those who are on the right path.[20]

In sum, accountability must be a clear and consistent strategy that needs to be constantly worked at and validated. It must start with leadership and be implemented at all times and to all involved. The main purpose of it is for organizations and actors to accept responsibility, acknowledge the consequences of their actions, and to not dwell in shame but take action. Turning failures into learning is perhaps the most important effect of accountability. Achieving this allows individuals to understand what they are accountable for and why it is important, creating a motivation for making visible commitments, following through on these commitments, and achieving business objectives and personal growth. Once this type of culture is achieved, the organizations across the value chain will hold themselves accountable for their outcomes consistently, resulting in improvements on higher-level goals. Figure 2.5 illustrates the panoply of activities that embody accountability.

Two companies that exemplify the quintet of M2W as presented in this chapter are Nestlé and Coca-Cola. Vignettes of the two firms illustrate their activities and achievements in this area.

Nestlé's Nespresso. Generating positive impacts for all stakeholders across the entire value chain,[21] Nespresso is one of the brands from the Nestlé Group. The company has made numerous efforts to increase welfare for farmers and improve their environmental performance, while remaining one of the most profitable brands for the company. Their strategy to accomplish this is by implementing innovative solutions to address socioeconomic and climatic challenges, identifying obstacles that posed threats to achieving their goal of

---

[20] Ibid.

[21] Nespresso CEO explains how the company's approach to creating shared value drives positive impact for coffee farmers. Retrieved August 24, 2020, from https://www.nestle-nespresso.com/newsandfeatures/nespresso-ceo-explains-how-the-companys-approach-to-creating-shared-value-drive-positive-impact-for-coffee-farmers.

Fig. 2.5 Achieving accountability. (Source: Authors)

supplying coffee of the highest quality, and at the same time ensuring the well-being of coffee farming communities. They found that farmers were exposed to price volatility, fluctuations of the currency exchange rate, lack of insurance for disability and accidents, decreased productivity, and lack of provisions for retirement.

To address these issues, Nespresso created their AAA Sustainable Quality Program through an innovative public-private partnership with the Colombian Ministry of Labor, Coffee Growers' Cooperative, coffee supplier Expocafe, and Fairtrade International. This program created a unique direct-from-farmer sourcing model that ensured quality, sustainability, and productivity principles. This project has identified failures and risks in smallholder coffee supply chains and worked with stakeholders to understand the issues and to design radical solutions that address them. Additionally, this initiative is providing the means for farmers to save for retirement while helping ensure the generational transfer of farms from parents to children. The results of this program are improved quality of coffee, decreased environmental impact, and increased income for farmers.

Nespresso also co-founded with local organizations a central mill or a community coffee-processing center to improve the quality of the coffee they purchased. This central mill created a centralized facility where farmers can transform coffee cherries into coffee beans instead of each farmer doing it on their own, with a clear delineation of responsibilities (i.e., ownership and accountability). The result: ensuring consistency in bean quality, reducing the occurrence of damages to the beans, and guaranteeing the highest quality coffee for consumers.

Jean-Marc Duvoisin, Nespresso's CEO, summarizes the company's approach to M2W and states that the main purpose of shared value for the company is to secure the future of the farmers they work with and to ensure they run sustainable businesses so that Nespresso can itself be sustainable. He also mentions that working closely with farmers is key to delivering on the brand promise of high-quality sustainable coffee for consumers. Duvoisin states that shared value has allowed the company to bring exceptional coffee experiences to customers while securing long-term supply that meets sustainability standards. More importantly, he mentions that in order for shared value to be created, the approach should be closely connected to the company's business model, and that for Nespresso, CSV is embedded in the company. The details of their implementation demonstrate the application of the quintet we propose under the M2W principle beyond the three basic ideas of the traditional shared value.

Coca-Cola. This firm provides an excellent example of measuring impact to unlock new value creation. After months of analyzing the needs of Brazil's middle class, Coca-Cola identified a key issue to focus on: skill development among low-income youth. The Brazilian government had been mostly successful in covering the need for primary education, but most young people could barely find jobs due to the limited number of job opportunities and their lack of skills. To address this issue, Coca-Cola devised its "Coletivo" initiative to work with local NGOs to train young people in various business areas like retailing and business development and pairing them with local retailers for their first job experience. This project allowed for participants to increase their skill base and provide them with practical experience.[22]

Coletivo also aimed to improve retailers' operations in areas like promotions and stocking, with the assistance of young trainees. Additionally, this would increase the sales and market penetration of Coca-Cola's products among consumers of the growing lower-middle class. The company implemented this initiative with the expectation that it could provide measurable results about young people's skills and employability, as well as measurable

---

[22] Coca-Cola Coletivo: Scaling Sustainable Communities. Retrieved August 24, 2020, from https://www.clintonfoundation.org/clinton-global-initiative/commitments/coca-cola-coletivo-scaling-sustainable-communities.

increases in sales and brand recognition in the targeted communities.[23] Details were explained to delineate the responsibilities.

When Coca-Cola started the program in 2009, a cornerstone of the project was measuring its progress on a monthly basis and creating progress reports to track the number of young individuals and retailers involved, the performance of retailers, and the costs associated with the program's implementation. Since its launch, Coletivo has trained thousands of young people in Brazil, with 130 more programs across the country. Approximately 30 percent of the individuals trained land their first job with Coca-Cola or one of its partners immediately after completion and 10 percent set up their own business with financial support from the company, through micro-credits. Coca-Cola found that the investments in the program were profitable after two years.[24]

Their rigorous measurement allowed for the identification and focus on the most effective approaches to develop the program. For instance, during its first year, the focus was on training related to technical skills;, however, data showed that young people continued to face difficulties in finding jobs due to lack of soft skills. As a result, Coca-Cola modified the content of the program to combine practical training with training in soft skills such as speaking, self-esteem development, and leadership. Data also showed that NGOs were a key success factor in the implementation of the program; therefore, Coca-Cola bolstered NGO's management capabilities by helping them obtain new and sustainable sources of funding. By doing this, Coca-Cola built stronger brand recognition across communities, which, in turn, helped to increase sales. Each participant clearly understood their responsibility, which was measured through the right metric to specify accountability.

Coca-Cola has understood the power of M2W and is clear on why shared value is a priority for the company. It believes that its business is only as sustainable as the communities in which it operates, and the M2W principle is a powerful tool to generate economic and social impact across communities and across business, which is at the core of their mission.

Figure 2.6 illustrates additional corporate examples of the M2W principle.

In sum, while proponents of shared value have focused on three ways of achieving economic and societal value—reconceiving products and markets, redefining productivity in the value chain, and building supportive industry clusters—the other equally important features must be added to the mix: ownership and accountability. These two features embody a more

[23] Pfitzer, & W., Bockstette, V., & Stamp, M. (2014, August 22). Innovating for Shared Value. Retrieved August 24, 2020, from https://hbr.org/2013/09/innovating-for-shared-value.

[24] Coletivo. (n.d.). Retrieved August 24, 2020, from http://reports.weforum.org/disrupting-unemployment/coletivo/?doing_wp_cron=1598279099.4019329547882080078125.

Nestlé	Dow Chemical	Mars
• Provides inexpensive micronutrient-reinforced spices • Helps malnourished families •Spirces are a fast-growing, profitable business	•Removed millions of kilograms of trans and sturated fats from the U.S. diet •Created a profitable business with the Nexera sunflower and canola seeds	•Created a cross-sector coalition to transform farms and communities in Ivory Coast •Avoided cocoa shortages

Novartis	Intel	Vodafone
• Created a social business model that became profitable within 3 years • Provided medicines and health services to over 40 million people in India	•Turned education into a proftiable business for the company •Trained over 10 million teachers in the use of technology •Improved educational oucomes	•Extended mobile banking services to over 14 million people in East Africa •Created M-Pesa, one the company's most important service offerings

Fig. 2.6 Companies under the quintet of M2W (FSG research note: Nestlé, Mars, Intel, and Becton Dickinson (BD) are FSG clients. Ibid. 15)

comprehensive meaning of competitiveness and enhanced governability (in the form of accountability) as indispensable characteristics of a sustainable and responsible shared approach for all stakeholders: the M2W principle. This understanding is extremely important as we investigate and critique the differences between shareholders and stakeholders in the following chapters.

3

Shareholders vs. Stakeholders

This chapter explains the fundamental differences between shareholders and stakeholders—terms which are often used interchangeably in the business setting. Although these terms sound similar, their meanings, roles, and interests in a company differ significantly. A shareholder is an individual or an organization that owns equity stock in a company, and therefore also holds an ownership stake in that company. Consequently, shareholders have the right to exercise a vote and to influence a company's management. As a result, shareholders tend to be perceived as "profit maximizers," with their main interest being focused on a company's profitability and its financial success. On the other hand, a stakeholder holds an interest in a company's performance that is unrelated to capital appreciation or stock performance. Companies have traditionally focused on satisfying the interest of shareholders and achieving profit. But recently, companies have been moving away from this approach and focusing on satisfying a wider range of stakeholders. Under this philosophy, the aim of companies has evolved from "making money" to creating shared value, operating under a more sustainable approach from a social and economic perspective.

Shareholders

Shareholders are individuals, companies, or institutions that own shares in a public or private company. They may be individual investors or large corporations who own at least one share of a company and have a financial interest in the company; their main goal is for the company's share price to increase.

Shareholders can be categorized as a subset of the wider stakeholder group and, as such, they are always stakeholders but stakeholders are not necessarily shareholders.[1]

Although they do not take part in the ongoing day-to-day activities involved in running a company, they have certain rights as owners of the company, which vary according to the laws and rules of the company and the shareholders' agreement. Generally speaking, shareholders have the right to buy new shares, sell their shares, receive dividends, nominate directors of the board, and vote on strategic decisions such as the selection of the board members, mergers, and changes to the corporate charter. Figure 3.1 illustrates the relationship between stakeholders and shareholders.

The investments made by shareholders in a company are usually liquid investments that can be withdrawn for a profit. The purchase of shares by shareholders is made as investments with the hope that shares will appreciate and they will receive a high return on their investment. If the company's share price increases, so does the shareholder's value, and if the company's stock price declines, so does the shareholder's value.

Shareholders buy a portion of a company's shares with the goal that its price will appreciate and that, consequently, they will receive a higher return on investment. Because of this, shareholders' interest is for the company's management to carry out strategies and activities that increase the profitability and financial success of the company, and thus increase share prices and the value of dividends distributed. Shareholders tend to encourage management to carry out activities such as acquisitions, expansions, and mergers that increase the company's overall profitability.

Fig. 3.1 Stakeholders and shareholders (stakeholder vs. shareholder—important differences to know (May 25, 2020). Retrieved July 06, 2020, from https://corporatefinanceinstitute.com/resources/knowledge/finance/stakeholder-vs-shareholder/)

[1] Landau, P. (2020, July 02). Stakeholder vs. Shareholder: How They're Different; Why It Matters. Retrieved July 06, 2020, from https://www.projectmanager.com/blog/stakeholder-vs-shareholder.

They are also able to sell part or all their shares in the company and buy shares from different and, at times, competing organizations. As a result, they are not necessarily focused on the long-term success and performance of a particular company. Nothing guarantees that shareholders will invest in the company for the long term. For the most part, shareholders' relationship with a company revolves around the view of "what is in it for me" and is strongly focused on profit maximization.

Focus on Shareholder Value

Rooted in political and economic causes as well as in academic research, shareholder dominance has become the prevalent philosophy in corporate America since the 1970s. Under this ideology, the shareholder became the center of the corporate world and high-level decisions revolved around them. The argument for this kind of thinking was that if corporations put shareholders first, capitalism would function better. We now know that there is an immense gap between this rhetoric and reality, and while shareholders can be effective and helpful in providing money, information, and discipline to corporations, focusing solely on their wants has caused the prioritization of short-term gains while potentially sacrificing long-term success. Extensive evidence has shown that companies focusing on achieving goals rather than maximizing shareholder value are actually more successful at maximizing shareholder value in the long run.[2]

Shareholders' primary concern and motive behind their decision to buy shares in a company is the generation of profits. Another priority for shareholders is the increase of a firm's overall value via strategies like expanding into new markets, increasing market share in existing markets, improving brand recognition, and boosting customer satisfaction. These strategies increase a firm's chances of long-term success, ensuring shareholders' continuous ability to reap profits. And while this is true, the relationship is a mutually beneficial one in which each profits from the activities of the other. Corporations benefit from shareholders because they provide funding to expand their business, enabling their means of growth and ability to build wealth. Corporations benefit shareholders by increasing shareholder value.[3]

---

[2] Kanter, R. (2014, November 04). How Great Companies Think Differently. Retrieved July 16, 2020, from https://hbr.org/2011/11/how-great-companies-think-differently.

[3] Brandenberg, D. (2019, January 10). What Are a Shareholder's Objectives? Retrieved July 15, 2020, from https://pocketsense.com/shareholders-objectives-2205.html.

Shareholder value is delivered to those who own equity at a corporation, obtained as a result of increases in sales and earnings, which, in turn, increases the dividends and capital gains obtained by shareholders. Overall, its value is based on a firm's ability to grow and be profitable over time. This is directly dependent on the ability of top management and board members to make strategic decisions that generate returns on invested capital. If this is achieved, eventually share prices increase and companies can pay larger dividends to their shareholders. Shareholder value is of critical importance for firms and can become a dilemma because it does not necessarily translate to creating value for other stakeholders like employees or customers. And although it has been commonly implied that directors and top management have the obligation of maximizing shareholder value, especially in the case of publicly traded companies, in reality it is not a legal duty of management to maximize profits for corporations.[4]

Shareholders and Stakeholders—The Emergence of CSR

Recently, corporations have begun to answer to both shareholders and stakeholders, unlike in the past, where they would mostly be interested only in shareholders. This is in tune with the emergence of corporate social responsibility (CSR), a business model that encourages companies to take into consideration the interest of a wide range of stakeholders and constituents in the business environment. Therefore, when making their decision-making process more engaging, companies might consider the impact of their choices on a variety of stakeholders rather than making choices based solely on the interest of shareholders.

While companies and large corporations have been long aware of the importance of creating value for shareholders, at first CSR was developed in the United States at the end of the nineteenth century from a conceptual standpoint. This was mainly due to the influence and importance of religion, which encouraged companies to engage in philanthropic activities through foundations. Additionally, the overarching mistrust toward the state and the expectation that the state will fail to fulfill its duty encouraged business people to carry out certain activities themselves.

---

[4] Hayes, A., & Scott, G. (2020, March 25). Understanding Shareholder Value. Retrieved July 14, 2020, from https://www.investopedia.com/terms/s/shareholder-value.asp.

Stakeholders

Stakeholders are individuals and organizations impacted by the performance or outcome of a company, and can be internal (e.g., shareholders, managers, and employees) or external (e.g., suppliers, vendors, the community, and public groups). They are impacted by a company or a project, both when in progress and once it is completed or ceases to exist.[5]

One of the main characteristics of the relationship between stakeholders and a company is longevity or a longer time horizon. Stakeholders are bound to a company by numerous factors that make them more reliant on one another, and this makes it more difficult for stakeholders to remove their stake in the company (e.g., employees' income and support to their families is tied to their relationship with the company). Stakeholders may not be as willing to remove themselves from the relationship as shareholders could. The success of a company or a project is just as important for stakeholders as it can be for shareholders.

However, stakeholders tend to have a greater need for the company's longevity and success in the long term. For example, employees and suppliers are interested in a company's long-term performance because poor financial performance could result in the loss of jobs for employees and loss of income for suppliers.

The focus on longevity by stakeholders means that they are less focused on a company's short-term profitability and have an increased interest in sustained performance and quality of service. For example, customers are interested in purchasing high-quality products and receiving good customer service. In order to meet this demand, the company needs to increase its investments and expenditures in raw materials and in a well-trained customer service staff, which do not necessarily increase profitability in the short term but can have a positive impact in the long run. Long-term performance ensures stakeholders like employees to ensure increases in their wages and salaries, and suppliers to ensure timely payments for goods and services sold to the company.

In sum, shareholders own part of a company, while stakeholders are interested parties who hope to see the company perform for reasons other than an increase in its stock price and dividends. As mentioned earlier, shareholders are part of the larger stakeholders' group, while the opposite is not always true. Additionally, shareholders do not necessarily need to have a long-term interest in a company and are able to sell their stock at any moment;

---

[5] Ibid., 1.

Nature	Impact	Viewpoint	Conflict of Interest
• Shareholders hold ownership of the company by purchasing equity stock • Stakeholders have an interest in the company either through a director indirect relationship	• Shareholders are affected directly by the financial performance of the company • Stakeholders may be directly or indirectly affected by what happens in the company	• Shareholders want a company to undertake activities that have a positive effect on the stock price or dividends • Stakeholders focus on long-term longevity apart from the financial performance	• Shareholders may want the company to focus on improving financial performance • Stakeholders want to incur expenditure that increases their value but does not necessarily add to short term profitability

Fig. 3.2 Shareholders vs. stakeholders (Borad, S. (2019, March 23). Shareholders vs. Stakeholders. Retrieved July 06, 2020, from https://efinancemanagement.com/sources-of-finance/shareholders-vs-stakeholders)

therefore, they are mainly concerned with a return on their investment. Stakeholders, on the other hand, are interested in the company in the long run and are focused on the company's performance and prosperity. Figure 3.2 summarizes the main differences between shareholders and stakeholders.

The Importance of Stakeholder Value to Top Management

Chief executive officers from some of the largest corporations (Apple, Pepsi, JP Morgan Chase, Walmart, among others) have recently been reconsidering the main purpose of the corporation with the aim of redefining the role of business in society. The Business Roundtable held in 2019 focused on debunking long-held notions that a corporation's sole purpose was to serve its shareholders and maximize profits. These CEOs agreed that corporations must also focus on their relationship with employees, the environment, their suppliers, and an overall commitment toward all of their shareholders. The main takeaway from these statements was that shareholder value is no longer the main focus of some of the United States' main corporations. Instead, they were committed to deliver value to all stakeholders as a means to ensure the long-term success of their companies, communities, and country. This shift is partially a result of accumulated unrest and distress over corporate America's role in societal issues including income inequality, poor working conditions, and products that are harmful to the environment. Corporations have come to the realization that only by investing in their workers and the communities in which they operate will they be able to succeed, and this necessitates fair compensation and training of employees; embracing sustainable production, distribution, and logistics practices; fostering diversity and inclusion; and taking actions that create prosperity.[6]

The purpose of corporations has started to shift from shareholder primacy to contributing to the solution of fundamental economic and societal issues. It is precisely the overarching stakeholder primacy ideology that has contributed to many of the economic inequalities and unsustainable practices that are present today. While each company will continue to serve its own individual purpose, they are also committed to incorporating stakeholders into their main objective. They will do so by "delivering value to customers, investing in employees, dealing fairly and ethically with suppliers, supporting the communities where they work, and generating long-term value for shareholders."[7] This statement marks a shift toward the primacy of stakeholders.

Freeman's Theory

Freeman's lens provides a different perception of companies and is based on three main points. First, Freeman proposes the "face and names" approach through which stakeholders are acknowledged as people with names, with whom the company must negotiate different issues. Second, Freeman argues that there are no absolute decision principles, meaning that companies must be willing to challenge each of its opinions in order to fully take its stakeholder's needs into account. However, this does not imply that a company must give up all its principles, but it should at least question their relevance. Finally, Freeman considers that even when conflicting interests arise between stakeholders, an agreement is always possible through compromises that will satisfy both interests.[8] Figure 3.3 summarizes the comparison between Friedman and Freeman.

---

[6] Gelles, D., & Yaffe-bellany, D. (2019, August 19). Shareholder Value Is No Longer Everything, Top C.E.O.s Say. Retrieved July 15, 2020, from https://www.nytimes.com/2019/08/19/business/business-roundtable-ceos-corporations.html.

[7] Fitzgerald, M. (2019, August 19). The CEOs of nearly 200 companies said shareholder value is no longer their main objective. Retrieved July 15, 2020, from https://www.cnbc.com/2019/08/19/the-ceos-of-nearly-two-hundred-companies-say-shareholder-value-is-no-longer-their-main-objective.html.

[8] Ed Freeman and his stakeholder theory. (n.d.). Retrieved July 06, 2020, from https://www.spidermak.com/en/ed-freeman-and-his-stakeholder-theory

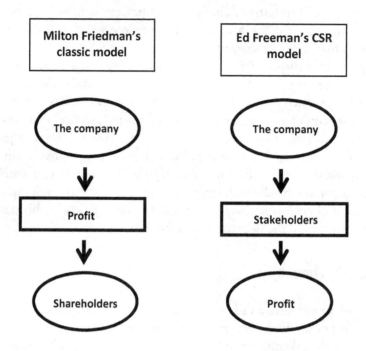

Fig. 3.3 Friedman vs. Freeman

Stakeholder Primacy and Freeman's Theory

This idea of distrust toward the state is what Ed Freeman, a philosopher whose work focuses on business ethics and moral philosophy, bases his stakeholder theory on. At the time this theory was developed the dominant model was based on Milton Friedman's ideology in which a company's main goal is to accumulate profit to be redistributed among shareholders. As such, Friedman's main premise is that companies should solely focus on its shareholders, and not on other groups affected by its activity, such as employees and customers. Freeman's stakeholder theory is now widely circulated in business schools and implemented by corporations as it is included in the ISO 26000, which provides the guidelines for corporate social responsibility.[9]

This theory was developed as an alternative view of the classic model of what a company's objective is. Stakeholder theory claims that Friedman's model is mistaken because profit is not a company's primary raison d'être, but

---

[9] Ed Freeman and his stakeholder theory. (n.d.). Retrieved July 06, 2020, from https://www.spidermak.com/en/ed-freeman-and-his-stakeholder-theory.

merely a consequence of the company's activities. Freeman argues that a company's aim is to meet the needs of its stakeholders, and if this done, then profit will come as a result.

Stakeholder vs. Shareholder Value

For a long time, large corporations have understood the necessity of creating value for all stakeholders, including employees, communities, investors, and suppliers. This recognition comes from two important facts. First, the case for creating stakeholder value has been proven—a company cannot make profits for its shareholders without creating value for a variety of stakeholders. When done strategically, creating value for stakeholders does not reduce profits for shareholders, but rather adds to it. Therefore, stakeholder value and shareholder value should not be seen as a zero-sum game. Second, companies that are falling into the trap of "short-termism" and are pressured to increase their profits more quickly are not likely to make strategic decisions that will allow them to prosper in the short term.[10]

When comparing some of the leading corporate executives in the United States, we see a clear differentiation between those who focus on shareholder value vs. those who have focused on creating value for stakeholders. Former General Electric CEO Jack Welch and AIG's Maurice Greenberg mainly focused on increasing their companies' stock prices, fixating their strategies on anything that would result in exceeding their prior earnings even if only by a penny per share. In order to achieve this, they created strict corporate cultures in which top-level managers were faced with insurmountable pressures to deliver results, and fired the bottom 10% every year. Another way they achieved this number-driven focus was through numerous acquisitions, as a way to generate additional earnings that were not being generated by the current business. However, these strategies tend to be unsustainable in the long run because companies and industries do not grow in a steady or predictable manner, making the promise of steady and predictable financial results almost impossible.

In contrast to Welch and Greenberg's approach is Warren Buffett's corporate philosophy. He made it clear that his main focus is on increasing the long-term value per share of his company and that he is not focused on

---

[10] Kline, M. (2019, August 26). Why the Debate Over Stakeholder Value Versus Shareholder Value Is All Wrong. Retrieved July 06, 2020, from https://www.inc.com/maureen-kline/why-debate-over-stakeholder-value-vs-shareholder-value-is-all-wrong.html.

Berkshire's short-term share price. Buffett is regarded as a more genuine and caring corporate leader and one of the wealthiest people in the world.[11]

Toward a Shift to Stakeholder Primacy

At the end of the last century, shareholders were considered the prime beneficiaries of companies—a shareholder-centric form of corporate governance also known as the shareholder primacy model. However, a few decades ago the shift toward including the non-shareholder interests began to surface. The model came under criticism as a result of a wave of hostile takeovers in the 1980s in which shareholders significantly increased their wealth but which resulted in employees struggling to find work and institutions having to respond with aid. In the United States and Canada, shareholder primacy model came under more scrutiny after the burst of the tech bubble in 2002 and the financial crisis of 2008.

As a response, Canada made changes to the Canada Business Corporation Act (CBCA), which stated that directors and officers should not be limited to act in the best interest and benefit of the immediate shareholders but also to the interests of other stakeholders. Through Bill C-97, the Canadian government deviated from the shareholder primacy model and moved toward a more inclusive model in which directors may consider, but are not limited to, the interests of shareholders, employees, creditors, government, consumers, and the environment when informing their decisions. In the United States, approximately 180 CEOs released a statement in 2019 in which they acknowledged that companies have a fundamental commitment to all stakeholders and to create value for all of them, denoting a shift from a shareholder primacy model to a more stakeholder-centric paradigm.[12]

These actions set higher expectations for corporations and their behavior, emphasizing their ability to consider diverse interests. In doing so, companies deviate from an overemphasis in short-term interests that resulted in immediate shareholder gains. This does not mean, however, that companies should stop taking into account short-term interests; the aim is to reconcile the achievement of short-term interests without harming long-term value.

---

[11] Tilson, W. (2020, March 03). The differences between Buffett, Welch, and Greenberg. Retrieved July 06, 2020, from https://empirefinancialresearch.com/articles/the-differences-between-buffett-welch-and-greenberg-jack-welch-inflicted-great-damage-on-corporate-america-ge-shed-about-78000-workers-in-2019-steve-ballmer-laughs-at-the-iphone-steve-jobs-vide.

[12] Stakeholders' primacy: Paradigm shift confirmed. (n.d.) Retrieved July 06, 2020, from https://www.iasplus.com/en-ca/news/regulations/2019/stakeholders2019-primacy-paradigm-shift-confirmed.

Achieving a shift toward stakeholder primacy requires implementing this mindset in all of the firms' activities and strategies. For instance, value chain strategies should also move from prioritizing short-term gains to emphasizing long-term value creation. This involves considering between vertical integration and horizontal integration and assessing which of these strategies result in increased profitability while also allowing to simultaneously address other stakeholders' interests.

A Paradigm Shift in the Value Chain—Vertical (Shareholders) vs. Horizontal (Stakeholders) Integration

Companies' strategies are a reflection of whether they focus on creating value for shareholders or for stakeholders. Some of the approaches commonly used by firms include horizontal and vertical integration. The former involves one company taking over or acquiring another company that operates at the same level in the value chain in a given industry. For example, a supermarket chain may choose to acquire another supermarket chain in another country to begin operations in a foreign market. The latter involves the acquisition of a company at another level of the value chain or another stage of production. For example, a computer manufacturer may choose to acquire a company that manufactures microprocessors.

When a company undergoes horizontal integration, its main objective is to acquire a similar company in a similar industry. An example of this is Facebook's 2012 acquisition of Instagram, both of which operate in the social media realm. By horizontally integrating, companies can expand their size, diversify their product and service offerings, increase their customer base and their presence in new markets, access overseas markets, achieve economies of scale, and reduce competition. Therefore, when done successfully, horizontal integration allows businesses to increase their revenue by limiting their competitors' share of the pie, and reduce costs by sharing production, marketing, research and development, distributions, and so forth. Horizontal integration is not without its limitations and issues from a business perspective. When merging two companies that operate at the same level of the value chain, competition can be reduced to the point where it may lead to a monopoly. In this case, one company plays a dominant role in a given industry, and holds full control of the supply of products and services and their prices, significantly reducing the choices available to customers. As a consequence, horizontal integrations are subject to anti-trust laws in the United States aimed at protecting consumers from monopolies where a sole company has high market concentration and influence over a given industry.[13]

When a company undergoes vertical integration, its main objective is to acquire a company that operates in the production process of the same industry. This involves the acquisition or merger with a company that is situated before or after in the value chain. An example of this is Ikea's 2015 purchase of forests in Romania to supply raw materials for its furniture. By vertically integrating, companies can strengthen their supply chain, reduce production costs, access additional distribution channels, and capture profits at different stages of the value chain. In order to achieve this, companies can undergo backward or forward vertical integration. In backward integration, a company acquires another company that makes an input for the manufacture of the acquiring company's product. An example of backward integration is an apparel company acquiring a textiles company. Such a strategy enables a manufacturer to ensure a steady supply of its inputs in order to continue the production of its final product. Forward integration involves the acquisition of a company in the post-production stage of the value chain. An example of this is an e-commerce retail company that chooses to acquire a shipping company. By doing so, the company becomes closer in proximity to the consumer and also provides an opportunity to reduce costs associated with distribution, and ultimately a revenue increase.[14]

When considering horizontal and vertical integration, companies should bear in mind the pros and cons of these strategies and the implications for their bottom line. When done correctly, horizontal integration can result in reduced competition, increased synergies, achievement of economies of scale, and expansion of market share. It also allows companies to broaden their consumer base, increasing their access to a larger pool of consumers, and, in turn, increase its revenue and profitability. However, as mentioned earlier, horizontal integration may also result in a reduction in flexibility and in antitrust issues, and can end up destroying value instead of creating it. Becoming a larger organization results in additional personnel and processes, creating the need for more accountability and transparency, but can also reduce flexibility and result in red tape that hinders decision-making and action. This strategy can also result in increased government scrutiny, with the aim to prevent large

---

[13]Tarver, E. (2020, March 13). Horizontal vs. Vertical Integration: What's the Difference? Retrieved July 06, 2020, from https://www.investopedia.com/ask/answers/051315/what-difference-between-horizontal-integration-and-vertical-integration.asp.

[14]Tarver, E. (2020, March 13). Horizontal vs. Vertical Integration: What's the Difference? Retrieved July 06, 2020, from https://www.investopedia.com/ask/answers/051315/what-difference-between-horizontal-integration-and-vertical-integration.asp.

corporations to engage in monopolistic practices where one company dominates the market and takes advantage of consumers by reducing the product and service offerings and increasing prices. Additionally, horizontal integration may end up destroying value and stunting economic growth when synergies between companies never materialize.[15]

Overall, both horizontal and vertical integration present advantages and disadvantages for firms in terms of economic gains and benefiting multiple stakeholders. Firms should account for the pros and cons of each strategy to decide which offers a better path toward achieving long- and short-term gains. These considerations are also necessary in other essential firm activities such as planning. Different time frames in planning can lead to overemphasizing stakeholder interests and deemphasizing other stakeholders' interests. As such, firms must thoroughly adjust their approach to planning in a way that allows them to achieve sustained performance while generating long-term value.

A Paradigm Shift: Long- vs. Short-Term Planning[16]

When developing their plans to achieve goals and objectives, business people find it useful to differentiate between distinct phases of planning. Separating plans allows companies to track immediate results and improvements while simultaneously monitoring and evaluating progress toward long-term goals and targets. Accounting for different time frames when developing plans is a way to include both time-sensitive goals and long-term goals in the planning process and adjust the inputs and outcomes for such goals accordingly. This kind of planning enables companies to achieve short-term goals and tasks while keeping long-term goals in mind.

Many companies develop strategic planning by separating short-, medium-, and long-term planning. Short-term planning usually focuses on the current characteristics of the company and develops strategies to improve these within a year. A good example includes planning for improvements in employees' skills and product quality. In order to address such issues, companies develop short-term solutions that set the stage for solving larger or more comprehensive issues in a longer time frame.

---

[15] Tarver, E. (2020, February 05). Horizontal Integration: Benefits and Drawbacks. Retrieved July 06, 2020, from https://www.investopedia.com/ask/answers/051415/what-are-advantages-and-disadvantages--horizontal-integration.asp.

[16] Markgraf, B. (2019, January 25). Short-Term, Medium-Term & Long-Term Planning in Business. Retrieved July 06, 2020, from https://smallbusiness.chron.com/shortterm-mediumterm-longterm-planning-business-60193.html.

Medium-term planning focuses on developing more permanent solutions to short-term issues. For example, when addressing employees' skills, companies should consider revising their employee trainings to include regular training programs in the medium term. Also, when addressing quality issues, companies can respond in the medium term by revising and reinforcing their quality control programs. Overall, medium-term planning involves implementing strategies and solutions that keep short-term problems from becoming recurring.

Long-term planning involves the permanent solution of problems and the achievement of overall targets and objectives. This planning is usually set for four or five years in the future and assesses the competitive situation of the company in regard to its social, political, and economic environment. This kind of planning includes the implementation of policies and procedures that enable the company to adapt to its environment and shape its position to meet top managements' objectives. When companies develop successful short- and medium-term plans, long-term plans tend to build on those accomplishments to ensure sustained performance and continued progress. As such, long-term planning provides a sustainable approach for companies to succeed and enhance their value, while short- and medium-term planning are usually more focused on solving immediate tasks and maximizing short-term profit, offering a more myopic view of the company's strategy.

Strategy

Long-Term Planning and Strategy[17]

When developing their strategic planning, long-term strategy paves the way for the future of the company and delineates the steps to reach that future. This kind of planning integrates the organization's major goals and the company's decisions and actions into a cohesive pattern or route map. This set of decisions enables companies to utilize their resources in a way that enables them to achieve their organization's objectives and obtain sustained performance rather than just a positive variability in firm performance.

Long-term or strategic decisions can be measured in terms of their magnitude, timescale, and commitment. *Magnitude* is related to importance of

---

[17] Contributor Guest author. (n.d.). What are the Points of Intersection between Your Strategy and Social Responsibility? Retrieved July 06, 2020, from https://www.inclusivebusiness.net/ib-voices/what-are-points-intersection-between-your-strategy-and-social-responsibility.

such decisions that affect an entire or a large part of an organization and usually entail interaction with the environment around it. *Time-scale* involves decisions that set the direction for the company in the long term while also affecting its performance and objectives in the short term. What constitutes short and long term will often vary between industries as some move faster than others. *Commitment* is related to the large investment of resources, which cannot be easily reversed.

In order for a company's strategy to be "good" it must consider its environment and adapt to it while remaining internally consistent; this is also known as "fit." Its strategy must also be distinctive from that of competitors in a manner in which it enables the company to develop a unique position and identity that stakeholders can perceive. Sustainability is also another important aspect of a company's strategy because it allows the company to survive and progress in the long term.

Once a company has fully incorporated a stakeholder primacy mindset into its value chain and strategic planning approach, its overall strategy should also be focused on satisfying a wider range of stakeholders. By moving into this direction, a company's main objective evolves from simply achieving profits to creating value or, more specifically, to creating shared value. This reasoning requires rethinking firm strategy to enable the achievement of social and economic progress.

Integrating Shared Value Into Strategy

Corporate strategy used to be focused solely on economic benefit with the marginal incorporation of corporate philanthropy that made no attempt at conferring any competitive advantages to the organization. Strategy expert Michael Porter and CSR practitioner Michael Kramer claim that approaches to CSR are disconnected from business and strategy, blocking the opportunities for companies to benefit society. These authors argue that companies should analyze the opportunities for CSR by using the frameworks that guide their core business choices; only then can CSR become a source of innovation and competitive advantage rather than just a cost or constraint. In doing so, Porter and Kramer advocate for "shared value" in which the connection between social progress and business success is established. They call for an integration of business and society in both business decisions and social policies, resulting in corporate choices that benefit both sides.[18]

---

[18] Kramer, M., & Pfitzer, M. The Ecosystem of Shared Value (2016). Harvard Business Review. Retrieved from: https://hbr.org/2016/10/the-ecosystem-of-shared-value.

The question that remains is how companies can find the intersection between economic and social benefit. Companies can no longer prosper at the expense of the community, and in order to remain legitimate they must perceive themselves as agents of social change and embark on initiatives that create shared value. To do so, companies must *determine the areas of intersection*—the areas in which the company influences and affects society through its core business and the external conditions that influence the company's operations. Following this, companies must *select the social issues they want to focus on*; this selection must be made on the basis of issues that present an opportunity to create shared value. Companies must *integrate their social agenda into the core of their business* model and firm strategy, while ensuring the business remains viable and profitable. Finally, companies must avoid limiting their social actions to responsive CSR that is disconnected from its strategy and that does not benefit both society and business.

In the view of Claudio Muruzábal, president of SAP for Europe, Middle East, and Africa: "Ensuring that a company's CSR initiatives are closely aligned to its strategy is important to deliver value to a company's multiple stakeholders, including customers, business partners and employees. A strong alignment across the trifecta of sustainability, diversity and purpose is key to business success."[19]

Corporations must also strive to integrate investors into the conversation of shared value strategies. The failure to integrate shared value into corporate strategy has also resulted in communication gaps between corporates and investors in regard to the environmental, social, and governance information. Investors focus on company's long-term value creation plans and the reception of rigorous and credible information to support risk assessments, and corporations tend to fail in the delivery of this kind of information to investors. What investors are looking for is to understand corporations' sustainable long-term value creation strategies and the related risks. Companies need to articulate their strategies around key issues like talent development and sustainability and show investors how these actions allow them to remain competitive; this will ensure credibility with investors. Corporations must embed environmental, social, and governance factors into their strategy and risk discussions with investors. This discussion must show investors a value creation story that allows for the management of environmental, social, and

---

[19] Email correspondence from Claudio Muruzábal, May 24, 2021.

governance (ESG) issues and mitigation of risks, shaping the narrative around corporate brands and practices.[20]

Overall, moving from a shareholder to a stakeholder primacy mindset is the first step for a company to incorporate a shared value philosophy into its strategy. Throughout the evolution of corporate strategy, companies have moved from focusing solely on shareholders' interests to delving into philanthropic efforts, to establishing formal CSR practices and metrics, to finally more and more firms fully incorporating a shared value mindset into their strategy. Figure 3.4 summarizes the role of business in society.

In sum, considering a wider range of interests and moving from focusing on short-term gains to focusing on long-term value and fully incorporating shared value into a company's strategic thinking is a process that must permeate all activities and all individuals involved in the company. By doing so, companies can take advantage of their resources and capabilities to achieve economic gains while simultaneously addressing social issues and interests of multiple stakeholders. To conclude this chapter, we present insights from company leaders who have moved past shareholder primacy into a shared value creation philosophy.

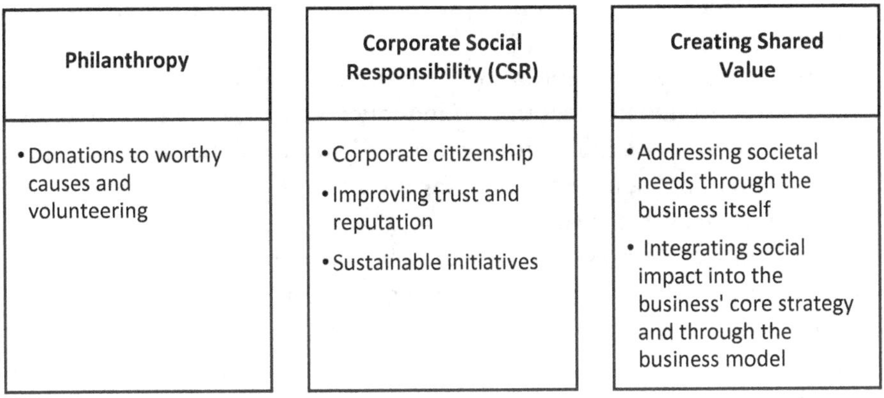

Philanthropy	Corporate Social Responsibility (CSR)	Creating Shared Value
• Donations to worthy causes and volunteering	• Corporate citizenship • Improving trust and reputation • Sustainable initiatives	• Addressing societal needs through the business itself • Integrating social impact into the business' core strategy and through the business model

Fig. 3.4 The role of business in society

[20] PricewaterhouseCoopers. (n.d.). ESG Governance: Understanding the issues, the perspectives and the path forward. Retrieved July 15, 2020, from https://www.pwc.com/us/en/services/governance-insights-center/library/esg-environmental-social-governance-reporting.html.

Shared Value Leaders[21]

FSG, a consulting firm guiding business and foundation leaders in their understanding of how to create social impact, discussed three common traits found in shared value leaders from different organizations and what they think is crucial in creating shared values. These CEOs' insights provide great advice and useful information on the implementation of shared value across companies.

Carolyn Miles, president and CEO of Save the Children, mentions the importance of having two bottom lines: one focused on social outcomes. The other focused on a business outcome. She mentions that developing plans with these two in mind can have powerful results that leverage the organizational skills while addressing important social issues. She warns that companies must be willing to be patient and stick with these strategies for years rather than expecting quick results.

Ole Kjerkegaard Nielsen, director of corporate sustainability at Novo Nordisk, disentangles the meaning of shared value. "S" includes seeing the value leaks in your business interactions. "H" involves harnessing the creative power in the organization. "A" means aligning with social needs. "R" involves reaching out to partners who see the opportunity and share the problem. "E" is related to engaging in partnerships. "D" involves driving the change and capturing the impact.

Mark Thain, vice-president of social innovation at Barclays, mentions that creating shared value involves unlearning much of what we know about our current business models. This involves creating unconventional partnerships and implementing new ways of doing business. He emphasizes that the rewards of shared value are enormous, but that the barriers are equally high.

Allan Pamba, vice-president for East Africa of GlaxoSmithKline, recommends taking a moment to empathize with key stakeholders; this allows to learn from them and to put oneself in their shoes. He mentions that company leader must try to look at the organization through the lens of stakeholders' eyes. This exercise will provide insights on how to be a better partner to your stakeholders. Pamba emphasizes that when implemented in a sound manner, shared value should deliver a competitive *edge*. *Companies* that do so will be at the cutting edge of change, although it will feel riskier and even disadvantageous in the competitive business environment at first.

---

[21] Peterson, K. (2015, September 17). Advice from 4 Shared Value Leaders. Retrieved July 06, 2020, from https://www.fsg.org/blog/advice-4-shared-value-leaders.

What Type of Capitalism?[22]

More recently, the World Economic Forum has been debating the trade-off between all these concepts, releasing what has been known as the Davos Manifesto. It centers on the debate over what type of capitalism we should have if we want to sustain our economic system for future generations. As such, three models are presented: "shareholder capitalism," which aligns with our concepts of "shareholder value" (i.e., corporation's primary goal is to maximize profits), "state capitalism," where the government sets the direction of the economy (e.g., China), and "stakeholder capitalism," which is aligned with our concepts of "stakeholder value" and the M2W principles.

In this chapter we have presented the fundamental differences between the concepts of shareholders and stakeholders as they apply to the main idea presented in this book regarding the required shift in organizations to make shared value, as the core of the M2W principles, a business imperative. The evolution of these concepts, as well as the different perspectives taken on their influence in business, will be developed in the remainder of the book.

---

[22] https://www.weforum.org/agenda/2019/12/why-we-need-the-davos-manifesto-for-better-kind-of-capitalism/.

4

M2W and Globalization

This chapter centers around the role globalization has played in normalizing, or at least in setting expectations for better living standards around the world. David Brooks presented this statement in an op-ed in *The New York Times:* "The percentage of people in the world living on $1 a day has declined by 80 percent since 1970s, adjusting for inflation. That's the greatest increase in human possibility in human history. The primary cause is globalized capitalism."[1] While the flow of goods, labor, and capital has contributed to the increase in welfare, globalization is also associated with some costs. Inequality between countries has been decreasing, but inequality *within* countries has worsened. The wage and income gaps between rural and urban areas are dramatic, especially in less developed nations. For example, workers in Nairobi and Bangkok can earn four times more than those in the countryside.[2] In Brazil, the per capita income in São Paulo state is six times more than the nation's three poorest states.[3] Therefore, the movement of goods, labor, and capital requires some vigilance in practice, increasing the need for shared value to become a cornerstone of all corporations.

---

[1] David Brooks, "Capitalism for the Masses," *The New York Times,* February 20, 2014.
[2] Knoema statistical database.
[3] Ibid.

Globalization as a Catalyst for Shared Value

The world is a more interconnected and interdependent place because of globalization, and, as a result, shared value has also been "globalized." Globalization is now changing and redefining the way companies compete, where they compete, and the regions and countries where workers are being benefited by such economic activity.

It is important to dispense with two unfortunate myths that have garnered widespread belief: globalization is a late twentieth-century phenomenon, and it is withering, for both political and economic reasons. To address the first myth, we in the West believe that the birth of globalization took place in the late fifteenth century when Spanish, Portuguese, British, and Dutch explorers sailed to the New World and around the Cape of Good Hope; however, that is not the case. As Yale historian Valerie Hansen notes in her extensive opus titled *The Year 1000,* most trade in the early 1000s resembled that of the twentieth century. People living in China could buy sandalwood tables from Java, ivory figurines from Africa, and amber vials from the Baltic region.[4]

The second myth—that globalization is dying—is not validated by fact. There are myriad of ways in which globalization has been changing.[5] Among the most prominent are those dealing with trade in goods and services, labor, research and development, and the regulation of trade. For example, cross-border scientific collaboration in the quest to develop a coronavirus vaccine provides a compelling case for global connectedness. Different countries have collaborated (not only financially) for the development of the vaccine, and in September of 2021 there were over 67 vaccine candidates in various stages of clinical trials around the world.[6] Cross-border internet traffic jumped nearly 50 percent from mid-2019 to mid-2020, twice the annual rates seen in the previous three years, and trade overall is running just 3 to 4 percent below pre-pandemic levels according to the WTO. While global trade in merchandise goods may be on a downward slope, trade in services, including financial services, is on the upswing, and data have become the new shipping container.[7]

---

[4] Valerie Hansen, *The Year 1000—When Explorers Connected the World and Globalization Began*, New York: Scribner, 2020.

[5] Five hidden ways that globalization is changing (2019). Retrieved July 21, 2020, from https://www.mckinsey.com/featured-insights/innovation-and-growth/five-hidden-ways-that-globalization-is-changing.

[6] https://www.cnet.com/how-to/coronavirus-vaccine-pfizer-moderna-and-how-many-vaccine-doses-are-coming-in-2020/?utm_source=morning_brew.

[7] Gillian Tett, "Reports of Globalisation's death are greatly exaggerated," *Financial Times,* December 3, 2020.

Before 2007, countries were exporting a higher share of the goods they produced. Now, global exports as a share of output have decreased. Accordingly, multinationals who ship a majority of their exports to their foreign affiliates have seen a drop in their share of global profits, while their foreign direct investment (also a platform for import-export trade) has tumbled from 3.5 percent of global GDP in 2007 to 1.3 percent in 2018.[8] This is a reflection of the development of emerging economies like China, which are now consuming a larger proportion of the goods they produce. The volume of trade growth has also slowed down, and the United Nations Conference on Trade and Development (UNCTAD) predicts that the volume of global merchandise trade will fall by 5.6 percent in 2020 compared with 2019, while trade in services—typically a better performer for more advanced economies—could fall by 15.4 percent compared to a year earlier.[9] This is surprising and unfortunate since many service sector industries such as telecoms and IT have been growing twice and, in some cases, even three times as fast as trade in goods.

As for labor costs, they have become a less important determinant of trade flows. The majority of goods traded used to move from low-wage to high-wage countries, but now only less than a quarter of the world's trade follows this pattern.[10] Other factors such as access to natural resources, skilled labor, infrastructure, and proximity to customers have become more important in determining trade flows.

R&D and innovations have gained significant importance in the global economy, with companies in different sectors investing heavily in intangible assets and intellectual property. Among the top spenders are Samsung, Alphabet, Volkswagen, Microsoft, Huawei, Intel, and Apple. Collectively, they invest over $93 billion into research and development.[11] This trend will continue to significantly favor developed countries where intellectual property protection is enforced more vigorously, access to highly skilled labor is available, and innovation ecosystems and clusters are common.

The regionalization of trade has increased as well, meaning that trade has become more concentrated within specific geographical areas. This trend has been most visible in the European Union and the Asia-Pacific region, but is also significant in Latin America. Intraregional trade in Latin America is 21.7

---

[8] Jeffrey Feffer, "'Slowbalisation': Will the slowing global economy be a boon or bane?," *Business-Standard*, August 21, 2019.

[9] UNCTAD, "Covid-19 drives large international trade declines in 2020," December 9, 2020.

[10] This would seem counter-intuitive, but the explanation is that an increasing amount of merchandise trade consists of higher value products (that many countries cannot manufacture) while lower value-added goods are manufactured *and* distributed locally rather than exported.

[11] Christo Petrov, *Top R&D Spenders: The Biggest Investors of 2020*, Spendmenot blog, August 3, 2020.

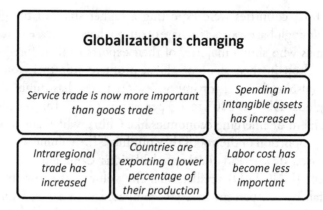

Fig. 4.1 The new globalization

percent, in Asia approximately 59 percent and in Europe 69 percent.[12] This increase is a reflection of companies prioritizing speed when it comes to market goods and services and proximity for customers. The latter reflects growth in the middle-class demographic and greater expenditures among the lower classes. Figure 4.1 summarizes the key features of the "new" globalization[13].

Shared Value and a New Era of Globalization

Globalization is, in general terms, a good thing, leading to an increase in wealth and knowledge. Despite this, it has faced immense criticism since its inception, and some of this criticism is justified. In particular, globalization's detractors argue that it has caused loss of jobs, deterioration of the environment, and widening of the gap between the rich and the poor. For example, the US trade deficit with China resulted in the loss of 3.4 million US jobs between 2001 (when China was admitted to the WTO) and 2018.[14] It is an undeniable and unfortunate reality that the benefits of globalization are not always spread equally and fairly, causing this phenomenon to ultimately harm some communities. These changes have created a fresh set of challenges and

---

[12] UN Economic Commission on Latin America and the Caribbean statistics; Dhruv Gandhi, "Increasing intra-regional trade in Africa," The Brookings Institution, *Africa in Focus*, February 22, 2019.

[13] Based on five hidden ways that globalization is changing. (2019). Retrieved July 21, 2020, from https://www.mckinsey.com/featured-insights/innovation-and-growth/five-hidden-ways-that-globalization-is-changing.

[14] Robert E. Scott and Zane Mokhiber, "Growing China trade deficit cost 3.7 million American jobs between 2001 and 2018," *Working Economic Policy Brief*, Economic Policy Institute, January 20, 2020.

opportunities for companies. The new globalization has brought to the forefront the benefits and costs associated with it and the need for companies to adopt a shared value approach as part of their strategy. Overall, there is consensus that globalization has been very positive, but not without an implicit cost. As presented extensively in our previous book, rather than discussing the positives and negatives of globalization, a more relevant question is how to take advantage of globalization. Shared value has allowed companies to take advantage of the benefits globalization provides, while the M2W guarantees a more sustainable development. Figure 4.2 summarizes the positive and negative sides of globalization.[15]

It is no surprise then that this current era is faced with an economic and social climate characterized by protectionist policies, populist political groups, anti-globalization, and anti-immigration movements, not to mention increasing concerns about inequality and environmental issues. Corporations are facing groundbreaking innovations that disrupt the way in which goods and services are produced and distributed. New technologies have resulted in the

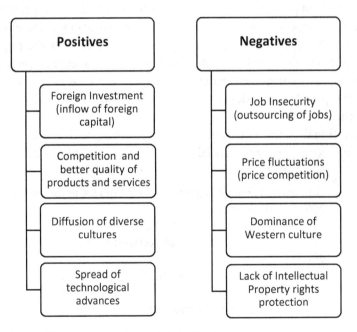

Fig. 4.2 The positives and negatives of globalization

[15] Ltd. (March 18, 2019). Positive and negative effects of globalization. Retrieved July 21, 2020, from https://www.ukessays.com/essays/economics/positive-and-negative-effects-of-globalisation-for-business-economics-essay.php.

proliferation of lean start-ups, the rethinking of new and more agile business models, and the disruption of entire industries. These innovations have also impacted the labor market, with automation and artificial intelligence reducing the amount of human labor involved in different stages of the value chain.[16]

Additionally, macroeconomic imbalances have been growing. The 2008 financial crisis resulted in the bailout of financial firms and an overall distrust of the global economic order. Liquidity injections into financial markets resulted in a significant increase of government debt, while also bringing forth wage stagnation for a wide range of employees and cutbacks to workers' benefits like health insurance, welfare, and retirement. Consequently, less educated and less skilled workers saw reductions in their standard of living. The economic growth and productivity of many countries saw slow improvements and, in some cases, remained stagnant. Figure 4.3 captures some of the key impacts of the 2008-2009 recession.

This situation created significant economic imbalances and more pronounced inequality gaps. In 2018, the Organisation for Economic Co-operation and Development (OECD) reported that income inequality was at its highest point during the past century in member countries, with the wealthiest members of the population having an average income that is approximately nine times that of the poorest 10 percent of the population. The relative and absolute Gini index (in which 0 represents complete equality and 1 represents complete inequality) indicate that inequality has exploded during the past few decades, creating an environment of social unrest and discontent.[17]

Unquestionably, the new landscape of globalization is ridden with challenges of economic and social inequality, decreased social mobility,

- The national unemployment rate **rose from 5%** in December 2007 to **10%** in October 2009
- GDP **declined by 4.3%** from 2007-2009
- Mass Layoffs involved **over 320,000** workers in just February of 2009
- **3M** households were for eclosed on from 2005-2009
- In 2007 The Dow Jones Industrial Average **declined by 50%**
- The S&P 500 **declined by over 55%**

Fig. 4.3 The great recession in numbers

[16] Pezzuto, I. (2019). Overcoming the Challenges of the New Era of Globalization Creating Shared Value. Retrieved July 21, 2020, from https://www.thestreet.com/economonitor/europe/overcoming-the-challenges-of-the-new-era-of-globalization-creating-shared-value.

[17] Inequality. (2017). Retrieved July 21, 2020, from http://www.oecd.org/social/inequality.htm.

environmental and sustainability issues, and geopolitical pressures and tensions. In order for the world to experience the benefits of globalization, corporations must operate under a mindset of shared value whereby social issues are treated as a source of economic opportunity, differentiation, and competitiveness for business rather than as an additional cost or social obligation. By adopting shared value as a cornerstone of business, new opportunities (as well as more aggressive competition) are likely to increase. This can ultimately result in a boost for innovation, R&D investment, collaboration, knowledge sharing, and technological improvement, while also increasing economic growth and prosperity.

Current conditions beckon immediate action via the creation of policies and reforms that advocate for the well-being and improvement of conditions for all stakeholders. However, it must be acknowledged that they cannot be tackled by individual nations and governments alone, regardless of how powerful they may be. It requires a response from institutions and organizations, including individual companies. Such reforms require a new approach to cooperation, a clear purpose, and an engagement in the undertaking of social and sustainability issues. Companies must restructure their way of thinking and operating to reflect a consciousness and shared responsibility of the issues faced by the world.

Focusing on social issues has the potential to unite and create relationships between companies, NGOs, and governments, while fostering common goals toward addressing social issues. Embracing the shared value approach is a necessity in this new era of globalization that is ridden with a myriad of social and economic challenges. As cited previously, the concept of shared value sets a way of thinking in which corporations can create measurable impact for society without compromising its competitiveness; this idea of shared value resets the boundaries of capitalism by connecting companies' performance and success with the improvement of societal issues. Porter and Kramer state that shared value has the power to unlock innovation and growth in companies, all the while reconnecting economic and community success, a concept that has been lost in light of the predominant short-term mindset and narrow managerial thinking.[18]

---

[18] Porter, M. E., and M. R. Kramer. "Creating Shared Value. Harvard Business Review, January-February" (2011).

Exploiting Differences in the World to Calibrate Shared Value

Due to a highly interconnected and interdependent global business environment, firms wishing to engage in international business can find exciting and dynamic opportunities. This is especially true for businesses that are highly innovative, competitive, and willing to engage in knowledge-sharing networks and the implementation of smart technologies. At the core of today's dynamic business environment are adaptable and revolutionary business models that employ digital transformation. In order to remain competitive, businesses must be willing to embrace the disruption of their industries and new groundbreaking technologies.

Companies are faced with additional challenges in the new global economy in addition to the ever-changing business environment. Global economic growth and increased worldwide trade do not necessarily result in increased benefits for all of humanity and the environment. Therefore, managers in a globalized world need to ensure benefits are not reaped by shareholders only. The aim should be to increase the well-being of all society and reduce poverty. Even for firms that embrace a shared value approach, implementing these policies worldwide can be difficult. Globalization might not create the same "shared value" principles in different parts of the world. The idea of tackling societal issues without compromising performance is universal; however, the implementation is different because of varying factors such as diversity, local cultures, and many other soft (i.e., managerial) and hard (i.e., structural) differences between regions and countries.[19] The same can be said regarding the ideas of ownership and accountability that are part of the quintet of M2W. The two concepts might have different degrees of intensity as a function of the varying factors previously mentioned, but they are needed for the required shared responsibility and the sustainable benefits of the M2W principles.

Globalization and Cultural Diversity

The effects of globalization on culture and cultural diversity have been a source of debate for decades. Technological advancements have enabled globalization by decreasing international boundaries, due to improvements in transportation and communication which have facilitated the movement of goods and

---

[19] Blair, T. (2016, September 20). What can values do for globalization? Retrieved July 21, 2020, from https://insights.som.yale.edu/insights/what-can-values-do-for-globalization.

services. Technology has opened cultures to a new arena of interconnectedness and increased information availability. This creates a dichotomy in terms of the relationship of globalization and cultural diversity. On the one side, globalization can stimulate the creation of a collective identity fostered by increased socialization and mobilization of people across the globe. On the other side, globalization can be detrimental in terms of generating a loss of group identity.

In light of the aforementioned, globalization seems to have both positive and negative implications for cultural diversity, which can exacerbate existing global issues. Globalization can result in what some detractors deem as a monoculture, in which countries and cultures seem to merge into a single identity, where tastes and preferences converge, and groups lack autonomy or a sense of cultural identity. These is especially true for Generations X, Y, and Z whose taste preferences, vocational aspirations, and lifestyle predilections converge, regardless of whether the individual is from Buenos Aires, Botswana, the Balkans, or Baltimore. Supporters of globalization claim that, on the contrary, this phenomenon brings distinct cultures into contact with one another in a harmonious manner in which individuals can engage in smooth interactions despite differing political forces and governments.[20]

Positive Effects on Culture

Globalization can create heightened levels of information sharing through technology, allowing for increased self-representation of various cultures and providing cultural groups a platform via which to expand the knowledge through their stories and heritage. Apps and language programs such as Babbel, Rosetta Stone, and Duolingo, along with e-learning venues like National Geographic, are dynamic vehicles for educational enlightenment and cross-cultural understanding. Additionally, communication tools have provided previously unseen cultures a voice on relevant issues, as well as increased awareness of their identities, enabling the preservation of their cultural artifacts, symbols, and overall cultural property. Having control over their own images allows for these different cultures to avoid misrepresentation and to manage their cultural property appropriately.

Globalization has actually allowed the revitalization and preservation of cultures, with technology empowering the existence of distinctive cultures and enabling groups to raise their voices on global and local issues. More

---

[20] Globalization and its Effect on Cultural Diversity (n.d.). Retrieved July 21, 2020, from http://etec.ctlt. ubc.ca/510wiki/Globalization_and_its_Effect_on_Cultural_Diversity.

cultures can now come together through the dispersion of products like food (sriracha sauce from Thailand and Vietnam), movies (*Parasite*, a South Korean Academy Award winner), and music (Shakira from Colombia, Daddy Yankee from Puerto Rico). Customers have become acquainted with cultural expressions from all around the globe to which they would otherwise never have been exposed were it not for globalization and the international flow of goods and services. In addition, the migration of individuals from one country to another in search of job opportunities and the hiring of multinational corporations in diverse markets have allowed people to come into contact with and appreciate cultures other than their own.[21]

Negative Effects on Culture

Unfortunately, there are some cultural drawbacks to globalization as well. The interconnectedness and interdependence resulting from globalization have resulted in unprecedented access to cultures all around the world. However, without proper monitoring and vigilance, these increased interactions can result in a loss of cultural identity, misrepresentation, stereotyping, and the lack of protection for intellectual property. In the case of multinational corporations, globalization has enabled these firms to have an immense influence on societal values and consumer culture, as well as the exploitation of markets and workers. Note the worldwide appeal of brands such as Nike, Polo, BMW, and Samsung. Increased exposure to media and a wider range of products and services can ultimately dissolve local cultural influences on consumer tastes and preferences.

Most critics argue that globalization tends to encourage Western ideals and create a homogenous set of beliefs. Technologies and gadgets are generally determined by a dominant Western culture and are commercialized to the masses, creating a worldwide desire to obtain products such as Echo Dot, Sonos, and Fitbit, even among individuals who are not financially equipped to obtain them. Additionally, education systems in which e-learning has become increasingly common focus on the cognitive styles of a dominant Western culture and reflect its ideals and philosophies. This poses challenges for populations such as sub-Saharan Africa that lack access to these technologies,; there is an overarching, incorrect assumption that the values and ideas of Western cultures are suitable for developing economies. Furthermore, globalization has enabled access to intellectual and cultural property. This is evident in many products appropriating symbols, rituals, and other artifacts that

---

[21] IBID

are considered integral parts of cultural heritage, oftentimes misrepresenting these cultures in the process. The commercialization of products that utilize cultural property fails to acknowledge this as theft that has been enabled by globalization, which has caused such appropriation to become difficult to monitor and prevent.[22]

Globalization—M2W in Human Resource Management

Globalization has enabled firms to have operations around the world, creating the necessity to rethink how they manage employees from diverse cultural backgrounds and experiences. Multinational corporations are now, more than ever, facing the complexities of cross-cultural management: with locations across the global marketplace, more and more corporations are hiring employees from diverse cultural backgrounds and distinct patterns of behaviors. Despite Western culture, language, and behavior setting the patterns for international business, top management must still remain cognizant of distinct regional attitudes, beliefs, and ideas that can impact productivity, sense of ownership, and efficiency of workers. However, most firms do not spend a lot of time planning how to manage their employees; this can harm business performance. Because the primary interest of employers is to hire and retain skilled, talented workers and motivate them to be their most resilient, effective, and productive selves, multinational corporations must establish a set of best practices when it comes to managing their human resources.

Setting standards in human resource management that can be applied globally can help firms establish solutions to complex issues that may arise, developing what is known as a global mindset. Top management teams need to think about human resource management as a strategic issue, in which long-term plans need to be established in order to achieve specific outcomes. As organizations expand their global reach and become more complex, it becomes necessary to think about human resource management standards that can anticipate issues that are likely to arise in a global business arena that is more unstable, turbulent, and highly competitive. For businesses to survive, they must establish plans of action and the appropriate accountability and set of metrics to better understand and develop talented employees, who are

---

[22] Globalization and its Effect on Cultural Diversity (n.d.). Retrieved July 21, 2020, from http://etec.ctlt. ubc.ca/510wiki/Globalization_and_its_Effect_on_Cultural_Diversity.

perhaps one of the most critical assets for multinational companies facing complex global problems.[23]

Global vs. Glocal—Is M2W Different?

Progress toward sustainability and societal progress requires corporations to focus both globally and locally. Tangible improvements toward sustainability and prosperity can only be achieved by developing actionable strategies at the regional and national levels. Why? Because even if countries claim policies and movement toward sustainability and development, no real gains can be obtained if certain areas within a country still struggle with poverty and environmental degradation. Failing to think locally results in increased disparities around the world.[24] This is especially true in the case of developed and developing regions both between and within countries.

For example, smallholder farmers (i.e., small farmers who may own and control the land they farm), who at times have been ignored by corporations, constitute an essential part of the global food system. According to the Food and Agriculture Organization of the United Nations, they account for approximately 80 percent of farms in Latin America and the Caribbean region. This is important because Latin America and the Caribbean are two of the world's leading regions when it comes to food production and exporting, due to their natural resources, wealth, and growing agricultural industry primarily made up of family-owned farms. Unfortunately, the region has continued to experience social challenges such as extreme intergenerational poverty and hunger. This brings to light the need for action from both the public and private sectors in order to spur economic growth and reduce the vulnerability of this population. Smaller farmers face challenges associated with reduced access to markets and to financing, lower technical support and productivity, vulnerability to market volatility, middlemen, and a reduction of suitable land as a result of climate change.[25]

Another important example of the need for balancing global and local actions is represented in China, a country that, despite experiencing rapid economic growth during the last decade, still faces enormous disparities

---

[23] Purcell, D. (n.d.). Globalization and the Role of Standardization. Retrieved July 21, 2020, from http://www.strategicstandards.com/files/SES2000.pdf.

[24] All global sustainability is local (2020, January 01). Retrieved July 21, 2020, from https://www.sciencedaily.com/releases/2020/01/200101144029.htm.

[25] Food and nutrition security in Latin America and the Caribbean (n.d.). Retrieved July 21, 2020, from http://www.fao.org/americas/prioridades/seguridad-alimentaria/en/.

between developed regions and those that are still developing. Even when progress is being made, it is important to examine what is happening at the local and regional levels in order to detect where attention and resources should be directed so as to achieve more even development.[26] Smallholder farms are some of the most valuable suppliers in global value chains and should, therefore, be brought to the spotlight when it comes to creating shared value locally.

M2W and the Supply Chain

In order to put the shared value approach into action, Porter and Kramer have identified distinct ways through which companies can create shared value; one of these focuses on the productivity in the value chain. They argue that corporations have often addressed their supply chain with a narrow focus, failing to find congruence between productivity along the value chain and societal progress. Approaching the value chain through a shared-focus approach is necessary to ensure cost reductions along its different activities while simultaneously reducing its footprint.

Managing the supply chain in the current global business environment, characterized by market uncertainties and demand volatility, requires managers to focus on cost efficiency, integration, and transparency. In order to achieve this, managers must review their entire supply chain from beginning to end, from suppliers to all the way to the final customer. Only by doing this can corporations achieve a flexible and competitive supply chain that is well equipped to address the current turbulent global business environment while ensuring practices that drive societal well-being.[27]

It is worth noting that an increasing number of corporations have recently made initial efforts to address issues like sustainability through corporate social responsibility (CSR) programs, mainly due to pressures and expectations from various stakeholders such as NGOs and customers. Unfortunately, most of these initiatives have failed to take advantage of interdependencies and opportunities that can have a stronger impact on sustainability.

Supply chain performance is closely intertwined with sustainability, and in order to create shared value, managers must enhance productivity without falling into the trap of short-term reductions that are unsustainable in the long term. This requires a purposeful integration of suppliers, NGOs, local

---

[26] Ibid. (12).

[27] D'heur, M. (2013, September 19). Global supply chains will deliver the shared value revolution. Retrieved July 21, 2020, from https://www.sharedvaluechain.com/global-supply-chains/.

communities, and governments into the discussion in order to tap into different stakeholders' perspectives and find opportunities for improvement. Proactivity allows firms to find a spot where stakeholders' interests are balanced and shared value is achieved.

Corporations evaluating the performance and societal impact of their value chains must find solutions for small suppliers and approach relationships with them as a way to ensure timely and high-quality supplies while also delivering financial benefits to suppliers that support long-term development of these communities. For example, businesses can encourage and assist suppliers in obtaining certifications that can be beneficial to both parties; firms can obtain higher-quality and more sustainably produced inputs, while suppliers can gain access to global markets where consumers expect more sustainably sources products. Standards such as the "Fair Trade Certification" can have a meaningful impact on supplier development while also benefiting firms that purchase from these suppliers, as these certifications are expected to adhere to strict social, environmental, and economic standards that ensure higher quality and sustainable products.[28]

Regarding the two additional elements of ownership and accountability required for M2W, supply chains are the perfect example where shared responsibility is definitely mandatory and easily enforced through ownership and accountability. Ownership is ingrained in the new battleground that requires a "my supply chain versus your supply chain" approach rather than the traditional "my company versus your company." Each member of the supply chain needs to embrace a deep sense of ownership regarding their responsibility in the performance of the entire supply chain. Accountability is implemented through the development of metrics that go beyond intra-company performance to inter-firm coordination.

M2W and Cluster Development

Companies do not operate in a vacuum, and a significant part of their success depends on the local businesses supporting it. Opportunities for innovation and value creation are largely influenced by clusters or geographic concentrations of firms. In essence, a cluster is a collaborative group of interconnected actors (government, academia, and businesses) gathered in a common geographical territory. When one thinks of clusters, Silicon Valley in California,

[28] Rice, P. (n.d.). Spotlight on Smallholders: Creating Shared Value in Global Supply Chains. Retrieved July 21, 2020, from https://agrolac2025.org/spotlight-on-smallholders-creating-shared-value-in-global-supply-chains/.

Greater Boston, and North Carolina's Research Triangle typically come to mind. However, clusters are predominant in all successful regional economies across the globe as illustrated in Fig. 4.4, and include firms, infrastructure, suppliers, distributors, service providers, and institutions that can play an essential role in driving innovation, productivity, and competitiveness.

The interconnectedness of companies, R&D centers, suppliers, service providers, and financial entities creates a dynamic and symbiotic enrollment that all start-ups and later-stage companies, not just established ones, use to innovate and accelerate the development and commercialization of their products and services.

Unfortunately, the existence of certain clusters can systematically result in the infringement or the diminishing of rights and progress for diverse stakeholders. For example, if cluster activities involve the extraction of natural resources and the use of land, their existence can result in the displacement of indigenous communities. Additionally, clusters located in developing nations where law enforcement is weak can violate labor rights and engage in unethical practices including poor working conditions, child labor, gender discrimination, and unfair remuneration. Issues such as these create the need for multinational corporations interested in sourcing from suppliers located in clusters and developing relationships with other businesses located in these clusters to adopt strategies that ensure progress for all stakeholders involved.[29]

- ❖ Taiwan (Hsinchu Park)
- ❖ UK (Silicon Fenn, Cambridge)
- ❖ Netherlands (Technopolis Innovation Park, Delft)
- ❖ Israel (Silicon Wadi, Tel-Aviv)
- ❖ France (Aerospace Valley, Toulouse)
- ❖ Canada (ICT, Waterloo)
- ❖ Chile (Santiago, technology and "Start-upChile")
- ❖ India (Bangalore, IT)
- ❖ Singapore (IT)
- ❖ Brazil (Campinas, IT)
- ❖ U.S. (Albany Technology Valley, NY, nanotechnology)
- ❖ Colombia (Medellin, multi-sector clusters)

Fig. 4.4 Industrial and technology clusters worldwide

---

[29] Federica, N. (2016). Creating genuine shared values in industrial clusters: The contribution of the human rights approach. Retrieved July 21, 2020, from https://www.mesopartner.com/fileadmin/media_center/JMS_Scholarship/JMS-Scholarship-No05.pdf.

Although companies have traditionally used clusters to support their growth, this has been seldom explored from an M2W approach. In doing so, firms can recognize and take advantage of the companies and organizations in geographic proximity to their business interests in order to drive economic and societal development.

The positive features that clusters provide far outweigh the negative ones. The agglomerations foster regional economic development and competitiveness by increasing productivity via improved access to specialized suppliers and access to skills and information. They also stimulate innovation, facilitate production process cycles, and present opportunities for entrepreneurial activity.

Local stakeholders who participate in and are associated with clusters often lack the knowledge regarding best practices in regard to critical issues such as working conditions and sustainability. Multinational businesses that develop relationships with clusters around the world have the opportunity to raise awareness among cluster participants and stakeholders about working and production practices based on international standards. Businesses must set ethical codes of conduct and environmental standards as a requisite to establish business relationships with clusters. By setting these guidelines, organizations involved in clusters can determine long-term strategies that enable its members to achieve sustainability goals and boost prosperity among its stakeholders and local communities. This involves investing in the promotion and training of local stakeholders that, although costly, can increase the efficiency and competitiveness of the cluster, generating a win-win situation.[30]

For example, the cooperation between INNOVACC (Catalan Association of Pig Meat Sector Innovation) and CWP (Catalan Water Partnership) from Spain adopted a shared value approach focused on sustainable water consumption and treatment practices which increased the efficiency and competitiveness of the local firms while simultaneously enabling better environmental conditions for local communicates. Evidence from this initiative showed that sustainable practices lead to economic benefits by optimizing resource consumption, reducing costs, and achieving overall environmental improvements for local communities.[31] The allocation of responsibilities and the definition of the correct interorganization metrics satisfy the conditions of ownership and accountability required by the M2W approach.

---

[30] Pezzi, A., & Amores, X. (2020, July 13). Shared value through clusters. Retrieved July 21, 2020, from https://www.clustercollaboration.eu/news/shared-value-through-clusters.

[31] Marse, M., Sierra, M., & Roig, O. (n.d.) Generating shared value through clusters. Living examples in Catalonia. Retrieved July 21, 2020, from http://redvalorcompartido.com/TEXTOS/SharedvalueandClusters_Tci.pdf.

Overall, clusters provide firms with intangible resources such as networking with companies from different stages of the value chain and with other organizations including universities and research centers, increasing the likelihood of potential collaboration and cooperation in projects that can create economic and societal value. Additionally, inter-cluster relationships create opportunities for the development of projects and initiatives across different clusters that can target shared value goals associated with employee well-being, community development, and efficient use of natural resources. Companies within, across, and adjacent to clusters have growing opportunities to come together to define strategies that prioritize welfare, environment, and progress while simultaneously improving cluster competitiveness. Figure 4.5 portrays clusters as an ideal environment for shared value[32]:

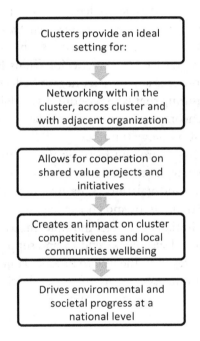

Fig. 4.5 Clusters and shared value

[32] Marse, M., Sierra, M., & Roig, O. (n.d.) Generating shared value through clusters. Living examples in Catalonia. Retrieved July 21, 2020, from http://redvalorcompartido.com/TEXTOS/Sharedva lueandClusters_Tci.pdf.

Please note that these clusters will be incomplete unless M2W is also incorporated in its design. It is here that the accountability and ownership required by all stakeholders play a key role in closing the loop along the lines of the elements discussed in previous chapters.

By its very nature, globalization makes the implementation of M2W both a challenge and an opportunity based on the different trade-offs presented in this chapter. However, when properly implemented (i.e., by incorporating the quintet of shared values), it offers vast opportunities for truly enlarging the size of the potential pie in a long-term sustainable manner.

The M2W paradigm, recognizing the world as interconnected and interdependent, is anchored to a moral compass by which ethical considerations reign supreme. In cross-border transactions, companies must be aware of the impacts of their actions to ensure they are positive for both the firm's shareholders and the broad array of stakeholders. The most obvious pertain to environmental and labor activities—two arenas that have grown in importance in structuring trade agreements such as the USMCA and the Comprehensive and Progressive Agreement for Trans-Pacific Partnership (CPTPP). While such concerns aim to deter negative effects, such as harming the environment and ensuring that labor conditions are fair and humane, the M2W paradigm also encompasses proactive initiatives such as corporate knowledge-sharing and technology transfer.

In summary, the challenges brought forth by globalization require managers to think about new strategies to effectively and proactively deal with market uncertainties and demand volatility. One way is to focus on managing supply chains in a more transparent and cost-efficient way with a clear global mindset. This requires initiatives across multiple industries and actors to ensure a more integrated and sustainable end-to-end supply chain, from component acquisition processes to all the way to product launch. Another proactive way to create shared value is to focus on cluster development by pushing forward initiatives that take advantage of complementarities and similarities of cluster members. By focusing on supply chain management and cluster development, companies can make significant advances in moving toward a "stakeholder mentality" with an M2W approach, in which economic and societal progress go hand in hand.

5

M2W and Competitiveness

The relationship between shared value and competitiveness is often overlooked; yet shared value can play a vital role in a firm's ability to compete effectively by enlarging its ecosystem and considering all members of the supply chain. Shared value increases the size of the pie for everyone involved by creating synergies, and by taking a more socially conscious approach to business, firms can ultimately increase their economic profit and their competitiveness. Figure 5.1 presents some of the most competitive companies—customer-centric ones— that embrace shared value.

In this chapter, we explore how some companies develop a competitive advantage by taking the lead on shared value. Clearly, some industries are better suited to take advantage of shared value, but in all, the opportunity of developing the M2W approach through the shared responsibility that it conveys generates a sustainable advantage, both financially and operationally.

What Industries Can Benefit the Most from Shared Value?

Unfortunately, a great many corporations are saddled with a bad reputation in regard to creating value for society. We think about companies in the energy industry contributing to air and water pollution, apparel companies reducing costs by using questionable manufacturing practices, and companies in the food industry using unsustainable packaging and farming practices. However, there are firms in all these industries that have found and implemented

Fig. 5.1 Competitive firms that embrace shared value

practices that create value for society and business. We now illustrate the results in some industries.

Food. In the food industry, companies like Nestlé and Mars are proving that shared value creation is possible. Mars, one of the world's leading companies in the manufacture of confectionery, pet food, and other food products, has proven that shared value is possible. This firm has committed to reducing the weight of its packaging by 10 percent, claiming that a small reduction can make a big difference when it comes to the environmental impact.[1] In addition to this, reducing their packaging will also have positive implications on shipping costs and the optimization of the value chain. By making changes in their sustainability practices, Mars is also ensuring sustainability in their growth, creating shared value and positive externalities of production. Nestlé, on the other hand, has focused on a few key societal issues: enhancing the quality of life and overall health of individuals and families using their products, reaching zero environmental impact of their processes, and improving the livelihoods of the communities directly connected to their operations. In the environmental domain, Nestlé has reduced the use of water resources and cut back the use of plastic. In doing so, they have created more

---

[1] *Sustainable Packaging*, Mars, Inc. 2019 https://www.mars.com/sustainability-plan/healthy-planet/sustainable-packaging.

environmentally sustainable practices while establishing more cost-efficient and productive production practices.[2,3]

Grocery Stores/ Supermarkets. Another company leading the way in the incorporation of shared value is Whole Foods Markets, the well-known supermarket chain with annual sales exceeding $16 billion.[4] Its focus on natural, fresh, organic, and healthy items has not only proven profitable by catering to customers with specialized nutritional requirements and educated consumers who are passionate about health and wellness, but has also fostered its success by creating societal benefits. Each Whole Foods store carries local produce and has the authority to contract with local farmers and provide these suppliers with low-interest loans. By creating these partnerships with local farmers, Whole Foods can deliver high-quality products while supporting community development and ensuring sustainable practices of their suppliers. In doing so, the company has proven how to successfully tackle societal needs while ensuring sustained profitability and growth.[5]

Insurance. The insurance industry is one in which societal progress and well-being are essential for economic success. This industry inherently benefits society by protecting individuals and companies from adversity. Therefore, when societal conditions improve, it directly benefits and monetizes by decreasing economic, security, health, and other risks. Unfortunately, most companies in the industry have taken a passive stance when it comes to tackling the societal issues that are most likely to affect their business. Companies in the insurance industry must focus on preventing adverse events before they happen and aim to incentivize beneficiaries to take on behavior that reduces risks. A great example of a firm that is implementing actions that create shared value is the South African financial and insurance firm Discovery. Its goal is not only to sell short-term insurance but also to make individuals engage in behavior that increases their health. Discovery uses technology to achieve this, taking advantage of technologies like smartwatches that track health information and use data analytics to facilitate customers with behavior and advice

---

[2] Health & Sustainability Commitments Results in New Report: Mars, Incorporated. (n.d.). Retrieved July 06, 2020, from https://www.mars.com/news-and-stories/press-releases/principles-in-action-2016.

[3] Nestle—Our approach: Creating shared value. (n.d.). Retrieved July 06, 2020, from https://www.nestle.com/csv/what-is-csv.

[4] Russell Redman, "Amazon finishes strong fiscal year with lackluster physical-store sales," *Supermarket News*, January 31, 2020.

[5] Adding a Social Dimension to Strategy. (n.d.). Retrieved July 06, 2020, from https://www.isc.hbs.edu/creating-shared-value/csv-explained/Pages/adding-a-social-dimension-to-strategy.aspx.

that can improve health. The results have yielded decreased mortality and morbidity rates and a reduction in the cost of claims.[6]

Consumer Goods. Unilever, the British-Dutch multinational consumer goods company, has engaged in shared value in several ways. In India, for example, the company has rethought its distribution system by creating a direct-to-home distribution, managed by female entrepreneurs. In doing so, Unilever has been able to reach Indian villages that were once difficult to access while simultaneously providing employment and income opportunities for underprivileged women. This distribution system is called Project Shakti, and it has benefited hundreds of women by providing them with training and skills that can double their income. This system has resulted in increased access to hygiene products for consumers in rural villages and the reduction of diseases by using such products, thereby creating social value. Additionally, by using their abilities to access consumers that were considered difficult to reach, Unilever has not only increased their revenue in India but has also built their brand image in regions where traditional marketing channels and media do not penetrate, resulting in overall economic progress and value creation for the company.[7]

Pharmaceuticals. Pharma companies have an immense potential to grab hold of social issues that are at the core of their business and integrating their strategy and operations to solve these problems. Novartis, a Swiss multinational pharmaceutical company, has found a way to use its resources and capabilities to tackle issues that are aligned with their strategy. It identified an opportunity in selling its pharmaceutical products in rural India where more than 50 percent of the country's population lives. Interestingly, it found that pricing was not the main issue in delivering these products to customers. It was the more predominant lack of health-seeking behavior by individuals and the lack of healthcare providers with adequate training and reliable supply chains that created impediments for Novartis in these regions. They approached these challenges by hiring hundreds of health educators, creating training camps for health providers, and building a distribution system to supply over 50,000 rural clinics. Creating this business model proved essential to Novartis' future, as customers in emerging markets have been growing steadily. The

[6] Ensuring Shared Value: How Insurers Gain Competitive Advantage by Better Addressing Society's Needs. (2020, January 31). Retrieved July 06, 2020, from https://www.sharedvalue.org/resource/insuring-shared-value-how-insurers-gain-competitive-advantage-by-better-addressing-societys-needs/.

[7] Porter, M. E., and M. R. Kramer. "Creating Shared Value. Harvard Business Review, January–February" (2011).

result was access to a vast customer base and an improved level of healthcare for India's rural population.[8]

E-commerce. Massive platforms connecting buyers and sellers around the world can also implement strategies that create shared value. The Alibaba Group, one the most famous Chinese e-commerce sites in the world, is adding value to the community by creating new uses for its map service Auto-navi. Alibaba has added a feature to the Auto-navi service to attract users to travel to economically less developed areas, highlighting the locations of restaurants, stores, gas stations, and other points of interest, in order to draw interest to small towns and countryside villages that are usually overlooked. This feature can help bring economic growth to more remote locations in the country from the influx of visitors while also attracting more customers to use its map service.[9]

Banking and Finance. Recently, microfinance has proven to be a cost-efficient model for shared value, and a way to distribute financial services to small businesses and individuals who would otherwise lack access to these resources. Microfinance can leverage a financial institution's capabilities and strengths to meet previously unserved financial needs in both developing and developed markets. Figure 5.2 provides examples of microlenders around the world.

Rank	Name of Microfinance Institution (Country)	Cost per Borrower (%)	Return on Assets (%)
1	Asa (Bangladesh)	1.17	14.4
2	Bandhan, Society and NBFC (India)	0,70	9.1
3	Banco do Nordeste, Crediamigo (Brazil)	1.52	17.2
4	Fundación Mundial de la Mujer Bucaramanga (Colombia)	3.37	8.5
5	FONDEP Micro-Crédit (Morocco)	2.62	19.2
6	Amhara Credit & Savings Institution (Ethiopia)	3.65	7.9
7	Banco Compartamos SA, Institución de Banca Múltiple (Mexico)	1.80	23.2
8	Assoc. Al Amana for the Promotion of Microenterprises (Morocco)	2.67	4.4
9	Fundación Munda Mujer Papayán (Colombia)	2.45	7.7
10	Fundación WWB Colombia – Cali (Colombia)	3.45	5.2

Fig. 5.2 The top ten microlenders. (Source: The Microfinance Information Exchange; MicroRate; Micro-Credit Rating Intl. Ltd)

[8] Kramer, M. (2012, April 25). Better ways of doing business: Creating Shared Value. Retrieved July 06, 2020, from https://www.theguardian.com/sustainable-business/blog/creating-shared-value-social-progress-profit.

[9] 5 businesses that are creating value for society (2019, September 11). Retrieved July 06, 2020, from http://drivinginnovation.ie.edu/5-businesses-that-are-creating-value-for-society/.

Banks can complement their conventional banking practices by creating banking systems that make small loans to economically depressed individuals and organizations. Among the most notable are Rank Raykat (Indonesia), Banco Real (Brazil), Sogebank (Haiti), Equity Bank (Kenya), and Banco del Pinchincha (Peru). By providing microcredit and financial training to small entrepreneurs, farmers, and artisans, individuals can increase their incomes and their living standard, while financial institutions can increase their customer base and ensure debt collection by using future purchase orders as collateral.[10]

Supply Chains as a Needed Conveyor of Shared Value

The supply chain area has received significant attention given that a company's value chain is affected by societal issues and simultaneously impacts them. Many companies have globalized their supply chain, searching for improvements in competitiveness. Because societal problems can create costs in the firm's value chain, this area has received a lot of attention. Particularly notable has been the problem related to the working conditions in sweatshops in the apparel industry, especially in Central America and Southeast Asia. Some of the biggest name brands have been cited, fined, and boycotted due to their unfair labor practices.

Poor practices and inefficient use of resources in the value chain are costly to businesses. Thus, this creates an incentive for companies to find congruence between societal progress and productivity in the value chain. This begins by companies evaluating their value chains from an efficiency perspective, and subsequently exploring ways of enhancing their productivity without falling into the trap of short-term reductions that are unsustainable in the long term. For example, significant improvement in environmental performance can be achieved through marginal investments in technology that can result in cost reductions in the long run through a more efficient use of resources and decreased waste. Two examples are Texterra of Canada that delivers advanced gasification systems to self-generate clean, low-cost heat and power using waste fuels, and Blue Sphere, an Israeli company that develops waste-to-energy plants that generate biofuels from food and farm waste.

Companies can transform their value chain and create shared value by focusing on areas such as procurement, resource use, distribution practices,

---

[10] Porter, M., & Kramer, M. (2011). Creating Shared Value. Harvard Business Review.

and energy.[11] In the words of Romaine Seguin, president of Global Freight Forwarding for UPS: "Companies that have the best relationships with all participants in the value chain will be in the best position to perform well in the chaotic times of uncertainty with the supply chain."[12]

In reality, competition between firms has evolved into a new battlefield where the focus is no longer on *my company against your company* but on *my supply chain against your supply chain.* By servicing as conduits linking all players in a business, supply chains provide an opportunity for firms to move beyond a shareholder approach, to a stakeholder mindset. This results in a shift from the optimization of individual players to the optimization of the entire ecosystem. In doing so, firms create synergies in the entire chain that can ultimately generate competitiveness for the firm.[13] According to Garner, some of the very best firms that embody the kind of synergies that ignite competitiveness are Cisco, Colgate-Palmolive, Johnson and Johnson, and Schneider Electric.[14]

By working closely on optimizing the forward flow and reverse flow of the supply chain (i.e., acquisition and inventory management, packaging, assembly, warehousing, internal and external transportation), companies can create shared value for numerous stakeholders. Working closely with suppliers and the entire hierarchy of an organization involved in the production and distribution of goods can allow manufacturing companies to ensure improvements and ultimate value creation in terms of: environmental practices, working conditions and human rights practices, occupational health and safety, and sustainability. For example, consumer goods companies have an enormous opportunity to reduce the environmental impact of providing goods and services to customers by working closely with the organizations involved in their supply chain. Some exemplary firms are CVS Caremark, General Mills, and Warby Parker, as well as Outerknown, a Los Angeles-based men's brand of sustainable clothing.

Firms committed to optimizing their supply chain must help suppliers in managing their impact and assist them in this process by helping suppliers design and implement practices and programs that align with their own objectives. For example, Walmart has helped thousands of its suppliers from China

---

[11] Porter, M. E., and M. R. Kramer. "Creating Shared Value. Harvard Business Review, January–February" (2011).

[12] Correspondence with Romaine Seguin, June 2, 2021.

[13] Tozan, Hakan, and Alper Ertürk, eds. Applications of Contemporary Management Approaches in Supply Chains. BoD–Books on Demand, 2015.

[14] Patrick Burnson, Gartner Announces Rankings of the 2020 Supply Chain Top 25, May 22, 2020. https://www.scmr.com/article/gartner_announces_rankings_of_the_2020_supply_chain_top_25.

to reduce energy consumption by launching an online monitoring tool to measure their consumption. In doing so, Walmart has contributed to thousands of suppliers reducing their energy consumption by approximately 10 percent. These kinds of actions contribute to reducing the overall impact of supply chains while significantly reducing costs across activities in the supply chain, enhancing economic and social progress.[15]

A high-functioning supply chain requires firms to work closely with their suppliers. Fortunately, digital technology has contributed to facilitating firms' monitoring performance of their suppliers and holding them accountable to it. For example, Unilever uses a digital tool developed by a university in the UK that allows the collection of data on farmers' sustainable practices, enabling the firm to procure its agricultural inputs from sustainable sources.[16]

For firms to properly implement the M2W ideas, it is important to redefine productivity in the value chain and to focus on accessing and utilizing resources, energy, inputs, logistics, and employees in a different and more productive manner. This includes implementing comprehensive programs to reduce energy usage and increase the use of renewable sources, reduce water consumption and minimizing packaging, and reduce waste to ensure a more sustainable production process.

A best-case example of M2W integration is Siemens's work for Chang Gung Memorial Hospital (CGMH), Taiwan. The hospital has nearly 4000 beds and a total of 29 specialty centers. Siemens equipped the hospital's Proton and Radiation Therapy Center with its building management system to make the building's operations more intelligent and energy-efficient. As a result of its efforts, CGMH received LEED for Healthcare Platinum certification in 2014. Platinum is the highest level possible. CGMH is Asia's first and the world's second hospital to receive LEED for Healthcare Platinum certification. The Proton and Radiation Therapy Center is now 42 percent more energy-efficient than regular buildings. Every year they save 2 million kilowatt hours of electricity consumption and reduce 1224 metric tons of CO_2 emissions. In addition, the wastewater recycling and reclaimed water system reduce water consumption by 61 percent or 18,750 tons of water annually.[17]

Additionally, prioritizing local sourcing can contribute to improving the local economies and generating well-being in the communities where they

[15] Bové, A., & Swartz, S. (n.d.). Starting at the source: Sustainability in supply chains. Retrieved July 06, 2020, from https://www.mckinsey.com/business-functions/sustainability/our-insights/starting-at-the-source-sustainability-in-supply-chains.

[16] Ibid.

[17] Siemens: Products and Services, Chang Gung Memorial Hospital, Taiwan (no date). https://new.siemens.com/global/en/products/buildings/references/chang-gung-memorial-hospital.html.

operate. In terms of employees and human resource involved in the supply chains, firms must be willing to raise wages of lower-incomes associates, increase their benefits, and implement health and wellness programs. Clearly, it should not be a one-way approach, requiring participants to embrace ownership and accept the accountability of the new arrangement. These strategies will result in improved efficiency, product quality, and sustainability, creating shared value.

Figure 5.3 summarizes the previous examples as they affect the different processes involved in supply chains.

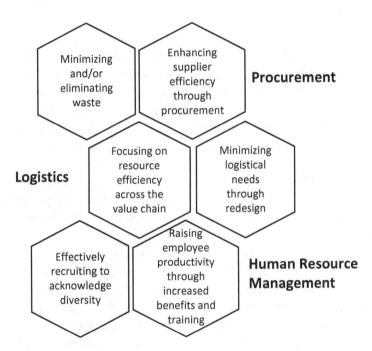

Fig. 5.3 Shared value in the value chain. (Source: Based on Michael Porter, "Competing to Change the World: Creating Shared Value," ZfU Seminar Zürich, Switzerland, May 18, 2016)

How M2W Creates Competitive Advantage

For the last 50 years or so business people have discussed and analyzed how companies can engage with society. And while most businesses agree that they want to add value to the world and contribute to societal issues, the question of how to operationalize this has not been an easy one. M2W is the viable approach to allow firms to make an impact in a meaningful and profound manner that transcends simple generosity. Tackling societal needs and societal issues with a business model that generates profits, firms can create a powerful force and achieve their full potential. And it is the stakeholder mentality that provides a guidepost for companies to address societal issues in new ways, modifying their operations accordingly to ensure societal progress and productivity.[18]

In its inception, shared value challenged the traditional notion of value creation, which focused on solely generating shareholder value. At its core, it provides an approach where shareholder value can grow while benefiting society, calling companies to rethink the old notion of where a company's responsibility begins and ends. Companies' role in society should no longer be constrained to philanthropic activities that have no clear strategic purpose or that do not leverage their core strengths. For example, by investing in wellness programs companies can not only ensure that employees and their families are healthy, but also reduce employee absences and increase productivity. In this manner, a company can address a societal concern while yielding productivity benefits that ultimately increase its profitability and economic success.

To illustrate, Accenture, a multinational professional services company, provides for both the minds and bodies of its employees. The business management consultant company offers employee assistance programs, which provide confidential support for issues like stress, substance abuse, depression, and anxiety. Additionally, employees are offered Tele-doc services, where they can ask a physician any health-related question 24/7. As for fitness, Accenture's innovative wellness program allows employees to set health goals and offers rewards for completing healthy activities. They make it pretty easy to do, too, as the company offers special rates and discounts for gyms and fitness centers as well as an online fitness program, so employees can work out anytime. Google, Intuit, Draper, and Microsoft also offer a host of wellness activities for their employees.

---

[18] Highlights of Michael Porter's 2012 Shared Value Summit Keynote. (2018, July 17). Retrieved July 06, 2020, from https://www.fsg.org/tools-and-resources/highlights-michael-porters-2012-shared-value-summit-keynote.

Returning to shared value, implementation involves strategic thinking and the creation of the kind of value that results in growth, profitability, and increased market share. In order to implement M2W, firms should steer clear from investments in sustainability activities that do not utilize the company's strengths and philanthropic causes with no clear purpose, as it will not lead to a shared value outcome; in fact, they need to enforce the principles of ownership and accountability.

From Corporate Social Responsibility to Shared Value

Over the past several decades many have argued that the environmental and socioeconomic climate has deteriorated. Many individuals and groups place the blame at the doorstep of the private sector, particularly multinationals companies. Not surprisingly then, these firms have lost much of their legitimacy in the eyes of these constituents. Being signaled as one of the major causes of social ills, corporations turned toward corporate social responsibility in an attempt to gain legitimacy and rebuild trust among customers and stakeholders. However, philanthropic endeavors and good citizenship have not been successful in enabling firms to become more competitive.

Corporate social responsibility (CSR) has not proven to lead to sustainable economic growth and profitability and societal progress because it generally involves a separation from a business' profit-driven core practices and is also limited by budget constraints. Shared value, however, calls for a rethinking about the consequences and effects of charitable funds and finds ways to achieve more through meaningful value propositions that catalyze social progress in the communities where firms operate while also increasing shareholder value. Shifting from a CSR mindset to a shared value thinking is what allows firms to achieve competitiveness in the long run.[19]

A company's role in society should no longer be constrained to philanthropic activities that have no clear strategic purpose or that do not leverage its core strengths. For example, by investing in wellness programs companies can ensure not only that employees and their families are healthy but also that there is a reduction in employee absences and an increase in their

---

[19] Keys, T., Malnight, T. W., and Van der Graaf, K. (n.d.). Making the most of corporate social responsibility. Retrieved July 06, 2020, from https://www.mckinsey.com/featured-insights/leadership/making-the-most-of-corporate-social-responsibility.

productivity. In this manner, a company can address a societal concern while achieving productivity benefits that ultimately increase their profitability and economic success.

From Traditional Shared Value to M2W

As discussed in Chap. 1, shared value as presented by Porter and Kramer was a very important step in supporting the need for a sustainable business approach to sharing benefits throughout the stakeholder ecosystem. However, the unidirectional and hierarchical focus does provide for a fair share of responsibility. The two additional elements that we introduce in this book, accountability and ownership, add to the competitiveness dimension by closing the required loop of full shared responsibility required by all players. Figure 5.4 depicts M2W and competitiveness, highlighting the business and social value dimensions from the traditional shared value plus the complete shared responsibility provided by the M2W approach.

M2W and the New Competitive Advantage

By implementing M2W as part of its strategy, a company can look at needs in a different way. As such, the firm discovers new opportunities and markets ripe for opening. In addition to a novel way to configure the value chain,

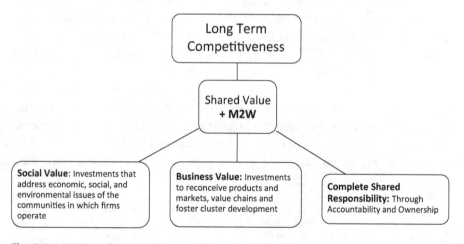

Fig. 5.4: M2W and competitiveness. (Source: Authors)

M2W shifts the focus to some of the external factors that constrain companies' productivity, hold it back from increasing its efficiency, and hinder quality in the business. Companies have traditionally focused on internal operations and have forgotten about the external environment. Essentially, shared value pushes firms to look outside as well.[20]

This way of thinking enables firms to reap social and business value by finding opportunities to differentiate themselves from the competition. Shared value, in its extended way through M2W, solves the fundamental problem of companies, which involves figuring out how to compete in a particular industry. This competition is done by creating and sustaining a competitive advantage. Among the notable firms to achieve this are Land's End, Samsung, and Whole Foods.

So how does M2W contribute to firm competitiveness? This approach enables firms to serve customers in a unique way, which, in turn, expands the size of the available pie while sharing the required responsibility for all stakeholders involved. This is the core idea of competition and strategy and is one of the greatest challenges faced by any business, because competition is a constant and relentless process for organizations looking to differentiate themselves from competitors. Shared value and shared responsibility (through M2W) open up firms to a new way of thinking about the business they are in and answering questions, such as *what do we do, what do we produce, who is our customer, what do we sell, and how do we operate*, under a new lens. By using this approach firms ultimately increase their value, as opposed to sacrificing value.[21]

Companies like Nestlé have embraced the expanded shared value approach by focusing on meeting nutritional needs rather than solely focusing on selling food products. They have also shifted their focus to rural development and water, which are key to their supply chain and sourcing, and ultimately a very significant part of their business costs. For example, Nestlé is a strong advocate of multi-stakeholder platforms (MSPs) that bring together companies, local governments, and other relevant stakeholders to create water solutions. They target their efforts in the areas where they operate; Nestlé is a member of MSPs in countries such as Bangladesh, Peru, South Africa, and Pakistan.[22]

---

[20] Porter, M. E., and M. R. Kramer. ": Creating Shared Value. Harvard Business Review, January–February" (2011).

[21] Highlights of Michael Porter's 2012 Shared Value Summit Keynote. (2018, July 17). Retrieved July 06, 2020, from https://www.fsg.org/tools-and-resources/highlights-michael-porters-2012-shared-value-summit-keynote.

[22] Creating Shared Value and Meeting Our Commitments, Progress Report 2019, Vevey, Switzerland: Nestlé, 2020.

By tackling these types of issues throughout their business portfolio, they create value by linking their products to larger societal issues. This kind of example is a proof that some industries facilitate the opportunities to make businesses profitable while also making enormous progress in society and in issues that matter in the world.[23]

Another great example of M2W can be seen in cooperatives. Co-ops are businesses inherently focused on the well-being of its employees, suppliers, and supporting organization; therefore, they are aligned with the concept of shared value. This thinking allows co-ops to focus more deeply on their impact in society and the well-being of their stakeholders, in comparison to firms that do not have this ownership structure. FSG co-founder Mark Kramer worked closely with cocoa farmers in Ivory Coast, where small farmers organize through a cooperative model. He identified inequality and climate change as two societal issues co-ops could contribute to reducing. In terms of inequality, he argues that co-ops present a very interesting model because they redistribute the rewards in a way that benefits not only shareholders and investors, but also all members. This enables a business model that is profitable and fosters societal improvement.[24]

Adding a social dimension to firm strategy creates new opportunities and new ways of thinking about the business, resulting in new ways of positioning the business and new competitive advantages. Incorporating the concerns and needs of stakeholders into firm strategy helps companies differentiate themselves from competitors beyond a pricing or product quality. By focusing on shared value, firms tap into a more sustainable advantage that is not based on cost reduction or product differentiation. A clear awareness for societal issues and a hands-on approach to ensure societal progress open up new opportunities for economic growth and profitability. This, in turn, attracts more skilled and productive employees, shareholders, business partners, suppliers, and supporting organizations. The elements of accountability and ownership guarantee a more direct involvement from the bottom-up in addition to the traditional top-down approach. And at the core of it is the fundamental requirement of shared responsibility.

In fact, the concept of focusing on shared value, and not solely on shareholder value, is penetrating the minds of CEOs across the globe, with many of them arguing that societal issues will be essential for business success in the near future.

---

[23] Nestle- Our approach: Creating shared value (n.d.). Retrieved July 06, 2020, from https://www.nestle.com/csv/what-is-csv.

[24] Harner, A. (2018, July 17). Shared Value in Côte D'Ivoire: Creating a Vibrant Cocoa Sector. Retrieved July 06, 2020, from https://www.fsg.org/blog/shared-value-c%C3%B4te-divoire-creating-vibrant-cocoa-sector.

FSG, a nonprofit consulting firm that advises businesses on how to adapt to social change, finds that companies are looking at social issues through a different lens and recognizing that business and society are not in opposition, but rather businesses depend on social progress to thrive, creating tremendous opportunities for firms to contribute to society. FSG finds that "Companies are uncovering new sources of growth, profit, and competitive advantage by building an intentional social impact into their strategy and operations."[25]

Often executives view shared value (or even M2W) as another source of pressure and expense. This is especially true during periods of economic decline when firms must contend with a significant fall in consumer spending as well as for natural resources companies when hit with a fall in commodity prices. However, as employees, customers, suppliers, and other stakeholders increase the importance of corporations' impact on society, corporate leaders have started to use this approach as an opportunity to strengthen their business' competitive positions while tackling societal issues. With the bottom-up elements that we propose, employees will be more directly involved and contribute to the required changes and adjustments, not as a unilateral imposition but as a shared responsibility for the outcomes. Using M2W as a strategic way of thinking forces business leaders to creatively address both key business and societal matters. Unfortunately, developing an approach that can deliver on both ends can be a challenge, and yet many have managed to do so successfully. For example, Bank of America began a program to attract new clients and help businesses move forward with their environmental initiatives. Their "green bonds" project, launched in 2013, has raised over four hundred billion dollars and has been successful in connecting investors with businesses working on green projects and renewable energy innovations. This project has allowed Bank of America to play a key role in fostering green business practices while increasing their profits in a new area of businesses.[26] Another example is the popular shoe manufacturer Adidas. The company has partnered with Muhammad Yunus' microfinance organization, Grameen Bank, to manufacture a low-cost shoe for the poor in Bangladesh.[27] Through this program, Adidas can provide an affordable alternative for customers at the bottom of the pyramid while also catering to a new segment of customers. Innovation and partnering are key components toward the implementation of

---

[25] Hills, G., and Hawkins, E. (2018, October 15). Advancing Strategy. Retrieved July 06, 2020, from https://www.fsg.org/tools-and-resources/advancing-strategy.

[26] 5 businesses that creating value for society. IE University. Retrieved from: https://drivinginnovation.ie.edu/5-businesses-that-are-creating-value-for-society/.

[27] Klein, P. (2011). *Three Great Examples of Shared Value in Action*. Retrieved from: https://www.forbes.com/sites/csr/2011/06/14/three-great-examples-of-shared-value-in-action/?sh=65d1eb10595d.

M2W. By partnering, companies can develop creative solutions that leverage the complementary capabilities of multiple organizations to foster business and societal impact.[28]

Another example comes from Fibria, a Brazilian manufacturer of chemical pulp, which partnered with small-scale producers near its mills. The goal was to integrate planted eucalyptus trees with native habitats to dramatically reduce the land required for wood fiber cultivation. Fibria provided the small-scale producers with technical training and inputs. By doing this, it improved sustainability by reducing the land and water needed when compared to traditional plantation methods; they achieved the preservation of more land as native forests and allowed more small-scale producers to become their suppliers, thus increasing employment and household income in the area.[29]

Figure 5.5 summarizes three spheres of activity that contribute to the competitiveness of a company as illustrated in the previous examples.

Exploring societal needs will allow companies to determine opportunities to differentiate and reposition themselves in existing markets as well as potential opportunities in new markets. The opportunities to meet these needs are constantly changing, as economies grow and develop, technologies change, and societal priorities evolve. The focus on the extended shared value concept through M2W creates opportunities for innovation and opportunities to create better products and services with a full, truly vested involvement of all stakeholders. Companies must embrace M2W and its implications—the idea that social issues can be incorporated into a business' core strategies while appropriately sharing full responsibility, resulting in benefits for society and in enhancement in a firm's competitiveness and performance.

---

[28] Shared Value and Long-Term Competitiveness (2018, August 02). Retrieved July 06, 2020, from https://www.sustainablebusinesstoolkit.com/shared-value-and-long-term-competitiveness/.

[29] Fibria 2017 Report: A Forest of Opportunities (n.d.). (2018). Fibria Celulose. Retrieved July 06, 2020, from http://r2017.fibria.com.br/wp-content/uploads/2018/04/Fibria-2017-Report-1.pdf.

- Worker safety
- Workforce skills and education
- Employee Health

- Energy efficiency
- Water use
- Environmental Improvement

- Financial Access and Inclusion
- Jobs for lower income citizens

Fig. 5.5 Forces that drive competitiveness. (Source: Based on "Creating Shared Value Explained," from Harvard's Institute for Strategy and Competitiveness. Retrieved from: https://www.isc.hbs.edu/creating-shared-value/csv-explained/Pages/default.aspx)

6

M2W and Government

In this chapter we emphasize the idea from our previous book that government can either help or hinder in everything, including the effective implementation of M2W as a catalyst for the cooperation between all players in the ecosystem. Although most of the time the government is not directly involved in the actual "business" of companies, it is a key player as it can provide the incentives for a better redistribution of benefits across all players in an ecosystem. Therefore, the "We" in M2W must include the role of government as a significant stakeholders in the shared value relationship between the firm and all stakeholders.

There are many instances where the government participates as the provider of policies and regulations for the rules of the game and acting as an active "partner" in situations such as public-private partnerships. For example, the city of Kentucky closed in 2015 a $275 million PPP to build a 3000-mile statewide broadband network, and the city of Long Beach, California, closed a $530 million P3 to build a new civic center in 2016. On the other hand, the private sector can influence its participation in the government through lobbying. In effect, aligning shareholders and stakeholders with the active participation of government represents a win-win for all.

© The Author(s), under exclusive license to Springer Nature Switzerland AG 2022
R. Ernst, J. Haar, *From Me to We*, https://doi.org/10.1007/978-3-030-87424-7_6

Where Is the Line Between Private and Public Interests?

The private sector has traditionally pushed for the primacy of shareholder interests, while the public sector has traditionally defended the primacy of stakeholder interests. The distinction between public and private interests has sparked discussions since ancient times and has been deeply rooted in Western political tradition. Roman philosophers argued that the power of the state should be used in benefit of the interests of the people, which aligned with their definition of a republic: "the property of the people." John Locke, the seventeenth-century English philosopher, emphasized that the functions of the state should be limited to serving the interests of the general public and should not exceed its assigned purposes to benefit the interests of private individuals. Nowadays, political theorists from varying political views seem to align with this idea, arguing that the power of the government should be used to promote public rather than private interests. The distinction between public and private interests has also been important in the American political history. In congruence with Locke's thought, many of the Founding Fathers agreed that the government should use its power to promote public interests as opposed to promoting the interests of individuals or factions.

Using public goods as a proxy for public interest has some limitations and can exclude private goods that advance public interests. For example, health, which is a prime example of a public good, functions like a private good because in countries where there is no universal health coverage, non-paying individuals (for health insurance) may not be able to achieve good health. Another example is the internet. Many have argued that it should be considered a public good; however, the costs of access and devices present significant access barriers, making it function more like a private good. In addition to this, public goods theory assumes that public goods are always underproduced by the market in the absence of government intervention. However, scholars have found various mechanisms through which optimal levels of public goods production can be reached even in the absence of government intervention. For example, private "planned communities" produce public goods such as security and pollution control at optimal levels, in which case it is not in the interest of the public for governments to provide these public goods given that they are already being effectively produced by the market.

In essence, differentiating between public and private interests is challenging because the distinctions tend to be based more on normative rather than on empirical concepts. While the social sciences can help us understand if certain goals can be better achieved by the market or the government, it is difficult to prove whether this is in the interest of the public.

Public and Private Interests: Do They Align?

It has been widely accepted that private interests dominate market decisions. For example, most people who invest their money in firms from the food industry do so because they expect those investments to increase their income, and not because they are primarily concerned with solving nutritional needs of society. However, some companies have managed to target private and public interests. For example, Heinz launched a "micronutrient campaign" to combat the threat of iron-deficiency anemia and vitamin and mineral malnutrition among infants and children in the developing world, providing more than five million children in 15 developing countries with sachets of vitamin and mineral powders. Furthermore, farmers do not plant crops because they are concerned with world hunger, but because they expect farming to provide an income for themselves. Although investors and farmers claim that they are concerned with these societal needs and most people do feel better when they contribute to helping society, in reality market economies do not motivate people to sacrifice private interests for the general good of the public. Market economies tend to motivate people to pursue their private interests in ways that can also promote public interest.

The decisions of government, on the other hand, are thought to be motivated by public interests and society's well-being such that the main concerns are centered around alleviating poverty, reducing environmental damage, increasing the quality and coverage of education, and promoting economic prosperity. However, government decisions, just as market decisions, are made by individuals.

Understanding who the stakeholders for the public and private sector is essential. Although the stakeholders for government include all citizens, in reality, governments have a very complex set of stakeholders, and decisions must balance the interests of citizens, the legislature, oversight groups, politicians, and a variety of interest groups. For businesses, although the common belief is that they only focus on the interests of shareholders, in reality, businesses must balance interests of employees, partner organizations, communities in which they operate, government, and interest groups as well. Recognizably, attempting to make everyone happy is a complex task. As such, decisions in both realms must aim to understand and acknowledge the needs of all these stakeholders.

In order to achieve more in terms of societal goals, it is necessary to shift from attributing societal well-being to government decisions alone and acknowledge the role of the market in moving society forward. In fact, scholars have advocated for a partial merging between public and private interests, given the interdependence between them. Research has found that public and private interests interact in several ways, and this interaction is conducive to shared value creation or the creation of strategies that are conducive to achieving public welfare and private goals.

Private-Public Partnerships

Public-private partnerships (PPPs) can play a significant role as a catalyst for shifting the view from shareholders to stakeholders. PPPs are the conceptualization or product resulting from aligning two drivers potentially pushing in opposite directions. Rather than thinking of the private sector and the public sector as enemies, they should be seen as partners, bringing different elements to achieve goals in a sustainable manner.

These cooperative arrangements and typically of a long-term nature and involve one or more governments working together with one or more businesses to carry on a project or provide a service to the population, as illustrated in Fig. 6.1. These partnerships have been implemented all across the globe mainly for large infrastructure projects such as construction of hospitals, schools, water systems, and transportation systems. For example, in the 1990s the UK implemented a large-scale project to upgrade aging healthcare facilities and expand capacity of its National Health Service (NHS). Within 12 years of its implementation, at least 100 new NHS hospitals had been built

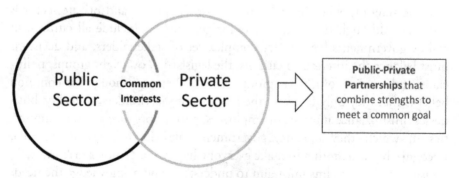

Fig. 6.1 Public-private partnerships (PPPs). (Source: Authors)

through these partnerships. A PPP typically entails a private partner taking on financial, technical, and operational risks, and being held accountable for specific outcomes. For the government a PPP provides an alternative source of financing to develop infrastructure projects and delivery of services.

PPPs have sparked some controversy as funding tools, mainly because the returns on investment are thought to be lower for the public investor than for the private investor. Additionally, because of a general lack of understanding about the financial details involved in PPPs, it is difficult to evaluate their success, resulting in issues of accountability and questions regarding the overall efficiency and costs of PPPs. However, supporters of PPPs contend that they are catalysts for innovation and allow for risk-sharing in projects that require larger investments. Overall, evidence on the success of PPP performance is mixed.

In the United States, PPPs have been gaining traction as governments have been increasingly turning to these partnerships for infrastructure projects. Unfortunately, the World Economic Forum has ranked United States' infrastructure below that of comparable nations such as Singapore and the United Kingdom. This signals a need for greater investments in infrastructure projects, and since governments are faced with fiscal constraints, PPPs present a viable option for filling financial gaps and expanding what governments can do on their own. PPPs can increase the likelihood of meeting cost and delivery objectives when compared with projects financed and managed solely by the government, especially when it comes to large and expensive public works projects. However, there is still some hesitation from public officials about enabling private businesses to finance and manage public assets through long-term projects.

Advantages and Challenges of PPPs

Using a PPP approach for larger projects such as those related to infrastructure can present some advantages and has the potential to mitigate the challenges of delivering larger projects, when executed correctly. PPPs in which private businesses control and operate projects that are subject to government regulation can help bridge the gap between the need for large-scale projects and the financial ability of governments to fund these projects. Because of the multiple difficulties that these partnerships can entail, PPPs need to clearly delineate governance, allocate risk, integrate resources, establish best practices, determine long-term costs, and establish accountability measures. For the private sector, the main concerns are related to managing risks across the development of the project. Additionally, other challenges can arise for all parties involved.

One of the most common issues that arise in PPPs includes a lack of clarity in terms of responsibilities, which, in turn, has a negative impact on effective delivery of projects. Addressing this challenge requires having documentation that explicitly states responsibilities, performance standards and measures, risk-allocation mechanisms, and penalties in case of failing to adhere to the aforementioned responsibilities and standards.

Overall, developing PPPs requires managing a broad set of risks across the execution of the collaboration. BCG has delineated some of the common risks that can arise in public-private partnerships and which, if not addressed, can pose significant challenges to successful partnerships.

Some of these challenges arise from the environment in which the project operates: politically based decisions and regulations, length of time for making decisions, changing legal or tax framework, and backlash from the community. Others are related to the financing and operational aspects, such as inflation or deflation, changes in exchange rates, interest rates, refinancing availability, changes in prices of commodities and the cost of labor, new technology, and changes in demand forecast. Finally, on the execution of collaborations, some risks include time delays, budget overruns, acquisition of permits, disputes with subcontractors, and poor performance of subcontractors.

Although these are only a few of the challenges that can come up in the execution of PPPs, and these partnerships will not tackle all these challenges consistently, evidence shows that PPPs can solve many of the issues associated with budget and delivery of large projects. For example, a study of more than 50 projects in Australia found that only one percent of PPPs exceeded their budget and delivered before their expected schedule, beating it on average by three percent. Canada has also been witness to numerous success stores in public-private partnerships, with a mature PPP market that has established an agency that oversees and enforces accountability of PPPs to deliver projects. Canada's PPP market offers an example of best practices and standards in transparency, which have ultimately led to the success of its PPPs. The United States has also found success in PPPs, with transportation projects such as interstate highway I-595, demonstrating the ability of properly managed and executed PPPs to deliver tangible benefits and optimal results. Figure 6.2 illustrates the most important conditions that determine the success of PPPs.

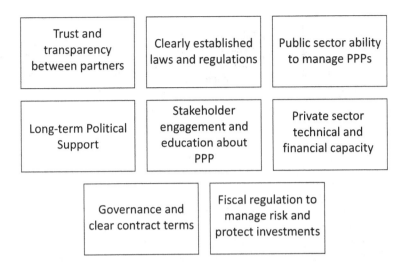

Fig. 6.2 Key conditions for successful PPPs. (Source: Based on PWC. PPPs in healthcare models, lessons, and trends for the future. 2018)

PPPs and M2W

Public-private partnerships present not only a more efficient way to deploy resources but also the potential to tackle many of our current and most pressing issues. These partnerships can help confront societal challenges such as poverty, environmental deterioration, and health by leveraging private businesses, research institutions, and governments' knowledge and resources for a common good, that is, to address public problems. PPPs offer a way for businesses to identify opportunities to take advantage of their existing operations and business models to make an impactful positive change in the world, while achieving business objectives. This is the basis of shared value. Using existing business models to create positive social impact can help balance interests of shareholders and stakeholders alike. The public sector has recognized that businesses can contribute their capacity and capital to achieve development priorities, while also giving these businesses opportunities for economic growth.

These collaborative agreements have the potential to achieve societal progress at a large scale and through innovative ways. Admittedly, successfully executing PPPs is not an easy task because it requires managing many of the challenges mentioned previously, as well as building trust relationship and

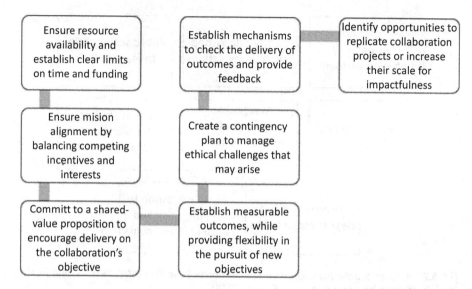

Fig. 6.3 Public-private partnerships (PPPs) aligned to create a M2W framework. (Source: Authors, based on information from McKinsey)

mitigating risks. One of the most important enablers of successful PPPs requires achieving stakeholder alignment at outset of the partnership. This means that all relevant stakeholders must align to a shared value statement to ensure long-term commitment by all parties; doing so is critical to deliver impactful results. Therefore, we propose the importance of the elements of ownership and accountability to guarantee full shared responsibility. Figure 6.3 illustrates the alignment of public-private partnerships in order to create shared value.

The Role of Lobbying

When related to the public sector, the main purpose of lobbying is to influence decision-making and decisions already made. The term refers to a time when individuals would wait in lobbies to talk to legislators. Usually, lobbyists are professionals hired to advocate for particular groups before Congress, in order to persuade legislators to pass specific laws favorable to their interests or to prevent the passage of laws inimical to their interests. These groups range from corporations and private businesses to nonprofit organizations and labor unions. As such, lobbying represents an active and legal mechanisms through which the private sector can influence the public sector. Lobbying can potentially have a positive impact in accomplishing the shift from shareholders to stakeholders.

When lobbying is done ethically and legally, it can be advantageous for the private sector. It allows certain groups, whose interests are not represented by elected government officials, to advocate for themselves. Lobbying helps to reduce the power of the majority and increase fairness in the passing of legislations so that they not only satisfy the interests but also reinforce the views of those in charge. In essence, lobbying can help represent the interests of large groups of people, giving these individuals a stronger voice in government.

Using Lobbying for Enhanced Shared Value Creation: Generating Profits and Making a Positive Impact

As a mechanism to influence the public sector and the passage of legislation, lobbying has the potential to drive positive changes in society. The private sector can use their influence and voice in government to pass legislation that is more closely aligned to the needs of consumers and other groups of stakeholders. These stakeholders want more sustainable products and practices and support companies that are committed to "doing good" and enacting change in the world. Excellent examples are global companies such as IKEA, SAP, GE, and Visa. The main question that organizations in the private sector must ask themselves is whether their lobbying is generating positive or negative impacts for society.

The private sector must approach lobbying with a new conviction under which advocating for legislation is done with the purpose of enabling profit opportunities and making the world a better place. Shared value objectives should act as a guiding force for lobbying, such that lobbying activities must align with businesses objectives to improve societal well-being and act as a mechanism to facilitate shared value creation. Because customers are now more inclined to believe that businesses have a responsibility to be involved in societal issues and act in favor of a wider range of stakeholders, lobbying for positive change can bring increased revenues for companies that use lobbying as a tool to generate positive change.

While successful advocacy is sometimes only a matter of sending a letter, making a phone call, or participating in a committee, sometimes more impactful lobbying requires sending an army of lobbyists. For this reason, many nonprofits that have traditionally been very active in engaging in lobbying activities have found that partnering with corporations who have ample political influence is a very effective path toward being key legislators and building effective advocacy. For example, the container shipping corporation has partnered with NGOs Forum for the Future and WWF to advocate for the "Sustainable Shipping Initiative" that seeks to achieve sustainability of the shipping industry.

Evidence shows that firms lobby not only against regulations, but also to change regulations that are perceived as being too rigid or that do not align to the current socioeconomic context in which firms operate. These regulations are connected to enormous economic interests and therefore it is not surprising that companies are spending thousands and even millions of dollars to petition governments to modify regulations. Data from the Center for Responsive Politics show that from 2009 to 2014, more than $3 billion dollars were spent on lobbying, specifically on environmental regulations. Companies are even getting customers involved; for instance, Airbnb contacted hosts to aid in their lobbying efforts in New York.

This kind of lobbying has several purposes: gaining positive reputational effects, changing the legislation to ensure that it is profitable to engage in more sustainable practices, and leverage new regulations to gain competitive advantage over their rivals. These examples show how companies in the energy industry are taking initiatives in making positive changes. This means that they are no longer expecting companies in other industries to change and take charge of environmental issues. They are making sure the change starts with them.

Corporations such as Mary Kay are increasingly leveraging their government contacts to enact legislation for positive change. Since the 1980s, Mary Kay Inc. has focused on the issue of violence against women by not only making donations to the cause but also advocating for additional federal funds to combat domestic violence, stalking, and sexual assault; they used their lobbying to educate legislators about domestic violence through their government relations department.

These and many other examples defy the common misconception that all corporate lobbying is based on self-interest. Some companies are using their connections with government officials to lobby for important social issues as part of their shared value strategy. Although nonprofits have been typically associated with this kind of lobbying, corporations can also use their lobbying activities to advocate for social good. Examples include companies like Pacific Gas and Electric (PG&E), which spent an estimated $27 million dollars lobbying on climate change, supporting a cap-and-trade system for carbon emissions; Exxon Mobil spent around $29 million dollars that same year in favor of greener regulations. Companies who shift their lobbying to align with their business operations, and social goals are best suited to make a positive differ-ence by using their voices and connections in the public sector.

Lobbying for social good is an important strategy in shared value creation. Lobbying for social good can target the conditions that influence firms' oper-ating environments and provide high strategic value for firms. For example, by lobbying for regulations to mitigate climate change, companies create improved standards for industries, and this, in turn, creates a competitive advantage for the companies in the industry. Among the companies active in efforts supporting environmental stewardship are Air Products and Chemicals, Disney, and Hewlett-Packard. Additionally, such lobbying results in a safer environment where safer and better products and services are delivered to consumers. Furthermore, lobbying for social good can create a business envi-ronment of transparency and fair business competition. This will lead to poli-cies that address social issues while simultaneously increasing firms' competitiveness. Lobbying for social good is a strategic means to enable the improvement of business and society simultaneously.

Effective Lobbying for Social Good

To lobby for social good, lobbyists must make sure their case is presented in the most skillful, knowledgeable, and confident way. Policy advocacy requires developing a lobbying campaign that can result in fundamental change and action toward social good.

Influencing legislators on an issue can be unpredictable and complex, but establishing a set of strategies for advocacy can yield effective results for busi-nesses' policy goals. Doing so can help private organizations identify specific actions to ensure their interests are reflected in public policies. Unfortunately, there is no magic recipe or single path that can ensure success from lobbying.

The Cartoon Network and Levi's provide vivid examples of the efficacy of lobbying for social good. Because sitting in front of a TV for hours had caused children to become more sedentary and more obese, Cartoon Network found itself as one of the culprits for such a negative impact on the youth. The com-pany launched a campaign titled "Rescuing Recess" to bring back a recess period which had been eliminated in many schools due to many reasons, including teaching needs, playground liability, and lack of budget. Taking advantage of the more than 90 million American homes tuning into the TV channel, Cartoon Network encouraged parents and kids to get involved in the campaign and send letters to school boards and teachers to support the return of recess. By doing this, Cartoon Network turned viewers into "lobbyists" by using public service announcements, on-air specials and events, as well as the help of organizations like the National PTA. The results of this campaign caused thousands of schools to register for "Rescue Recess" and caused politicians in several states to create a task force for this issue. The benefits for Cartoon Network included numerous awards and accolades, the endorsement of important stakeholders endorsing the campaign, as well as the boost in reputation for its network.

In the case of Levi's, the firm has been a strong advocate for labor laws in textile-supplying countries. As an illustration, Guatemala is one of Levi's suppliers for textiles and a country that is highly dependent on its trade with the United States for economic stability. In 2001, the US government found that Guatemala was not complying with labor regulations, which was one of the requirements for the country to enjoy preferential trade. This preferential trade enabled Guatemala to trade with the United States without having to pay duties. Levi's saw this as an opportunity to get to the root of the problem, which was weak and lax Guatemalan labor laws. Levi's sent a team of representatives from its government affairs departments to discuss this matter with the Guatemalan Ministry of Labor. These experts lobbied the Guatemalan government to enforce labor laws, and Levi's also encouraged local suppliers to join them in their advocacy toward stronger labor laws. As a result, the Guatemalan government passed stronger labor laws and was able to continue to enjoy preferential trade with the United States. By using their voice to advocate for a social issue, Levi's was able to improve the well-being of the communities that are part of its value chain and avoid disruptions to its value chain.

What Is Keeping Companies from Using Lobbying for Shared Value or M2W Creation?

Even though we have made a case for lobbying as an effective tool to tackle social issues, increase competitiveness, and create shared value, many firms refrain from using lobbying as a strategy to effect positive change. Organizations promoting corporate social responsibility barely mention lobbying as a way in which firms can persuade governments to change regulations for social good. No doubt this is due to the negative connotation attributed to lobbying per se. However, the discourse must change and organizations must promote lobbying for social good as a proactive way to engage in shared value creation.

This is not an easy endeavor, especially because many of the organizations with the greatest amount of assets and possibilities to influence government and policymakers tend to rarely advocate for social issues. Yet, large corporations have the potential to mobilize not only consumers but also numerous companies involved in their value chains and even entire industries to use their power to advocate for social good. Yamaha and Starbucks are leading examples. Furthermore, corporations can join forces with NGOs and non-profit organization in their advocacy efforts and help them overcome the constraints and restrictions they face in terms of using their funds for lobbying.

Why have companies overlooked the potential of lobbying for shareholder-stakeholder creation? Many companies are still under the impression that making monetary contributions is sufficient to mitigate the negative effects of their social and environmental footprints. When they do decide to proactively address social issues and environmental challenges, they tend to go for other strategies that do not involve interacting with government and the public sphere. Other companies are afraid that lobbying might have a negative effect on firm reputation, with the public thinking they have hidden motives to advocate for policy changes. Additionally, other companies are just fearful of crossing legal boundaries by getting involved with matters in the public sphere. This is unsubstantiated, because if companies are lobbying for social good they are not breaking the law. Using lobbying to advance social issues requires companies to look at lobbying as a way to enact change and benefit society and business rather than a way to defend the status quo. It also requires companies to overcome the fear of facing criticism from those who oppose corporate lobbying. Only by doing so will companies make use of their voice and power to create value.

Other companies are just focused on short-term, quick results and are not willing to commit to longer processes and strategies. Governments tend to take a long time to enact change, and influencing policymakers can take years and be quite complex. Lobbying can be too tedious when compared to funding a nonprofit or any other initiative that can be reported on quickly. Although influencing government can be slow, the payoff can be many times bigger than that of short-term initiatives. If companies want to really aim for long-lasting social change, lobbying is a proactive means toward achieving that goal. Lobbying for good can be an effective strategy to tackle social issues and ensure business competitiveness in the long run.

Advocating for Good and Building Relationships with Government

In order for companies to use lobbying for good, they must put their government affairs departments and experts to good use. Larger corporations such as Google tend to have a department dedicated to creating relationships with government, either internal or outsourced. These experts know how to use their voice and how to connect with politicians. Lobbying for good is a way to build long-lasting relationships with policymakers and show that they wish to advance the social issues faced by their constituents.

Using lobbying for good can help companies stand out among a sea of corporations making philanthropic efforts and can show government that companies have common goals with the government. Companies can show policymakers that private and public interests do align. Rather than just partnering with government for philanthropic events, lobbying for good requires building a deeper relationship between the private and the public sector and deeper engagement. Advocating for social issues can cause government to perceive certain companies as industry leaders when it comes to particular issues.

The role of government runs the gamut from regulator, facilitator, partner, and adversary. Its actions impact shareholders and stakeholders alike. One can expect that many companies will continue to lobby for social good, be it in the social, healthcare, and environmental domains, as their reputations will be impacted by their performance in this domain. In fact, the government has the capability of "enforcing" the switch from shareholder to stakeholders. If M2W does not evolve naturally from a PPP arrangement, the government could accomplish it through regulation. In the end, the principles of shared value plus accountability and ownership, which are the elements of the quintet presented in this book, provide the foundation for a genuine shared responsibility which guarantees sustainability over time.

7

Fair Trade as an Illustration

Abstract The emergence of organizations to "certify" that trade is fair provides buyers of consumer goods assurance that the manufacture, distribution, and sales of products comply with an agreed upon set of standards. This gives the "We" in "Me to We" the full equality it deserves in calibrating shareholder-stakeholder relations. The underlying philosophy of the Fair Trade movement is the idea that buyers have power, and therefore their decisions matter. The ideas of Fair Trade in any of its forms are directly related to the message of switching from shareholders to stakeholders. Fair trade and the certification of fair trade products, be they of an agricultural, agribusiness, manufactured, or services nature, have been growing in importance and will continue to do so. By accepting, embracing, and implementing sustainable M2W policies in an organization, shareholders and all stakeholders will benefit in both measurable and immeasurable ways.

When one thinks of "Fair Trade," Nike's use of sweatshops in China, South Korea, and Taiwan in the 1970s may come to mind. However, due to media attention and the widespread creation and mobilization of advocacy groups, significant progress has been made during the last two decades in particular. For those who share the belief in the concept and application of M2W, concerns over worker exploitation, especially of women and children, along with the environment and degradation of natural resources have raised awareness among stakeholders and shareholders that investment and commerce—especially transborder transactions—must be transparent, fair, and safe. The emergence of organizations to "certify" that trade is fair provides buyers of consumer goods assurance that the manufacture, distribution, and sales of products comply with an agreed upon set of standards. This gives the "We" in "Me to We" the full equality it deserves in calibrating shareholder-stakeholder relations.

What Is Fair Trade?

Initiatives like NGO Fairtrade International, a product-oriented multi-stakeholder group, aim to promote the lives of farmers and workers through trade, targeting the redistribution of benefits among stakeholders. This means a difference in how value is assigned, not on the size of the pie. But what exactly is Fair Trade, and why is it important to know about it? For many, it is just a movement that seeks to reduce poverty in developing countries. In reality, it is much more than that. Fair Trade attempts to redistribute the creation of value in a fairer way. It does this by making sure that purchasing power is exerted in a responsible way.[1]

The underlying philosophy of the Fair Trade movement is the idea that buyers have power, and therefore their decisions matter. We might not be aware of it, but in our everyday decisions, we all make important choices that determine other people's lives as well as our own. In our interconnected world, from the shoes we buy to the computers we use, our buying decisions shape the world we live in. A mobile phone uses different components that have been extracted and processed in various places located all over the world. Raw materials are usually extracted in developing countries, while processed technological components come from highly industrialized nations. In general, poor nations that only supply the raw materials will receive a smaller share of the phone's overall value. Richer nations, on the other hand, will receive a greater portion as a consequence of their complex and technology-based, value-adding process.

Figure 7.1 portrays the raw material composition of iPhone 6. Note that the total value of the elements amount to $1.03, although this model phone pre-owned retails for $150–180.[2]

The same occurs with other types of goods such as coffee beans. It is easy to buy an espresso from your favorite coffee shop, but have you ever wondered where the coffee beans come from? They most likely come from the work of

[1] World Fair Trade Organization (2020, August 07). Our Fair Trade System. Retrieved September 24, 2020, from https://wfto.com/our-fair-trade-system.

[2] Best Buy website, iPhone 6 s—Best Buy.

Materials that Make Up the iPhone: 129 Grams
Total Value of Elements: $1.03

Fig. 7.1 Materials that make up the iPhone. (Source: Statista)

farmers in a developing country like Vietnam, Brazil, and Ethiopia, and as in the previous example, farmers receive just a small portion of the end product's total value. Something similar occurs with a product like plant-based meat. Due to its sophisticated elaboration process, most of the value is produced at later stages of the value chain rather than in the early phases which tend to focus on raw materials. If no Fair Trade[3] measures are in place, we can almost be sure that there will be an asymmetric distribution of value among the different stakeholders involved in the process.

These differences in how a product's value is distributed can create significant benefit variations for the stakeholders involved. While some receive significant benefits, others receive considerably less. This is due to the nature of how certain business transactions are performed. Factors like negotiating power and the complexity of the processes involved can determine who receives what. However, this is being put into question for several reasons. In particular, the argument that to improve people's lives it is necessary to change how value is redistributed is very attractive.

---

[3] Through the rest of this chapter "Fair Trade" refers to the international network organization rather than the concept of fair trade itself, unless otherwise noted.

No matter where a product comes from, how value is distributed influences different stakeholders' lives. Under regular conditions, farmers will never be able to receive the same benefits as capital- and technology-intensive agribusiness. Therefore, whether it be canned food (meat, fruit, vegetables), yogurt, peanut butter, bread, or jam, the value-added will be far greater than the inputs/ingredients. Farmers tend to have less negotiating power to claim additional value from their raw goods. Due to the impact of unequal benefit distribution for different stakeholders within the value chain, movements like Fair Trade exist.

Simply stated, Fair Trade is a movement whose goal is to redistribute value. This means that fair trade focuses on how the pie is distributed rather than its size. As such, Fair Trade looks after the different stakeholders in order to make sure that everyone receives a fair portion of a product's value. While growth can occur with fair trade, most of the time this is an unintended consequence rather than a planned, strategic one.

One of the most common results of making sure that everyone involved in the value chain of a product or service is treated fairly is that sellers can charge consumers an increased price.[4] Many consumers are willing to pay an additional value if their purchase is referred to as fair. This applies to coffee beans, bananas, and flowers, just to name a few. Instead of the usual bananas for a given price, a fair trade banana can cost double the price of a non–fair trade banana. The difference in price for fair trade products comes from the cost of making the transaction "fair."

The Origins of Fair Trade

While the concept of fair trade has existed ever since the exchange of goods first began, it was only recently that it became a formal movement. Throughout history, the exchange of goods between parties has not always been fair to all involved. From the sixteenth to the eighteenth centuries, the mercantile system in Europe was focused on increasing the wealth of the state. Colonies that were operating to the benefit of the colonizing country were given privileges that protected them from competitors with the use of tariffs. For example, in order to protect the English colonies' sugar growers from competition with the other islands, the Molasses Act of 1733 imposed a tariff on molasses imported from French, Dutch, or Spanish islands.[5]

---

[4] Why Fair Trade—Why Buy Fair Trade (n.d.). Retrieved September 24, 2020, from https://www.fairtradecertified.org/why-fair-trade.

[5] Frank William Taussig, *The Tariff History of the United States.* New York: G.P. Putnam and Sons, 1931.

Additionally, individuals were forced into labor through slavery and were exposed to dire working conditions. Under these conditions, trade was not operating under the concept of fairness. By the 1960s, organizations began to advocate for supply chains that were fair to workers and producers, especially for agricultural products. (Manufactured goods came later, as mentioned in the beginning of the chapter.) This is when the Fair Trade movement began to take its initial steps. Criticism of multinational corporations and developed countries increasing their wealth to the detriment of developing countries was also a catalyst of the Fair Trade movement.

The coffee industry perhaps did the most to significantly bolster the Fair Trade movement into fruition. Because coffee crops are highly sensitive to environmental conditions, coffee is subject to tremendous price fluctuations and cycles of high and low growth. These rapid shifts in supply cause prices to be highly unstable, resulting in economic uncertainty for producers, who are in most cases located in developing countries. This resulted in the creation of the International Commodity Agreement (ICA) as a way to help stabilize the price of coffee. In 1950, following World War II, the ICA became more of a cartel in which the member countries, who were coffee producers, agreed to restrict coffee output during periods of high growth in order to keep higher prices, storing the surplus to sell during periods of low output.[6]

In 1989, the United States withdrew from the ICA, and its members failed to abide by the agreement, resulting in its eventual dissolution. At that time, fair trade activists in the Netherlands created a certification in which a label was given to products that met specific wage standards. The main objective was for farmers to obtain a reasonable pay for their labor. Similar organization came into existence in Europe, and in 1997 these organization merged into the Fairtrade Labelling Organizations (FLO) with the purpose of inspecting and certifying producers.[7]

As with many other movements, fair trade began to take shape as a way to address market failures and social injustice. Its main focus was on correcting the mercantilist system that gave privileges and special treatment to large businesses while leaving small businesses in an unfair position to compete. Its main purpose has been to help small growers improve their income and their well-being. Although there is still much to be done in this regard, fair trade has been growing significantly in the past decades.

---

[6] Haight, C., & Colleen Haight is an assistant professor at San Jose State University (n.d.). The Problem With Fair Trade Coffee (SSIR). Retrieved October 23, 2020, from https://ssir.org/articles/entry/the_problem_with_fair_trade_coffee.
[7] IBID.

To illustrate, in Costa Rica there are cooperatives and farmers' organizations representing a diversity of agribusiness activities, including dairy, coffee, and pineapple, such as Coopepiña R.L. and Probio in pineapple and Coocafe R.L. in coffee production. As noted by Esteban R. Brenes, former Minister of Agriculture of Costa Rica: "Fair trade is a great opportunity for farmers around the world, especially given the explosive demand for fair trade products by consumers. Nicaragua is a great example where there are over 20,000 farmers who are fair trade recipients."[8]

The Fair Trade Federation, a nonprofit trade association founded in 1994 that provides support to and promotes North American businesses committed to the principles of fair trade, has established a set of principles that are widely followed by companies. These fair trade principles[9] are ones that must be followed by buyers and sellers involved in fair trade.

The first principle pertains to *direct trade.* This entails cutting out the middlemen so that fair trade importers work with producers directly, or as directly as possible. This allows for the importers to pay farmers and producers a larger share of the money their products will sell for. It is also common for fair trade importers to work with collectives or groups of small-scale farmers who run their own farms. These collectives must be run democratically, with profits being split equally among members, and all farmers getting a vote. These characteristics must be present in collectives that meet fair trade standards.

Guaranteeing farmers a *fair price* is one of the most important benefits of fair trade. What this means is that even when the market price falls, buyers will still receive reasonable minimum price for their goods. Producers must commit to paying fair wages to their workers, and buyers commit to promptly paying producers for their crops. Buyers can also provide producers with credit by paying for crops in advance, ensuring that farmers will have resources to grow and harvest crops on time.

Good working conditions are also covered in Fair Trade Principles. Producers must provide farmers safe working conditions in which no child or forced labor is used. This means that farmers must not be subjected to any form of discrimination, abuse, harassment, including discrimination based on union membership. While these working conditions may seem like the bare minimum, many of these practices are still common in plantations across the world.

And these are related to *respectful relationships* between producers, buyers, and consumers and must promote respect and honest communication. Buyers must aim to build long-term relationships with producers, assist them with

---

[8] Correspondence with Esteban R. Brenes, June 1, 2021.

[9] Fair Trade Federation Principles – Fair Trade Federation. (2020, June 12). Retrieved October 23, 2020, from https://www.fairtradefederation.org/fair-trade-federation-principles/.

any issues that arise, and provide technical assistance and all the information about best practices, market conditions, and so forth.

Another set of principles governs *community development.* Here producers can also earn a premium to investing in their communities. For example, for crops grown organically, producers will earn an extra sum in addition to the regular price of their crops. These additional earnings will go toward initiatives like scholarships and programs for nutrition and healthcare. Producers can also use these funds to invest on improving their business through better irrigation systems and organic certifications that can help them earn more for their crops.

Related to community development is *sustainability.* Producers must use sustainable growing practices that make the most efficient use of water, soil, vegetation, and natural resources. Energy and water must be used efficiently, and waste must be managed appropriately, through practices of recycling, reusing, and reducing. Additionally, the use of certain pesticides and fertilizers is restricted, and the use of genetically modified organisms (GMOs) is banned for fair trade products.

Respect for cultures is the final key principle. Fair trade buyers must allow producers to follow their traditional practices and respect their cultural heritage. While they can teach growers about new growing practices and techniques, they must restrain from forcing them to adopt particular methods for growing crops.

Why Should We Care?

Fair trade has been around for some time now, with its impact having been strongly felt, particularly in developing countries. Fair trade grants people at the bottom of the value chain the possibility to improve their lives. In some cases, it requires paying farmers or those at the bottom of the value chain a just price for their labor. Usually, certain agents or middlemen in the value chain tend to receive greater gains because of how the industry operates. Farmers are usually underpaid even though they have to work very hard to produce food at reasonable prices. When it comes to gains, much seem to be concentrated in a few hands. The Fair Trade movement seeks to address these injustices. By allowing consumers to decide whether they buy a regular product or a Fair Trade one, sellers can offer an alternative that can help make things better for others involved in the process.[10]

---

[10] Shoenthal, A. (2018, December 14). What Exactly Is Fair Trade, And Why Should We Care? Retrieved September 24, 2020, from https://www.forbes.com/sites/amyschoenberger/2018/12/14/what-exactly-is-fair-trade-and-why-should-we-care/.

The Path to Certification

Fair trade certification acts as a guarantee that buyers and sellers will abide by the Fair Trade Principles. There are currently multiple organizations that certify fair trade product, each with its own standards. These organizations conduct regular inspections on farms to monitor that they are complying with the standards. While it is common to think about agricultural goods when it comes to the Fair Trade label, both Fairtrade International and Fair Trade USA certify manufactured products, including jewelry, wine, and clothing. Figure 7.2 lists some well-known products that are fair trade certified.

Even some luxury brands are moving into the fair trade space, such as Nanushka, a cutting-edge firm that produces affordable luxury products from vegan leather.[11] Most common, however, are non-profit organizations, including cooperatives, such as The Little Market, Global Goods Partners Fair Trade, and Change the World by How You Shop. These organizations feature accessories, clothing, food, toys, home décor, and office goods, with heavy representation from developing nations.[12]

The certification process is quite rigorous and it can take from six to nine months for a producer to obtain a Fair Trade Certified label. In many

Fig. 7.2 Some well-known fair trade companies

---

[11] Kate Finnigan, "How vegan leather brand Nanushka aced affordable luxury," *Financial Times*, November 20, 2020.

[12] See: https://www.changetheworldbyhowyoushop.com/,; https://www.thelittlemarket.com/;www.globalgoodspartners.org.

industries, leading companies will nominate their best suppliers to enter the program.[13] Then, an unbiased third-party auditor is enlisted to evaluate whether they meet the fair trade standards, culminating in the awarding of the certification. Audits are repeated on an annual basis, with local organization providing support to producers in order to make sure standards are maintained on an ongoing basis.

So, what does a fair trade certification mean? According to Fair Trade Certified:

> When you see a product with the Fair Trade Certified seal, you can be sure it was made according to rigorous social, environmental, and economic standards … The label ensures that the people making Fair Trade Certified goods work in safe conditions, protect the environment, build sustainable livelihoods, and earn additional money to empower and uplift their communities.[14]

The certifying process for fair trade is exhibited in Fig. 7.3.

In the United States, Fair Trade USA certifies a large variety of products in which inspections are performed by SCS Global Services, a third-party certifier. However, some differences in standards can be observed in the United States. For example, while Fairtrade International requires certain products like coffee to come from collectives of small farmers, in the United States Fairtrade also allows for coffee to come from plantations run by a single company.

As with any system, there will always be flaws and those who find ways around it. For instance, many of the intended benefits might not reach the farmers as intended by fair trade. For this reason, Fair Trade has been under criticism as another marketing tactic, with detractors claiming that while its intentions are good, they may not always have the desired impact. A study published in 2015 concluded that the benefits of Fair Trade were close to none due to an excessive supply of certification and because most of the fair trade products do not end up being sold in the countries where they were produced, making it difficult for some of the parties to earn back the costs of certification.[15] As illustrated in a study of Nicaragua, one of the main issues

---

[13] Shoenthal, A. (2018, December 14). What Exactly Is Fair Trade, And Why Should We Care? Retrieved October 23, 2020, from https://www.forbes.com/sites/amyschoenberger/2018/12/14/what-exactly-is-fair-trade-and-why-should-we-care/.

[14] Why Fair Trade—Why Buy Fair Trade. (n.d.). Retrieved October 23, 2020, from https://www.fairtradecertified.org/why-fair-trade.

[15] De Janvry, Alain; McIntosh, Craig; Sadoulet, Elisabeth (July 2015). "Fair Trade and Free Entry: Can a Disequilibrium Market Serve as a Development Tool?" The Review of Economics and Statistics. 97 (3): 567–73.

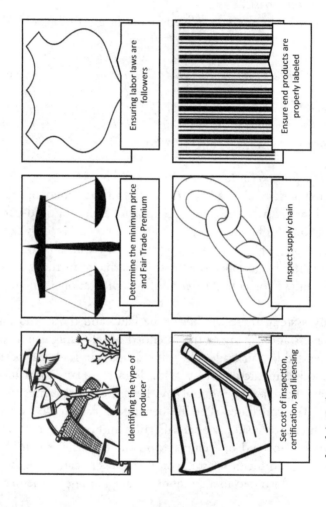

Fig. 7.3 Certifying process for fair trade

that have also been subject to criticism is the failure to enforce the standards and principles, causing many participants to evade them once they receive the certification.[16]

Other studies have pointed out that Fair Trade does achieve many of its goals, even if it does so on a small scale.[17] However, Fair Trade certification does force companies to stop and assess whether workers across their supply chain are treated ethically, have good working conditions, and whether suppliers are environmentally conscious. In essence, this is a way for companies to think beyond profits and shareholder value, to take into account a wider range of stakeholders' interests.

The Differences Between Fairtrade Mark, Fair for Life, and UTZ Certified

Fairtrade International is the largest fair trade organization and works with producers in over 70 countries. Its label, named Fairtrade Mark, may be found on over 25,000 products around the world, ranging from food to clothing and jewelry. Through an organization named FLOCERT, Fairtrade International enforces its standards and certifies its members. While the Fair Trade Mark is given to specific products that meet the standards, it is not concerned with other products the company produces. The Fair for Life mark on the other hand is concerned with companies that provide fair working conditions to all their workers and suppliers, and not just to the producers of certain products. The Fair for Life label can be used for almost any type of products made by companies who meet the organization's standards.

In addition to these labels, the UTZ Certified program also shares many of the principles of Fair Trade, yet it is not a fair trade certifier. UTZ promotes sustainable farming, opportunities and well-being of farmers and their communities, and good working conditions. However, the program does not guarantee producers a minimum price for their goods, but it does pay them a premium over the market price and helps them improve the efficiency of their harvest and the quality of their crops as a means to increase their price. UTZ monitors farms to ensure they follow the standards on their farming methods, working conditions, and environmental practices.

---

[16] Valkila, J (2009). "Fair Trade organic coffee production in Nicaragua—Sustainable development or a poverty trap?" Ecological Economics.

[17] Dragusanu, Raluca; Giovannucci, Daniele; Nunn, Nathan (2014). "The Economics of Fair Trade" (PDF). Journal of Economic Perspectives. 28 (3): 217–236. doi:https://doi.org/10.1257/jep.28.3.217. S2CID 31,724,677. Retrieved 1 April 2020.

The World Fair Trade Organization (WTFO) also plays an important role in global commerce. This network of small fair trade organizations around the globe has a guarantee system to monitor its members and to ensure that they abide by the principles and standards of fair trade. Its central office is located in the Netherlands and it represents over 350 organizations in over 70 countries.

Fair Trade and M2W

Significant increases in income inequality and the rapid deterioration of the environment have made it necessary for businesses to engage in actions and initiatives that aim at sustainability, income redistribution, and improvement of working conditions. Certifications such as Fair Trade that aims at alleviating some of the world's issues are great avenues for firms to create value for a wide range of stakeholders and move beyond a profit-centered focus. In 2018, Fair Trade presented its new charter reaffirming its principles and values and denounced the failures of the current system which it believes has increased inequality and poverty in general. This new charter emphasized their commitment to a "solidarity economy," or an economy that prioritizes people, the environment, and sustainable development over other interests.[18] This statement highlights their aim of putting the interests of a wide range of stakeholders first, as opposed to focusing on the benefits of a few interest groups exclusively.

Fair Trade is moving past a sole focus on economic profit and gives importance to sustainable production and social development based on respect, transparency, and open communication.[19] In this way, a fair trade certification is an important conduit for creating shared value and looking beyond stakeholders to assess the impact of the complete value chain network on society and the environment. Fair trade is concerned with the disadvantageous situation in which some members of the supply chain operate, making it difficult for these producers to increase their well-being and have just compensation for their work. This principle of equity is an important aspect that is also related to shared value because it acknowledges that all individuals and groups involved in commercial relations are entitled to equal rights, such that

---

[18] The International Fair Trade Charter (2018, September 01). Retrieved October 23, 2020, from http://www.socioeco.org/bdf_fiche-document-6271_fr.html.

[19] Fair Trade and Solidarity Economy: Shared values (n.d.). Retrieved October 23, 2020, from https://www.ripess.eu/fair-trade-and-solidarity-economy-shared-values/.

businesses must account for the well-being of multiple stakeholders and move away from stakeholder primacy.

Fair Trade's key objectives also focus on the environment and its protection. This calls for a recognition of businesses and all those involved in the value chain ecosystem to move toward more sustainable practices as a way to generate well-being to society and alleviate the effects of climate change. For example, banana growers complying with fair trade standards apply sustainable environmental practices that include waste and water management, reduction in chemical usage, biodiversity conservation, and avoidance of banned pesticides; additionally, banana workers and farmers must complete trainings on protection of the environment.[20] The shared value imperative also focuses on the importance of businesses finding more sustainable ways of producing and delivering their products and services as a way to increase profits and well-being.

Furthermore, Fair Trade emphasizes the power of working collectively and the importance of building respectful relationships based on trust, transparency, accountability, and equality. This principle is an important aspect for shared value as well, which calls businesses to collaborate with other members of the supply chain ecosystem, institutions, and members of clusters to create long-term relationships and carry on actions that have meaningful impact in society. While fair trade focuses on relationships with producers, shared value focuses on a wider range of relationships with other businesses, government, universities, NGOs, and so forth.

Another value of fair trade emphasizes the reinvestment of profits, which involves reinvesting the additional profits into projects for the community linked to education, health, infrastructure, and development. Cafédirect, a Fair Trade Certified coffee company from the UK, invests 50 percent of its profits into Producers Direct, a UK charity that works directly with farmers to help smallholder tea and coffee growers to build their expertise and improve their crop quality and yield.[21] This is closely linked to corporate social responsibility and the role of business in reinvesting some of its gains to help the advancement of the communities in which they operate. For example, in 2019, Microsoft committed to invest more than $500 million dollars over the next three years for affordable housing in the Seattle area, where the company is based.[22]

---

[20] Food and Agriculture Organization (2011). Impact of Fair Trade Bananas: Summary and Management Response. Retrieved from: http://www.fao.org/fileadmin/templates/banana/documents/IIWBF/contributions/FT_Banana_Summary1.pdf.

[21] Producers Direct. Partners. Retrieved from http://producersdirect.org/partner/cafe-direct/.

[22] Microsoft. News. Retrieved from https://news.microsoft.com/affordable-housing/.

Economic Consequences of fair trade	Non-economic Consequences of fair trade	Spillover effects to conventional farmers	Role of the cooperative
• Income from produce • Fair trade premium • Income sufficiency • Secondary income • Savings • Loans • Excess money	• Local development awareness • Education for producers • Education for children • Diet improvement • Household development	• Fair Trade premium • Local development awareness • Education	• Sales to fair trade market • Information and knowledge of fair trade • Motivation • Quality of organizational structure

Fig. 7.4 The effects of fair trade (Holmes, H. L. (2015). An analysis of the impact of fair trade: a case study of tea producers in the central province of Sri Lanka (doctoral dissertation, Manchester Metropolitan University)

In sum, there are multiple key words in the principles of Fair Trade that can be associated with the philosophy and purpose of shared value. Despite the aforementioned similarities in principles, fair trade has been mainly associated with corporate social responsibility and not related to shared value. One of the main arguments for this is that shared value focuses on increasing the size of the pie and redistributing the pie, while fair trade is mainly concerned with its redistribution. However, fair trade does create additional profits when compared to traditional production practices, and aims to redistribute it among producers, workers, and across supply chains and regions. Overall, there are undeniably a number of aspects in which shared value and fair trade align. If we analyze respect and improvement in working conditions, all of these concepts can be associated with shared value. Figure 7.4 illustrates the effects of fair trade.

Fair Trade Examples

Coffee. As we discussed earlier, this product started the fair trade movement, and it is still one of its most important products. Before abiding by fair trade principles, coffee prices were regulated by the International Coffee Organization in accordance with the International Coffee Agreement negotiated by the United Nations in 1962. Unfortunately, the prices of coffee had no basis on the cost of actually producing, thereby harming coffee growers around the world.

Currently, approximately seventy percent of the world's coffee comes from 20–25 million family farmers, with most coffee being grown in small farms of no more than 12 acres.[23] Because these small farmers produce reduced quantities of coffee, investing in more advanced processing equipment is usually not worth their investment. In Indonesia, for example, smallholder plantations continue to account for 98 percent of all area, averaging between 1 to 2 hectares per holding.[24] As a result, several farmers must process their coffee harvests together, making it difficult to trace coffee to individual farmers. These small farmers also lack the resources to transport their coffee to the processor, creating dependence on middlemen who purchase their harvest at whatever price they offer. The product from these millions of farmers then goes from these traders to roasters, and finally to one of the few companies who trade the world's coffee. Both the roasting and trading market for coffee are highly concentrated, with around 10 companies roasting approximately one-third of the world's coffee and five companies trading around twenty-five percent of the world's coffee.[25]

This high concentration within the industry means small coffee growers have little to no power in negotiating coffee prices. Additionally, the price of coffee has been highly volatile and has been steadily decreasing for the last decade. For example, coffee growers in Brazil saw their income drop by half between 2016 and 2019.[26] Lower prices have affected small farmers' well-being, forcing them to look for better working jobs. Furthermore, climate change and fungus have affected and decreased coffee crops tremendously. This situation has resulted in a crisis for coffee growers, but Fair trade has provided a way to address these issues and ensure farmers earn enough and are able to produce high-quality coffee.

Fair trade helps the coffee industry by setting the fair trade minimum price, based on a global benchmark on the production costs of coffee. The standard minimum price for washed arabica unroasted coffee is $1.40 per pound, or $1.70 per pound if the coffee is also certified organic.[27] When the market price falls below this minimum price, coffee growers can rest assured that they will receive at least the minimum price for their harvest. This system helps coffee growers during hard times.

---

[23] Fair Trade Certified. (n.d.). How Fair Trade USA helps the global coffee industry. Retrieved October 23, 2020, from https://www.fairtradecertified.org/sites/default/files/filemanager/documents/Impact%20Reports%20%26%20Research/COM_CoffeeArticle_V02_191030.pdf.

[24] U.S. Department of Agriculture, Coffee Annual: Indonesia, Washington, D.C.: U.S. Department of Agriculture, 2020.

[25] IBID.

[26] Ritu Prasad, "How the 2019 Coffee Crisis Might Affect You," *BBC News*, July 11, 2019.

[27] 5 Common Myths About Fair Trade Coffee (2019, September 16). Retrieved October 23, 2020, from https://www.fairtradecertified.org/news/fair-trade-coffee-myths.

Additionally, for every pound of coffee sold on fair trade terms, each coffee producer earns an additional 20 cents that are directed toward a community development fund. Cooperative members decide how these funds are used in the local community, in ways that help meet their social, environmental, and economic needs. These investments are aimed at helping the farmers' communities, the workers, and improving the infrastructure of their cooperatives. Overall, these additional funds can help coffee growers become more resilient in the face of issues like climate change and unexpected crises. Figure 7.5 illustrates the increasing growth of coffee volumes by Fairtrade USA.

Cocoa. In 1990, more than 80 percent of the cocoa used in the production of chocolates was produced by small farmers from Africa and Latin America who did not have the knowledge about how much their cacao beans were worth.[28] This resulted in these small farmers getting paid low prices for their harvest and an increased use in child labor as a way to counteract labor shortages from the increased use of fertilizers. Additionally, the price of cocoa beans

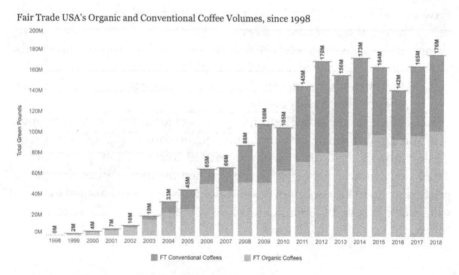

Fig. 7.5 Organic and conventional coffee volumes. (Source: Fairtrade USA)

[28] Leissle, K., & Leissle, K. (2013, October 05). What's Fairer than Fair Trade? Try Direct Trade With Cocoa Farmers. Retrieved October 23, 2020, from https://www.yesmagazine.org/issue/human-cost-stuff/2013/10/05/a-sweeter-deal-for-cocoa-farmers/.

has been volatile during the last decade because of increasing demand and the diseases that harm cocoa trees.[29] Similar to coffee, growers largely depend on local collectors and intermediaries to purchase and transport the cocoa to exporters and processors.[30]

Fair trade certification has become an important mechanism to overcome many of these issues. The fair trade model guarantees cocoa farmers a minimum price per ton for their product plus the community development fund or premium. These higher prices for farmers reduce the need for child labor. Additionally, third parties conduct annual inspections of farms to ensure that they meet child labor standards. Furthermore, the Fair Trade organization has focused on promoting environmental sustainability in the production of cocoa, prohibiting the use of GMOs and dangerous chemicals. The Fair Trade standard requires pest management and soil erosion mitigation practices, and regulates the use of pesticides and their disposal.[31] Figure 7.6 illustrates the case for fair trade in chocolate.

The ideas of Fair Trade in any of its forms is directly related to our message of switching from shareholders to stakeholders. Fair trade and the certification of fair trade products, be they of an agricultural, agribusiness, manufactured, or services nature, have been growing in importance and will continue to do so. The collective conscience of consumers in developing as well as developed nations stems, stoked by social media, advocacy organizations, and the ESG units of large companies, will play an even larger role in the production, packaging, and distribution of goods and services. Hopefully, the exploitation of women, children, the poor, and the environment will continue to dissipate across the world. The vision of a more inclusive, shared responsibility and full ecosystem stakeholder embrace guarantees its sustainability. By accepting, embracing, and implementing sustainable M2W policies in an organization, shareholders and all stakeholders will benefit in both measurable and immeasurable ways.

---

[29] Macrotrends, https://www.macrotrends.net/futures/cocoa.

[30] 5 Important Things to Know About Fair Trade Chocolate (n.d.). Retrieved October 23, 2020, from https://www.simplychocolate.com/learn-what-is-fair-trade-chocolate.

[31] IBID.

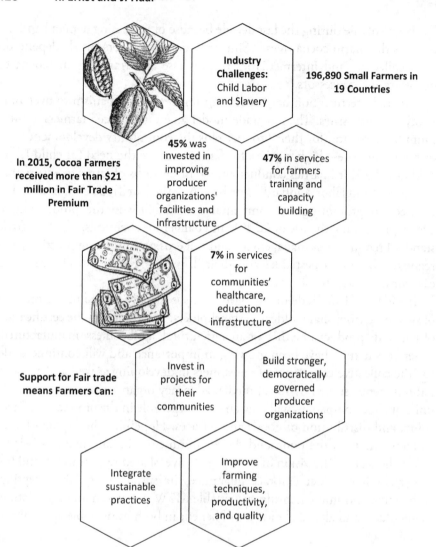

Fig. 7.6. The case for fair trade in chocolate (Chocolate and Cocoa. (n.d.). Retrieved October 23, 2020, from https://fairtrade.ca/en-CA/Buying-Fairtrade/Cocoa.html). (Source: adapted from www.fairtrade.ca)

8

M2W and the Bottom of the Pyramid

Perhaps no dimension of the transformation of business from a purely shareholder to a stakeholder focus (M2W) is more compelling and more vivid than that of the bottom of the pyramid (BOP). That segment of the wealth pyramid is the largest and poorest socioeconomic group worldwide (see Fig. 8.1). According to the World Bank, there are approximately 3.4 billion people who live on less than $5.50 per day, and 10 percent of the global population live in extreme poverty, earning a mere $1.50 per day.[1]

Traditionally, the BOP has been neglected, as neither local nor foreign producers considered this demographic group as a viable and promising consumer market. However, in 2004 a spark was ignited with the publication of *The Fortune of the Bottom of the Pyramid*, a seminal work by late C. K. Prahalad of the University of Michigan and Stuart Hart of Cornell.[2]

Their radical idea (for the time) was that the private sector, government, and non-governmental organizations need to alter their frame of reference and mindset to see the poor not as helpless victims but as value-conscious and entrepreneurial consumers and producers. Prahalad and Hart argue that there is tremendous financial potential for multinational companies especially (since they have the production scale) to serve emerging markets in ways that can meet the needs of the BOP market segment. They assert that co-creation of solutions to the problem of poverty and entrepreneurship on a massive scale are key to significantly improving the economic and social conditions of

---

[1] World Bank, *Poverty and Shared Prosperity*, Washington, D.C.: World Bank Group, 2018.
[2] C.K. Prahalad and Stuart L. Hart, *The Fortune at the Bottom of the Pyramid*, Upper Saddle River, N.J.: Wharton School Publishing, 2004.

© The Author(s), under exclusive license to Springer Nature Switzerland AG 2022
R. Ernst, J. Haar, *From Me to We*, https://doi.org/10.1007/978-3-030-87424-7_8

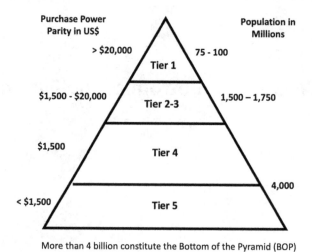

Fig. 8.1 The economic pyramid. (Source: U.N., *World Development Report*, 2017)

the very poor and emphasize that the BOP market also represents a major engine of growth and global trade.

That being said, Prahalad and Hart advocate that the BOP segment be incorporated as an integral part of the core business of companies with, where warranted, collaboration with government and non-governmental organizations. And by encapsulating innovative principles for operating in the BOP segment, consumers will have greater engagement in the global economy and increased dignity and self-esteem and will experience a lesser level of poverty.[3]

Returning to Fig. 8.1, one notes that tier 1 consumers represent the upper classes in developed nations and the elites of the developing world, while tiers 2 and 3 illustrate the middle class and tier 4 the working class. The bottom of the pyramid, tier 5, consists of a multitrillion dollar market that is growing worldwide and presently consists of over 4 billion people.

Just who are the individuals who reside at the bottom of the pyramid? Not surprisingly they are people who dwell in small rural villages, slums, and shantytowns (such as the *barrios* in Lima and *favelas* in Rio de Janeiro). They usually do not hold title to their property; do not have a bank account, credit, or steady employment; and are challenged in terms of educational level, health, and access to social services. For shareholders in companies that wish to see

---

[3] Ibid.

their companies penetrate this promising market, they need to be mindful of four critical elements.

First is the *creation of buying power*. This entails providing access to credit and boosting the earning potential of the poor. The key to unlock this, according to Peruvian economist Hernando de Soto, is for the poor to gain title to property, where they live (very often without a deed) or the small kiosk where they sell sundried—or both.[4] Another vehicle is microfinance which has grown significantly over the past several decades. Microfinance is increasingly being considered as one of the most effective tools of reducing poverty by enabling microcredit to the financial poor. Microfinance has a significant role in bridging the gap between the formal financial institutions and the rural poor.

Second is the *shaping of aspirations*. People at the bottom of the pyramid aspire to possess many of the goods those higher up on the pyramid can afford. An example is a refrigerator. If large local or multinational firms can produce an inexpensive, reliable (strong motor), compact, and low-energy consuming refrigerator, BOP consumers will flock to an appliance store to buy one. For example, some time ago the Mumbai-based firm Godrej and Boyce created Chotukool, a portable and mobile cooling system that consumes half the power of traditional refrigerators. The Chotukool is a chlorocarbon-free CFC-free, fan-cooled thermoelectric cooling system intended to conserve food and consume half the power of traditional refrigerators.

Third is *improving access*—both physically and financially. With large swaths of a country's population residing outside metropolitan areas, large companies lack the distribution systems to efficiently serve widely diffused populations. Small clusters of economically poor populations do not provide for an effective way to serve these communities via logistics systems. Nevertheless, recognizing the fortune at the bottom of the pyramid, both local and foreign companies—especially those in the personal care products industries such as Avon—have not allowed geography and disposable income level to deter them.

Fourth is *tailoring local solutions* for the BOP market. Invariably, this will mean that companies have to adapt their consumer products to the needs and preferences of underserved populations. This would include smaller packaging, due to limited shelf space in smaller dwellings for products like detergent, which, at the same time, would be prepared in a more concentrated format for the cost-conscious BOP consumer. The manufacture and distribution of single-size packets of shampoo, tea, aspirin, and other frequently used

---

[4] Hernando de Soto, *The Mystery of Capital*, New York: Basic Books, 2000.

consumer products are other ways companies can tailor local solutions to low-income consumers.

Since Prahalad and Hart published their book over a decade and a half ago, profound changes have been closing the gap between the BOP consumer and others, with marked progress in upward mobility from the lowest strata of society, and companies have more vigorously embraced the concept of a *new* fortune at the bottom of the pyramid.[5] In addition to a dramatic reduction in extreme poverty, two other factors have spurred optimism and contributed to the aspirations of managers and consumers alike. The first is technology, particularly the use of mobile telephony to lower the cost of communication and learning. This enables companies to develop, deliver, and scale many important services, such as bank payments, to mobile phones. The other is the concept, design, development, and implementation of innovation that improves the quality of life for BOP consumers, for example, a $28 prosthetic leg developed for India's BOP consumers in which they can squat, sit cross-legged, and walk on rough ground.[6]

Subsequently, Stuart Hart and Erik Simanis, both affiliated with Cornell University's Center for Sustainable Global Enterprise, advanced another approach to BOP, one that regards the poor as not only producers and consumers but also as business partners and innovators. Their framework is encapsulated in the base of the pyramid protocol, an entrepreneurial process that companies can avail themselves of for the purpose of developing partnerships with low-income communities—the aim being to co-create businesses and markets that mutually benefit the companies and communities[7] (See Fig. 8.2).

While there remains a fortune at the bottom of the pyramid, with great potential for both domestic and multinational companies, regardless of size, to succeed in this market segment is no easy road to hoe. In particular, it requires addressing issues around the macro-economic and business climate of the country, mispricing of risk, entrepreneurship, and a shift of focus away from multinational corporations to the small business sector, and the transaction costs that bedevil it.[8] Even firms that have achieved sales success in BOP

---

[5] Deepa Prahalad, "The new fortune at the bottom of the pyramid," *Strategy+Business,* Spring 2019, issue 94.

[6] Tim Mcgirk, "The $28 Foot," Time, October 1, 1997.

[7] Erik Simanis and Stuart Hart, "Innovation from Inside Out," *MIT Sloan Management Review,* Summer 2009, 77–86. The initial protocol was developed with the input of a consortium of social entrepreneurs, NGOs, academics, and four corporate sponsors (DuPont, S.C. Johnson, Hewlett-Packard, and TetraPak).

[8] Aneel G. Karnani, *Mirage at the Bottom of the Pyramid* (August 2006). William Davidson Institute Working Paper No. 835, Available at SSRN: https://ssrn.com/abstract=924616.

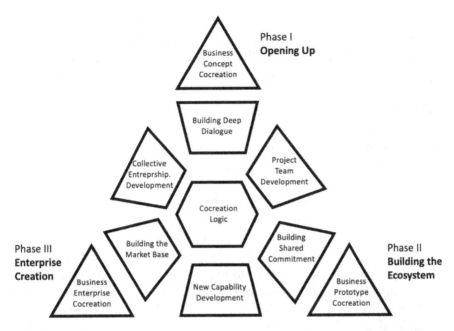

Phase I
Opening Up

Business
Concept
Cocreation

Building Deep
Dialogue

Collective
Entreprship.
Development

Project
Team
Development

Cocreation
Logic

Phase III
**Enterprise
Creation**

Building the
Market Base

Building
Shared
Commitment

Phase II
**Building the
Ecosystem**

Business
Enterprise
Cocreation

New Capability
Development

Business
Prototype
Cocreation

Fig. 8.2   The BOP protocol. (Source: Erik Simanis and Stuart Hart, "Innovation from Inside Out," *MIT Sloan Management Review,* Summer 2009, 77–86)

markets, such as Procter and Gamble, DuPont, and Unilever, have been unable to garner high margins and price points that corporate headquarters expect. In essence, BOP is a long-term play for shareholders, if they are willing to endure the patience and length of time required to attain satisfactory results.

Since the bottom of the pyramid is primarily a phenomenon of emerging markets, it is worth stepping back to place the BOP within that geographic context. Emerging markets—countries undergoing rapid economic growth and industrialization—have grown in importance dramatically over the last two decades. These countries are fast-growing and comprise nearly 60 percent of the world's population (or 3.5 billion) and 40 percent of the world's economic output (18.5 trillion in GDP).[9] China, Brazil, Russia, and India lead in the pack of emerging economics in terms of GDP. And these emerging economies are poised to grow faster than industrialized nations.

---

[9] International Monetary Fund, *World Economic Outlook, (April 2020),* Washington, D.C.: International Monetary Fund.

Interestingly, given the ups and down of emerging markets, these countries have often intervened more promptly and resolutely than developed nations to protect their hard-won gains.[10] The outcome of boom-and-bust cycles' impact on emerging markets is hard to predict—some can bounce back fast, like Asian nations in the late 1990s; others, like in Latin America in the 1980s, can lose an entire decade of growth and prosperity.

Whatever the case, most developing countries presently are stronger, richer, and more competitive than in the past and possess a resilience that allows them to manage and recover from economic and financial crises, be they internal, regional, or global.

Taking a long-term perspective, the prospects for the emerging markets were bright before the pandemic, although there will be exceptions such as Venezuela, on the downside, and India on the upside. These nations comprise four-fifths of the world's working-age citizens and have been the main driver of world growth in recent times. With sustained trends of population growth, mass urbanization, and increasing disposable incomes, despite short-term set-backs forces will propel emerging markets to the forefront of the economic and political stage. By 2050, up to six currently emerging nations, including China, India, Brazil, Mexico, and Indonesia, could be among the seven largest economies in the world, according to projections by PwC and others.[11]

Innovation and the Bottom of the Pyramid

Bring up the term "innovation," and one invariably associates the word with science and technology firms such as Pfizer, Microsoft, Amazon, and Samsung. However, besides its application and commercialization, innovation is a driver of economic productivity and social progress, impacting all geographic regions and functional dimensions of the world economy. While both industrialized and emerging markets are capable of producing market-disrupting innovation, each tends to produce innovation with distinct characteristics and aspects. For example, Syngenta, a Chinese-owned and Swiss-based agrichemical firm, has introduced innovative crop chemical packaging and training for smallholder farmers in Kenya.[12]

---

[10] "Early Morning in Emerging Markets," *Global Finance,* July 14, 2020. Also see International Monetary Fund, *World Economic Outlook Reports*, July 24, 2020.

[11] Ibid.

[12] Jerry Haar and Ricardo Ernst, eds., *Innovation in Emerging Markets*, Basingstoke, U.K.: Palgrave Macmillan, 2016.

For emerging markets, home to the vast majority of the BOP population, the major advancements that have driven innovative economic progress are the expanded access to finance (particularly microcredits and government-backed loans and grants), affordable technologies (such as mobile telephony), and the overall growth of developing economies. Because of its contribution to job creation and income growth, innovation is the single most important force driving economic evolution.

On the business side, innovation in developing nations has been driven by suppliers who strive to capture the growing demand of low-end consumers who are rapidly becoming the world's largest consumer segment. Companies know that affordability, flexibility, and functionality are essential in in the BOP market where the principal forms of innovation encompass product, process, service, and business model innovation. It is critical that shareholders of firms that do business with, or consider doing business with, emerging markets—with attention to the BOP segment—understand the fundamental differences between innovation activities in industrialized nations and developing ones.

For example, Unilever, a British-Dutch multinational consumer goods company headquartered in London, discerned that Indian consumers had a great desire to use shampoo but that the price point of purchasing an entire bottle—regardless of the size—was too high. So as not to miss out on serving and profiting from this huge and ever-growing market, Unilever began manufacturing sachets of shampoo and selling them for only 1 rupee, thereby making shampoo available and affordable to the lowest stratum in society. Needless to say, this was a win-win formula for Unilever and its shareholders and BOP Indian consumers.[13]

Turkey presents the case of a country where personal signatures are widely required—more so than most other nations. The country's laws mandate that signatures are required for certain processes such as receiving paychecks, holiday requests, and corporate travel reservations. In 2004, Turkey passed and implemented a law authorizing electronic signatures as the legal equivalent of "wet signatures." Subsequently, Turkcell created an innovation that resulted in a secure mobile signature solution service dubbed "Mobilİimza."[14] Eventually many other countries adopted this technological innovation.

When considering whether to enhance the economic opportunities and welfare of the poor, one must be clear in noting that innovation by itself is

---

[13] Vijay Mahajan, "How Unilever Reaches Rural Consumers in Emerging Markets," *Harvard Business Review*, December 14, 2016.

[14] "Signature in Turkey—A Case Study of Turkcell: Mobilİimza," *GSMA Newsletter*, July 3, 2013.

insufficient to improve living standards: "it must be inclusive, meaning that it must be accessible and affordable to those at the BOP (base of the pyramid) or help create better economic opportunities for them."[15] This *inclusive* innovation centers upon knowledge creation, acquisition, absorption, and distribution activities directed at meeting the needs of low-income populations. The emphasis on inclusive innovation is becoming ever more compelling, as more than 40 percent of the world's population falls below the international poverty line and inequality continues to widen, creating greater political, social, and economic instability in a number of locales.

Two categories of innovation are especially germane to emerging markets and the BOP segment: reverse innovation and sustainable innovation. Traditionally, innovation has been synonymous with the transfer of knowledge, products, services, and business forms from the developed world to developing countries. However, a disruptive business book titled *Reverse Innovation* by Vijay Govindarajan and Chris Trimble of Dartmouth's Tuck School of Business brought widespread attention to this unique form of innovation: one embodying the scaling of growth in emerging markets, and importing low-cost and high-impact innovations to mature ones. See Fig. 8.3 for a sample of reverse innovations.

Given the incredible growth and access to technology in the developing world, combined with wider availability of venture capital and angel

	Innovation	Description	Country
1	GE MAC 400 electrocardiogram machine	Portable, low-cost electrocardiogram machine	India
2	Lyft	Ride sharing/peer-to-peer taxi service	Zimbabwe
3	John Deere 5003 series tractor	Basic tractor model	India
4	The Odon device	Low-cost labor device	Argentina
5	Tata Nano car	Basic, low-cost car model	India
6	Allview tablets	Affordable tablet	Romania
7	Walmart Bodegas Aurrera	Small format stores	Mexico
8	Microsoft starter	Simple operating system	India/Thailand
9	Synoptix diagnostic device	Breast cancer early detection device	Saudi Arabia
10	Minute Maid Pulpy	Orange juice with pulp	China

Fig. 8.3 Reverse innovations. (Source: Authors)

---

[15] Carl Dahlman, Esperanza Lasagabaster, and Kurt Larsen, "Inclusive Innovation: Harnessing Creativity to Enhance Economic Opportunities and Welfare of the Poor," in Jerry Haar and Ricardo, Ernst, eds., *Innovation in Emerging Markets*, Basingstoke, U.K.: Palgrave Macmillan, 2016.

investment, not to mention governmental support of technology-based economic development, innovation hotbeds have sprung up in all emerging market regions. Consequently, innovation activities have gradually moved from the West to the developing world. In the past, products were innovated and produced for the developed world for eventual expansion to the developing world as production volumes increased and prices decreased. However, over time a greater percentage of innovations is adopted first in emerging markets to eventually spread to the developed world.

An excellent example of *reverse innovation* is GE Healthcare's MAC400, a low-cost, portable, battery-operated electrocardiogram machine in India that has since spread to numerous developed markets due to its functionality and attractive price. The machine can be easily transported to rural areas in the developing world and provides a crucial medical service at a fraction of the traditional cost. Mobility-impaired patients can have the procedure directly in their bed, preventing the pain and trouble caused by moving.[16]

As for *sustainable innovation,* it is not commonly known that developing nations are in the forefront of creating innovative solutions to recycle waste, thus gaining access to recycled materials and reducing contamination and ever-expanding landfills. One of the best examples is "bottle brick" technology, developed in Latin America and India as a method whereby plastic bottles are packaged with mud or sand to be used as a replacement for actual bricks in construction. The product is much cheaper and more durable than bricks and offers more heat shelter due to its thick perimeter. Guatemalan schoolchildren are instructed in building "bottle schools" by filling plastic bottles with plastic wrappers. These bottles are then stacked and covered in cement and serve principally as insulation, rather than structural support, and provide the students with classrooms.[17] See Fig. 8.4 for a summary of sustainable innovations.

Another example can be found in Lagos, Nigeria, where human waste is converted into biogas through a relatively simple addition of inexpensive retrofit entry waste pipes to existing underground septic tanks.[18] In this method, the waste pipes extract oxygen from the decaying waste and produce a combustible gas. This technique eliminates the problem of airborne disease and provides self-produced energy to fuel Nigerian households.

---

[16] Vijay Govindarajan and Chris Trimble, *Reverse Innovation*, Boston: Harvard Business Review Press, 2012.

[17] Rob Hopkins, "EcoBricks and education: how plastic bottle rubbish is helping build schools," *The Guardian*, May 29, 2014.

[18] George Webster, "How Human Waste Could Power Nigeria's Slums," *CNN*, September 26, 2011.

Innovation	Description	Country
Hug It Forward	Bricks of garbage-filled bottles	Guatemala
Polypropylene Box	Disposable refrigeration box	Brazil
Human Biogas	Energy from human sewage	Nigeria
Hippo Water Roller	Efficient transport of water	South Africa
Advantix AC	AC using salt and water to cool air	Israel
Easy Latrine	Simple, low-cost toilet	Cambodia
Bottle Light	Lightbulb created by bottle filled with water and bleach	Brazil
Mitticool Fridge	Nonelectric clay refrigerator	India
Soletek	Multisource renewable heating	Estonia
WiseSoil	Accelerator transforming organic waste into energy	Russia

Fig. 8.4 Sustainable innovations. (Source: Authors)

Finally, two Brazilian companies, SOL Embalagens and Braskem, innovated a new concept of disposable boxes for food transport (particularly for exports), since bacteria proliferation and breakage were a common issue with existing boxes and sanitary compliance was at stake. The commercialization of their innovation entails new boxes that are easy to assemble and made of 100 percent polypropylene. Light, extremely durable, and bacteria-resistant, they have an on-screen injection structure using heat exchange for cooling, leading to lower power consumption than traditional cooling boxes. They are easy to clean and can be reused over and over.[19]

Innovations aimed at, as well as developed by, communities at the bottom of the pyramid are and will continue to be an important feature of business in the global economy and one that shareholders and stakeholders alike will consider in deliberations surrounding corporate activities, in emerging markets in particular.

As noted by innovation and design strategy consultant Deepa Prahalad: "Business has already made the world a better place by creating shared experiences and aspirations. The challenge ahead will be in unleashing innovation to create shared prosperity."[20]

---

[19] "Sustainable innovation in plastic boxes unveiled for fruits and meat products," www.plastemart.com, June 6, 2009.

[20] Deepa Prahalad, "The New Fortune at the Bottom of the Pyramid," Strategy+Business, 94, 2019: 1–13.

The BOP Consumer

The bottom of the pyramid consumer is not a monolithic being. Apart from economic status (in which there are various gradations), BOP consumer behavior is shaped by cultural, ethnic, religious, nationality, and geographic factors.

Measuring and comparing different BOP markets is both complex and complicated due to issues such as variation in poverty-line benchmarks, exchange rate fluctuations, and the socioeconomic variations among countries.[21] Traditionally, the BOP has been considered the domain of governments, aid agencies, and nonprofit organizations and is overwhelmingly composed of the informal economy—a subsector that accounts for as much as 30 percent to 60 percent of the total economic activity in some developing countries.[22]

Eight characteristics align with BOP consumers, according to a study of global and local BOP characteristics to model country-specific consumer profiles.[23] These characteristics are as follows.

Significant buying power. Recognizably, BOP consumers have relatively low incomes compared to consumers in industrialized nations, but there is as much as $1.3 trillion buying power at the aggregated level. Just the South African market alone has a BOP consumer market worth nearly $41 billion annually, and these consumers have significant control over their spending power.

A life under pressure. Poor infrastructure and limited social and economic support are constraints on the lives of lower-income consumers. Unemployment, low and inconsistent income, high inflation, and price surges all impact spending patterns. They often have to pay more for the same products as wealthier consumers, lack consumer protection, and are hampered by poor and unreliable services for water, sanitation, and electricity.[24]

High rates of functional illiteracy. Since many BOP consumers are functionally illiterate, brand-related information in picture form is the optimal way to communicate with them to influence their purchasing decision- making,

---

[21] James Lapperman, Kristin Ransome, and Zach Louw, "Not One Segment: Using Global and Local BoP Characteristics to Model Country-Specific Consumer Profiles," European Business Review, 31, 3, 2019: 317–336.

[22] Ted London and Stuart L. Hart, *Next Generation Business Strategies for the Base of the Pyramid,* Noida: Pearson Education India, 2010.

[23] Lapperman et al.

[24] Ans Kolk, Miguel Rivera-Santos, and Carlos Ruffin, "Reviewing a Decade of Research on the "Base/Bottom of the Pyramid" (BOP) Concept," *Business and Society,* 55,3, 2013: 338–377.

although their choice encompasses one attribute only. Consumers who are functionally illiterate often trade economic value and convenience for emotional goals. To effectively handle the shopping experience, BOP consumers are most likely to shop at the same locations, frequent smaller stores, and buy only name brands and in small quantities.[25] Building personal relationships with store proprietors and store personnel is deemed extremely important in the mindset of the BOP shopper.

Strong sense of community and partnership. Social relationships and community interaction are paramount among the BOP. The norms of social capital and networks allow these citizens to establish and maintain strong bonds of cooperation and collaboration and mutual assistance whenever needed. It is embodied in the "extended family." A collectivist mindset lives side-by-side individual initiative and personal aspirations. The sense of belonging and supporting a particular social group, neighborhood, or a religious or political organization strengthens the idea of community.

Connectivity. The explosive expansion of mobile communications and digital technology has empowered BOP consumers to purchase goods and services—especially low-cost ones, like mobile phone services—which they had not imagined possible before. Fast-growing cellphone markets in Asia, Africa, and Latin America have created very attractive business prospects, not just for mobile devices and pre-paid SIM cards but for those consumer product companies that utilize mobile technologies to generate sales.

Dignity and self-esteem. BOP consumers place a high value on self-respect and dignity. They may not have a lot of money, but they have their pride and they expect others, regardless of socioeconomic status, to treat them with dignity.[26] As an aspirational segment of consumer markets, many BOP purchasers base their spending decisions on the desire to accumulate material possessions to put themselves on par with the rest of society and to gain self-esteem at the same time. This is not to say that BOP consumers will purchase goods and services that will put them in debt; on the contrary, most are judicious in terms of the amount of money they spend, but they will stretch to obtain the psychic and emotional satisfaction of demonstrating to others that they are on par with them as human beings.

Brand consciousness. BOP consumers are aware of popular brands and generally prefer them much more than non-popular ones. While price is a major

---

[25] Van R. Wood, Dennis A. Pitta, Frank J. Franzak, *"Successful marketing by multinational firms to the bottom of the pyramid: connecting share of heart, global 'umbrella brands', and responsible marketing," Journal of Consumer Marketing*, 5, 27, 2008: 393–401.

[26] Edgard Barki and Juracy Parente, "Consumer behavior of the base of the pyramid in Brazil," Greener Management International, 2006, 56, 2006: 11–23.

factor in their buying decisions, they also place considerable weight on trust, image, personality, and reputation. Branded goods, providing backing, confidence, and quality, are universally the first choice among BOP consumers.[27]

Lack of trust in big firms. BOP consumers may well value the products of multinational firms but at the same time disapprove of their "bigness" and the perception that they exploit low-income markets. This dichotomy—a strong affinity by BOP consumers for the brands of major firms while distrusting the companies themselves—is prevalent across geographic regions. Certain industries such as banking and insurance are held in low regard by BOP consumers.

There are many myths about emerging market consumers, and in a study conducted by Booz and Company (rebranded as Strategy& following its sale to PricewaterhouseCoopers), researchers investigated buying behavior and supermarket retail trade trends in six Latin American countries.[28] They found that although BOP consumers are poor, they spend proportionately more of their money (50–75 percent) on consumer goods than those in wealthier segments, and they buy premium-priced branded products—not only in staples but in "aspirational" products such as dishwasher detergent, condensed milk, canned tuna, makeup, and shampoo. At the same time, BOP shoppers take into account many other factors, besides price, in tallying up their shopping costs (e.g., transportation, child care); they shop daily and make small purchases due to their limited and unstable cash flow.

Two other characteristics of the BOP consumer should also be noted. First, these shoppers are fully satisfied with traditional retailers and not looking to move "upscale" to modern supermarkets. Small, neighborhood, independent stores make them feel more comfortable, and the social experience—interaction with the shop owner and staff whom they know well—is something they value greatly. They also enjoying shopping at street markets since they highly value "farm fresh" products. Second, while one would suspect that given their limited finances and unstable economic situation, BOP shoppers would be highly dependent on credit, this is not the case at all, as proven by research. These consumers use credit to *extend* their purchasing power. They tap the goodwill and long-term relationships with shopkeepers to provide them with short-term credit and in small amounts.

Finally, despite the monumental growth of metropolitan areas during the last half century, such as Shanghai, Mexico City, Lagos, Cairo, São Paulo,

---

[27] Mizan Rahman, Rajibul Hasan, and David Floyd, "Brand orientation as a strategy that influences the adoption of innovation in the bottom of the pyramid," *Strategic Change*, 22, 3/4, 2013: 225–239.

[28] Guillermo D'Andrea, E. Alejandro Stengel, and Anne-Goebel-Krstelj, "6 Truths about Emerging-Market Consumers," *Strategy+Business*, issue 34, Spring 2004.

most of the world's poor live in rural areas.[29] Here, too, there are fortunes at the bottom of the pyramid. In India where two-thirds of the population is rural, over half of all fast-moving consumer goods, including 45 percent of soft drinks, more than 50 percent of life insurance policies, and half of all motorcycles, are sold in rural areas.[30]

Microfinance

For those individuals and small businesses that do not have access to traditional banking services, microfinance provides a solution to their needs. These services, mainly in the form of microcredit, aim to reach precisely those at the bottom of the pyramid. Besides helping the poor and underserved with their specific financial needs, microfinance is yet another tool to promote economic development, employment, and growth via microenterprises and small businesses, be they urban or rural. According to Plan International Canada, over 2 billion adults and 800 million young people worldwide do not have access to formal financial services, and in sub-Saharan Africa less than 30 percent of women have an account with a financial institution.[31]

The benefits of microfinance for the BOP segment of society are multiple. To begin with, it allows people to provide for their families, provides access to credit when traditional lenders such as banks are reluctant to do so, and it serves those often overlooked in society, especially women whom research has shown to be far better credit risks than men. It creates the possibility of future investments. Microfinance can create jobs, encourage people to save, and offer better loan repayment rates than traditional lenders.[32]

Microfinance, then, may involve very small loans and financial services, but it has had a worldwide impact over the last four-plus decades. For a small business that needs just a bit of extra cash or credit to secure a new opportunity, microfinance may be just the ticket. And for a small lending or banking business looking for new opportunities, microfinance literally offers a world of opportunities—one small loan or financial service at a time.

---

[29] Homi Kharas, Constanza Di Nucci, Kristofer Hamel and Baldwin Tong, "To Move the Needle on Ending Extreme Poverty, Focus on Rural Areas," *Brookings Report,* February 21, 2020.

[30] "The fortune at the bottom of the pyramid," Financial Express Bureau, New Delhi, May 21, 2018.

[31] "Economic Empowerment: What is Microfinance?, https://plancanada.ca/microfinance-benefits.

[32] Louise Gaille, "12 Benefits of Microfinance in Developing Countries," *Vittana,* January 9, 2017; Sugato Chakravarty, S. M. Zahid Iqbal, and Abu Zafar M. Shahriar, "Are Women 'Naturally' Better Credit Risks in Microcredit?," presentation at the 2014 Annual Meeting of the American Economic Association, Philadelphia, PA, January 3–5, 2014.

Nevertheless, microcredit is not a panacea to endemic problems related to poverty. Geographically dispersed and highly mobile populations pose severe challenges for microlenders, as do borrowers with debilitating diseases such as diabetes and HIV/AIDS, or severe psychological problems, and those whose livelihood in agriculture depends on a single crop. Then there are the major issues of economic volatility, especially high levels of inflation, and the tax and regulatory burdens that are especially challenging for microenterprises and small business.[33]

Four cases are illustrative of microfinance for BOP populations.

Bangladesh. The Grameen Bank is the most prominent and most widely cited example of BOP microfinance in emerging markets. In 1976, Dr. Muhammad Yunus, an economics professor at Chittagong University, started a project by lending an amount of $27 to forty-two poor persons in a village near to his university. Due to a massive famine, Dr. Yunus visited the villages near to his university campus and found the village people suffering from extreme poverty. Yunus found that in order to survive, these people used to take loans from the local informal money lenders with difficult loan terms, since banks would not lend to them. The solution was for him to approach the bank and guarantee the loans and thus was born Grameen Bank. However, the success of the bank can be attributed to its mission and operations. First, the belief that the problem of poverty cannot be solved through charity and that charity creates dependency. Poor people can succeed if they mobilize their energy, creativity, and commitment, and that the more likely they are to pay back their loans to Grameen Bank, the more money the bank will loan to them. In other words, creditworthiness is everything. Additionally, the bank believes that it is more important to lend to women than to men as women can bring more benefits to the families.

Grameen Bank loans are not provided for consumption but to create self-employment. In general, three types of loans are given to the poor: income-generating loans, housing loans, and higher education loans for the children of the families of the borrowers. What makes Grameen Bank truly unique is its innovative lending policy. In order to get the loan from the bank, the borrowers have to form a group, generally consisting of five members. One important feature of group-based lending is the use of peer pressure as a substitute collateral, since the peers of the borrowers have to take the loan jointly.

---

[33] Leon Teeboom, "The Role of Microfinance Institutions," *Chron*, February 4, 2019.

So, as the loan is not given on an individual basis, there remains a joint responsibility for the repayment of the loans.[34]

Colombia. The Colombian microfinance sector is the largest in Latin America, both in terms of total active borrowers served and outstanding gross loans disbursed. The success of microfinance in Colombia is due in no small part to the strong partnerships between key governmental, non-governmental, and private sector actors. Since its inception in the early 1980s the sector has been growing steadily toward achieving scale and deepening access to finance. Downscaling commercial banks, commercial finance companies, financial cooperatives, loans and savings cooperatives, and NGOs are the major players in providing microfinance services in the market.

The country has a very well-developed, consolidated system of microfinance; however, the interest rates charged on microcredit are actually higher than interest rates on other financial products. This is due to the risk factor with respect to the borrower; however, microcredit is not particularly risky and the bad loan rate is low. Therefore, microcredit lending, with relatively high interest rates and good profit margins, provides an attractive opportunity for investors who, in turn, expand the pool of capital to loan to BOP customers.[35]

Kenya. Africa is a fertile terrain for scaling up microfinance initiatives, and the Kenyan Rural Enterprise Program (K-Rep) is a compelling example. It has been able to apply best practices and scales up to meet the objective of substantial welfare impact. K-Rep was able to achieve its goal of scaling up through commercializing. Its transformation from an unsustainable NGO project to a viable commercial bank with considerable outreach is evidence that implementing microfinance best practices, while engaging the regulatory environment and persevering through setbacks, can lead to a sustainable microfinance program with substantial outreach. The K-Rep program advances sufficiently high interest rates, high loan portfolio standards, a strong productivity orientation, effective liquidity management, and a diverse product mix.[36]

---

[34] Dewan Mahboob Hossain, "Social Capital and Microfinance: The Case of Grameen Bank, Bangladesh," *Middle East Journal of Business*, 8, 4, 2013: 13–21.

[35] Carmelo Intrisano and Anna Paola Micheli, "An Asset for an International Investor: The Colombian MFIs," International Business Research, 8, 8, 2015: 191–203.

[36] Catherine Burns, "Scaling Up Microfinance in Africa: Best Practices and a Case Study from Kenya," *SPICE: Student Perspectives on Institutions, Choices and Ethics*, 3, 1, 2008, article 1; Forah M. Obebo, Nelson H. W. Wawire, and Joseph M. Muniu "Determinants of Participation of Micro and Small Enterprises in Microfinance in Kenya," *International Journal of Management Sciences*, 7, 3, 2018: 1–5.

Finally, a word about microfinance and the multilateral lending institutions. Multilateral financial institutions play a significant role in financial small and medium-sized enterprise projects worldwide, be it the World Bank, International Finance Corporation, or the development banks of Latin America and the Caribbean, Asia, and Africa.[37] For example, on July 1, 2020, the World Bank Board of Directors approved a US$260 million loan for Ecuador's National Finance Corporation to promote access to financing for microenterprises and small and medium enterprises (SMEs) for productive activities.[38]

The bottom of the pyramid is precisely where M2W principles manifest themselves most clearly. As firms take ownership and accountability for the relationship with marginalized consumer segments of society, working with a range of stakeholders to do well and do good at the same time, more and more enterprises across the globe are shaping their commitments for greater involvement with this important, non-traditional segment of the market.

---

[37] See: https://projects.worldbank.org/en/projects-operations/project-detail/P095554?lang=en; https://www.adb.org/sectors/finance/microfinance; https://www.afdb.org/en/topics-and-sectors/initiatives-partnerships/microfinance-multidonor-trust-fund; https://www.iadb.org/en/topics/microfinance/microfinance-latin-america-and-caribbean; https://www.ifc.org/wps/wcm/connect/industry_ext_content/ifc_exte.rnal_corporate_site/financial+institutions/resources/ifc+microfinance+%2D%2D+creating+opportunity+in+emerging+markets

[38] World Bank, "Ecuador Will Receive US$260 Million from the World Bank to Finance Loans for Microenterprises and SMEs," Press Release, July 1, 2020.

9

M2W and the Multinational Enterprise

The multinational enterprise epitomizes the Me to We (M2W) nexus, given the myriad of relationships global corporations maintain with both business and non-business entities. While the flow of goods, labor, and capital has contributed to the increase in welfare among peoples and countries, there have also been associated costs. For example, despite the fact that inequality between countries has been decreasing, indeed, growing inequality is not a universal trend. The Gini coefficient of income inequality has declined in most Latin American and Caribbean nations as well as several African and Asian countries over the last two decades.[1] However, inequality within these countries has worsened.[2] Therefore, the movement of goods, labor, and capital requires some vigilance in practice, increasing the need for M2W to become a cornerstone of all corporations.

Despite the benefits and overall economic growth experienced mostly by developed countries as a result of the growth of multinational corporations (MNCs), governments and the public in both developed and developing nations have mixed feelings about the presence and contribution of these firms. Poor labor conditions, environmental degradation, and allegations of corruption are some of the reasons cited by critics of MNCs. The following question then arises: How should MNCs behave when they operate in a country where labor, business, and environmental practices and standards are lower than those existing in the home country of the MNC? Overall, these

---

[1] United Nations, *Inequality in a Rapidly Changing World*, World Social Report 2020, New York: United Nations, 2020.
[2] Kemal Derviş and Zia Qureshi. "Income Distribution Within Countries: Rising Inequality," Policy Brief, The Brookings Institution, August 2016.

R. Ernst, J. Haar, *From Me to We*, https://doi.org/10.1007/978-3-030-87424-7_9

practices have created a new set of challenges and opportunities for companies as well as a need to move to a new mindset. For MNCs to move past profit-seeking objectives they must adopt a M2W imperative approach as part of their strategy to contribute to the alleviation of global issues.

Related to M2W—a precursor, actually—is ESG. As spelled out by PricewaterhouseCoopers (PwC), ESG entails:

- **E (environmental):** carbon emissions, water and waste management, raw material sourcing, climate change vulnerability
- **S (social):** diversity, equity, inclusion, labor management, data privacy and security, community relations
- **G (governance):** board governance, business ethics, intellectual property protection.[3]

ESG factors have been growing in importance in shareholder-stakeholder relations. Ethical consideration and alignment with values are the common motivations of ESG investors; consequently, many corporate investors look to include ESG factors into the investment process alongside traditional financial analysis.[4]

According to Deloitte, 26 percent of professionally managed assets in the US had ESG mandates in 2018, up from 11 percent in 2012. Much is concentrated (25 percent) in the hands of several giant money managers such as Black Rock, Vanguard, and State Street; these firms are increasingly likely to support shareholder resolutions by ESG activists.[5] ESG can encompass such environmental issues as climate change and resource scarcity, social issues like a firm's labor practices, talent management, product safe and data security, and governance issues including board diversity, executive pay, and business ethics.

As companies respond, the results can show up tangibly in the marketplace. To illustrate, Burger King launched the "Impossible Whopper," featuring a vegan patty with 10 percent of the carbon footprint of a beef hamburger. After its success, it was soon followed by McDonald's "McPlant." GM pledged to sell only zero-emission vehicles by 2035; United Airlines promised that by

---

[3] PWC, *ESG Reporting*, PricewaterhouseCoopers, https://www.pwc.com/us/en/services/audit-assurance/esg-reporting.html?WT.mc_id%27CT3-PL300-DM1-TR1-LS3-ND30-PRG7-CN_ESG-Google&gclid=Cj0KCQjwo-aCBhCARIsAAkNQiuz6v50rPjVt17sD06DaWchpP7jJMLs3o5SIPYaFwcYm0AeGYunywUaApmAEALw_wcB&gclsrc=aw.ds.

[4] MSCI, *MSCI Investment Insights Report*, 2021. https://www.msci.com/our-clients/asset-owners/investment-insights-report.

[5] Sean Collins and Kristen Sullivan, "Advancing environmental, social, and governance investing: A holistic approach for investment management firms," *Deloitte Insights*, February 20, 2020.

2030, it would reduce its greenhouse gas emissions 100 percent.[6] For ESG to be truly meaningful and embody the concept of shared value, it must have *profit-driven* social impact. And when it is, the outcomes for companies can be dramatic. To give an example, research by Aaron Yoon, Mozaffar Khan, and George Serafeim found that when companies focus their sustainability efforts on material, social, and environmental factors, they significantly outperform the market.[7]

Both research findings and documented accounts of business practice bear out that a strong ESG proposition can create value for an enterprise, linking cash flow in five important ways: (1) spurring top-line growth; (2) curtailing costs; (3) minimizing regulatory and legal interventions; (4) enhancing the productivity of employees; and (5) optimizing investment and capital expenditures.[8] Figure 9.1 displays the links between ESG and value creation in five essential ways.

We present examples of different stakeholder relationships that vividly illustrate the connection between the multinational enterprise and key constituencies groups that form the "We" in the Me to We equation.

Multinationals and Suppliers

Multinationals have been increasing their efforts to work with suppliers that abide by environmental, health, and human rights standards. Ideally, MNCs would not only expect their direct supplier to comply with these standards, but would also expect them to ask their own suppliers to comply with these standards, and so on. This would create a ripple effect in which sustainable practices are amplified across multiple supply chains, enabling better practices across the supply network. However, this has been difficult in practice, with many companies coming under scrutiny because of their suppliers' actions. For example, Nike and Adidas were under fire because their suppliers were dumping contaminants into rivers in China.[9] So, the following question remains: How do MNCs work with suppliers, actual and potential, to ensure

---

[6] Michael O'Leary and Warren Valdmanis, "An ESG Reckoning Is Coming," *Harvard Business Review*, March 4, 2021.

[7] Mozaffar Khan, George Serafeim, and Aaron Yoon, "Corporate Sustainability: First Evidence on Materiality," (November 9, 2016). *The Accounting Review*, Vol. 91, No. 6, pp. 1697-1724.

[8] Witold Henisz, Tim Koller, and Robin Nuttall, "Five Ways that ESG Creates Value," *McKinsey Quarterly*, November, 2019.

[9] Villena and Dennis A. Gioia, V. H. (2020, February 19). A More Sustainable Supply Chain. Retrieved September 28, 2020, from https://hbr.org/2020/03/a-more-sustainable-supply-chain.

	Strong ESG proposition (examples)	Weak ESG proposition (examples)
Top-line growth	Attract B2B and B2C customers with more sustainable products Achieve better access to resources through stronger community and government relations	Lose customers through poor sustainability practices (eg, human rights, supply chain) or a perception of unsustainable/unsafe products Lose access to resources (including from operational shutdowns) as a result of poor community and labor relations
Cost reductions	Lower energy consumption Reduce water intake	Generate unnecessary waste and pay correspondingly higher waste-disposal costs Expend more in packaging costs
Regulatory and legal interventions	Achieve greater strategic freedom through deregulation Earn subsidies and government support	Suffer restrictions on advertising and point of sale Incur fines, penalties, and enforcement actions
Productivity uplift	Boost employee motivation Attract talent through greater social credibility	Deal with "social stigma," which restricts talent pool Lose talent as a result of weak purpose
Investment and asset optimization	Enhance investment returns by better allocating capital for the long term (eg, more sustainable plant and equipment) Avoid investments that may not pay off because of longer-term environmental issues	Suffer stranded assets as a result of premature write-downs Fall behind competitors that have invested to be less "energy hungry"

Fig. 9.1 A strong environmental, social, and governance (ESG) proposition links to value creation in five essential ways. (Source: *McKinsey Quarterly*, November, 2019)

they will be strong and dependable? This is an important topic because lack of commitment from suppliers, including direct and low-tier suppliers, can pose significant risks for the environment, for social safety and health, and for the MNCs.

One of the first steps in order for MNCs to ensure that suppliers along the value chain are dependable and committed to standards is to establish their own sustainability goals and objectives. Additionally, MNCs should work with their direct suppliers so that they can establish their sustainability goals as well. In doing so, direct suppliers become part of the sustainability process and MNCs can hold them accountable to the goals and objectives they have established for themselves. Additionally, MNCs need to consider the following actions[10]:

---

[10] Ibid.

- *Evaluating current practices*—the starting point to ensuring a more sustainable supplier network is to understand the state of current supplier practices and evaluate how these practices match or contradict the company's sustainability goals. This will help to obtain a general picture of the supply networks' practices.
- *Establishing a Supplier code of conduct*—MNCs must have formal documents where they explicitly state the principles under which suppliers are required to operate.
- *Setting performance indicators*—determining the standards expected from suppliers can be done by setting up performance indicators that can measure and assess whether suppliers are abiding to the expected standards. In doing so, direct suppliers are encouraged to also establish such standards from their own suppliers to make it possible to achieve performance indicators.
- *Training*—providing education on best practices and standards among direct suppliers can help foster learning and knowledge along the supply network.
- *Constant monitoring and surveying*—to achieve long-term sustainability objectives, MNCs must appoint a task force to constantly monitor and work closely with suppliers to ensure that they remain committed to the environmental, health, and safety standards. In doing so, MNCs are collecting information about their direct supplier but also about other members of the supply network.
- *Using data and technology*—collecting data can help track improvement and progress toward long-term sustainability goals. Additionally, using such data and taking advantage of technology can also contribute to new ideas and ways to practice sustainability.
- *Encouraging and rewarding new initiatives*—MNCs must set up a system that encourages suppliers to come up with new ideas and strategies to achieve sustainability and reach the established goals. Such initiatives should be rewarded and encouraged throughout the value chain.
- *Working with NGOs and organizations that promote sustainability*—joining organizations like the United Nations Global Compact and other organizations that promote best practices toward environment, health, and safety is a good way to encourage suppliers to join efforts and hold them accountable with these organizations.

Although these are some actions that MNCs can take as part of their process toward improving sustainability across the supply network, this is a long-term process and requires continuous action, commitment, and evaluation.

Developing sustainability beyond direct suppliers is not an easy task and can be faced with multiple challenges. Direct supplier must undergo an approval process and the same should be done with low-tier suppliers. Additionally, accountability must be the cornerstone of the supply network, with all supply chain members holding responsibility for actions that violate sustainability standards.

Best Practices in Supply Chains Around the World[11]

Supply chains have experienced significant, continuous improvement over the last decade, by way of notable advancements in manufacturing technology, information systems, and operations. Gartner, a global research and advisory firm, has ranked the top 25 supply chain firms, as illustrated in Fig. 9.2. (It is interesting to note that there is an ESG component in Gartner's reporting of results.)

Within the context of M2W, three firms—HP, Kimberly-Clark, and General Mills—are noteworthy. HP, most known for its printers and IT products, has focused on improving the sustainability of its company and global supply chain network. The company has set as a goal for 2025 to double the participation of their factories in sustainability programs and to significantly improve the well-being of their 500,000 workers. To do so, HP Inc. has set up transparency principles on their manufacturing processes, and sustainable practices and environmental standards in their global supply chain.

As for Kimberly-Clark, the personal care company whose essential consumer products are used by one out of every four people around the world on a daily basis, is focused on creating business partnerships that enable sustainability on their supply network. Their strategies include actively engaging in environmentally sustainable practices throughout their supply chain and social programs to improve the health and safety of their workers. Finally, General Mills serves as a beacon for sustainable supply chains with commitments and a timeline of measurable accomplishments through 2030. See Fig. 9.3 for the details.

---

[11]Victor, R. (June 09, 2017). Best Supply Chains from Companies Around the World. Retrieved September 28, 2020, from https://www.hollingsworthllc.com/best-supply-chains-companies-around-world/.

Rank	Company	Peer Opinion[1] (151 voters). (25%)	Gartner Opinion[1] (44 voters) (25%)	Three-Year Weighted ROPA[2] (20%)	Inventory Turns[3.] (5%)	Three-Year Weighted Revenue Growth[4] (10%)	ESG Component Score[5] (15%)	Composite Score[6]
1	Cisco Systems	470	574	300.7%	12.5	2.9%	10.00	6.25
2	Colgate-Palmolive	1113	532	68.8%	4.7	1.0%	10.00	5.37
3	Johnson & Johnson	885	454	77.6%	3.0	3.6%	8.00	4.65
4	Schneider Electric	567	453	63.0%	5.4	4.2%	10.00	4.48
5	Nestlé	1084	350	40.0%	4.8	1.2%	10.00	4.44
6	PepsiCo	857	385	47.9%	8.2	2.7%	10.00	4.42
7	Alibaba	991	316	106.7%	23.9	54.0%	0.00	4.39
8	Intel	583	488	37.4%	3.5	5.8%	8.00	4.12
9	Inditex	737	351	34.7%	4.6	6.8%	10.00	4.11
10	L'Oréal	677	252	71.1%	2.8	7.4%	10.00	4.01
11	Walmart	1333	324	13.2%	8.5	2.4%	7.00	4.00
12	HP Inc.	296	389	51.1%	8.5	5.5%	10.00	3.87
13	Coca Cola Company	1195	207	75.4%	4.4	0.0%	6.00	3.74
14	Diageo	403	280	41.4%	0.9	6.2%	10.00	3.49
15	Lenovo	397	307	16.9%	11.2	7.0%	10.00	3.44
16	Nike	768	265	47.2%	4.0	6.7%	6.00	3.35
17	AbbVie	128	30	262.4%	4.1	7.6%	5.00	3.20
18	BMW	575	182	24.8%	3.9	4.2%	10.00	3.17
19	Starbucks	799	202	52.6%	13.0	7.7%	4.00	2.99
20	H&M	412	161	22.4%	2.8	7.7%	10.00	2.95
21	British American Tobacco	154	56	85.6%	0.7	18.1%	9.00	2.90
22	3M	624	207	54.1%	3.9	1.1%	6.00	2.90
23	Reckitt Benckiser	265	14	99.0%	3.8	8.2%	9.00	2.79
24	Biogen	79	27	152.2%	2.5	7.8%	7.00	2.78
25	Kimberly-Clark	534	80	34.6%	6.6	0.2%	10.00	2.76

Fig. 9.2 The Gartner supply chain top 25 for 2020. (Source: "Garnter Announces Rankings of the 2020 Supply Chain Top 25" (May 2020), https://www.gartner.com/en/newsroom/press-releases/2020-05-20-gartner-announces-rankings-of-the-2020-supply-chain-top-25)

Commitment and Progress
2020
• Sustainable source 100% of our 10 priority Ingredients ✓ **Progress through 2019:** 91% achieved
2021
• Protect and establish 100,000 acres of pollinator habitat ✓ **Progress through 2019:** 207,000 acres restores or protected
2025
• Reduce absolute GHG emissions across our full value chain by 28% compared to 2010 ✓ **Progress through 2019:** 14% reduction • Champion the activation of water stewardship plans for the company's 8 priority watersheds ✓ **Progress through 2019:** 3 of 8 watersheds have active water stewardship in place • Achieve zero waste to landfill at 100% of our owned production facilities ✓ **Progress through 2019:** 24% achieved
2030
• Achieve 100% of packaging recyclable by design ✓ **Progress through 2019:** Approximately 88% of our packaging in the US (by weight) met the criteria • Advance regenerative agriculture practices on 1 million acres of farmland ✓ **Progress through 2019:** Measurement in progress

Fig. 9.3 General Mills' sustainable supply chain mode. (Source: Sustainability. (n.d.). Retrieved September 28, 2020, from https://www.generalmills.com/en/Responsibility/Sustainability.aspx)

Establishing a Supplier Code of Conduct

As previously mentioned, more and more MNCs are establishing supplier codes of conduct or formal documents in which the company explicitly states the principles under which suppliers are required to operate. This code of conduct is created to ensure that all suppliers' practices are environmentally responsible, safe for workers, and respectful toward them. A code of conduct must include these areas: environmental policies (i.e., components, raw materials, manufacturing processes, technology of transport to be used), labor practices (i.e., policies against child labor, discrimination, standards for workers' safety and health, compensation and rights), and ethics (i.e., policies against corruption and fair business practices).[12]

For a company that seeks to formulate and implement a code of conduct, a common place to start is to speak with other companies in the industry, as well as with suppliers who are working with other companies who have codes

---

[12] Supplier Code of Conduct Definition (February 28, 2020). Retrieved September 28, 2020, from https://ecovadis.com/academy/supplier-code-conduct/.

of conduct. This will provide useful guidelines and examples based on industry initiatives and industry practices. Whirlpool and Hershey are illustrative of companies that follow sound codes of conduct.

Whirlpool. The company established its Supplier Code of Conduct in which the objective is to do business with companies who are reputable and committed to the same practices and ethical standards as Whirlpool. This code sets the standards for all of Whirlpool's suppliers and the company has been explicit in stating that suppliers must aim to exceed the requirements of the code and work toward continuous improvement in their operations. One of the most important tenets of this Supplier Code of Conduct is that "*Whirlpool suppliers must not use any type of involuntary or forced labor; this prohibits, among other things, slave labor or business practices which in any way rely on, or encourage, human trafficking.*"[13]

To make sure that suppliers understand and abide to the Code of Conduct, Whirlpool has implemented a training system in which sourcing professionals are trained on the code of conduct through e-learning courses. These professionals are constantly required to review and retake the courses to keep them updated with changing circumstances. Through this training program, sourcing professionals can certify their knowledge of the code of conduct and be held accountable when audits are performed through third-party agencies. Failures to comply with the code can result in the termination of business relationships with suppliers.

The Hershey Company. With a history of more than 125 years, this company has established its commitment toward implementing high ethical business standards and integrity across its business partnerships and throughout the communities where they operate. To ensure that this holds true for their operations across the globe, they have set up a Supplier Code of Conduct delineating their expectations for suppliers to uphold their standards of integrity and business principles. The Hershey Company requires all suppliers to adhere to local regulations of the markets where they operate. However, in the case of markets where the national laws differ from their Supplier Code of Conduct, Hershey expects suppliers to abide to the more stringent standards. Additionally, the Hershey Company encourages suppliers to exceed the requirements established in the code and work toward continuous improvement.[14]

---

[13] Supplier Code of Conduct / Supply Chain Transparency. (2020, June 02). Retrieved September 28, 2020, from https://www.whirlpoolcorp.com/supplier-code-of-conduct/.

[14] The Hershey Company Supplier Code of Conduct (2019). Retrieved September 282, 2020 from https://www.thehersheycompany.com/content/dam/corporate-us/documents/partners-and-suppliers/supplier-code-of-conduct.pdf.

The M2W approach is also explicitly captured in many of these examples through the corporate and supplier protocols—an example of bottom-up shared value, whereby one entity establishes protocols that embody ownership by and accountability of members to meet standards of responsible corporate behavior, especially as it regards women and children in developing countries. In 2018, a total of 123 apparel and footwear companies signed a "AAFA/FLA Apparel & Footwear Industry Commitment to Responsible Recruitment," reflecting the industry's commitment to the fair treatment of workers in the global apparel, footwear, and travel goods supply chain.[15] Developed in conjunction with the American Apparel & Footwear Association and the Fair Labor Association, the Commitment is a proactive industry effort to address potential forced labor risks for migrant workers in the global supply chain. Each signatory commits to working with its partners to create conditions where no worker pays for their job; where workers retain control of their travel documents and have full freedom of movement; and where workers are informed of the basic terms of their employment before joining the workforce. The FLA counts some of the world's leading brands among its affiliates, organizations that have committed to ensuring fair labor practices and safe and humane working conditions throughout their supply chains. FLA holds participating companies accountable for monitoring 100 percent of their supply chains for compliance with FLA standards, and FLA conducts independent assessments of a random sample of each company's supplier factories. Firms like Hanes, New Balance, Nike, and Patagonia are all active members of the association.

MNCs and Universities

Research partnerships between companies and universities have become a common practice in the last decade, as a way for companies to reap the benefits of accessing the best minds for their research activities. These partnerships are beneficial to both parties. On the one hand, they help companies reduce their spending on the early stages of research by having universities perform those activities with the most talented minds. On the other, universities can overcome the challenges of conducting research with less support from the government by receiving support from private companies. Because

---

[15] "123 apparel and footwear companies signed the new AAFA/FLA Apparel & Footwear Industry Commitment to Responsible Recruitment," Fair Labor Association, October 22, 2018. https://www.fairlabor.org/blog/entry/123-apparel-and-footwear-companies-sign-new-aafa/fla-apparel-footwear-industry-commitment.

of these benefits, both parties have become more open to such partnerships and have focused on creating long-term projects that result in more productive collaborative relationships. However, these partnerships necessitate strong non-disclosure agreements that protect intellectual property without sacrificing flexibility in the collaborative projects. Figure 9.4 illustrates the expectations in academic-industry partnerships.

A noticeable example of these partnerships has been the collaborations between Silicon Valley and the universities in close proximity to it—Stanford University and University of California Berkeley, among others. These partnerships have provided companies in Silicon Valley with access to R&D talent, creating an innovative cluster in the region. The same holds for other university-company collaborative areas such as North Carolina's Research

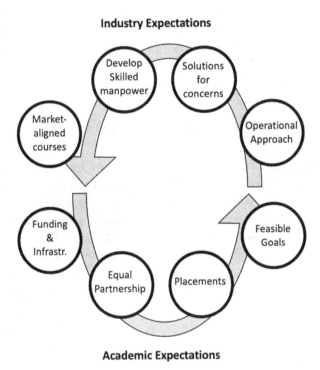

Fig. 9.4 Expectations in academic-industry partnerships. (Source: World Economic Forum, https://www.weforum.org/agenda/2018/11/3-ways-to-nurture-collaboration-between-universities-and-industry/)

Triangle, Greater Boston, Austin, Atlanta, and Boulder. Another example is the University of Minnesota and its research center on medical devices, which has also forged one of the strongest innovation ecosystems in the area of medical technology. The Boston area, which is home to more than 25 higher education institutions, has seen the establishment of companies like Pfizer and Philips Healthcare. Companies from other industries like the tech giants Facebook and Twitter have also established headquarters in the area or opened R&D headquarters and research centers in this part of the country to be at the center of this innovation ecosystem.[16] Moving to these locations shows great commitment from companies to move away from one-off projects to more durable, long-term collaborations that allow companies to forge strong relationships with these institutions and further multiple research projects as they emerge.

Why are these partnerships necessary? Our current society's challenges are evident and urgent, and combining the skills, knowledge, and resources available in universities and companies can foster innovative ways to address these pressing issues. These types of collaborations provide tangible benefits to the parties involved and to the society at large.

Benefits of Partnerships with Universities

Collaborative partnerships between companies and universities have become essential drivers of innovation, allowing for the creation of knowledge through focused research, innovative solutions, and the development of improved products and services. As noted by Osmar Zavaleta, interim dean of EGADE, Tec de Monterrey's graduate business school: "Through long-term corporate relationships, with companies such as Cemex, Ternium, Metalsa, among others, our students have had the opportunity to participate in relevant corporate projects and challenges that have complemented significantly their academic formation."[17] This is the case, as well, with Colombia's Universidad de los Andes, which enjoys a long-standing relationship and partnership agreements with private companies, particularly in the agribusiness and food industries, according to dean Veneta Andonova.[18]

---

[16] Lutchen, K. (2018, January 24). Why Companies and Universities Should Forge Long-Term Collaborations. Retrieved September 28, 2020, from https://hbr.org/2018/01/why-companies-and-universities-should-forge-long-term-collaborations.

[17] Correspondence with Osmar Zavaleta, June 1, 2021.

[18] Correspondence with Veneta Andonova, May 27, 2021.

By providing the most talented minds, these relationships have become an essential partner for companies wishing to create next-generation products that solve essential problems. Additionally, these partnerships have allowed for the development of regional innovation ecosystems where universities are key stakeholders in these knowledge networks composed of governments, companies, investors, and entrepreneurs.

Despite the evident benefits of these partnerships, putting them into practice entails several challenges when it comes to establishing and running the partnership effectively. Because of the multiple stakeholders involved in these innovation ecosystems, some of these challenges are significant because of the diverse (and at times unaligned) interests and ambitions of those involved. Differences in governance, culture, and expectation can create obstacles in achieving a real impact from these partnerships. For these partnerships to function, companies must focus on the goals that drive the partnership and select clear criteria to choose the partner university, making sure that the university's goals align with the company's goals and the talent pool matches the needs of the projects. Furthermore, the partnerships must be structured in a manner that the people and processes selected facilitate the achievement of goals. Establishing key performance indicators is also essential for monitoring the progress of these partnerships.[19]

For universities to develop successful partnerships they must actively work to develop industry connections. This requires strategically identifying companies facing specific challenges and engaging with these companies to inform how the university can potentially contribute to solving a particular industry problem. In doing so, universities are clear about the value they bring to the partnership. It is important that these relationships, especially in the early stages, are forged on the basis of commitment and authenticity, rather than solely on the basis of a transaction.[20] This way, collaborative relationships between companies and universities can result in the commercialization of processes and methods that are mutually beneficial. Figure 9.5 presents examples of the outcomes of university-firm collaboration.

Clemson University. In 2017, through a Venture Well Faculty Grant, bioengineering students from Clemson University became part of a program to assess medical device needs in Tanzania. This was possible because of Clemson

---

[19] Lars Frølund, F. (2017, December 06). Developing Successful Strategic Partnerships With Universities. Retrieved September 28, 2020, from https://sloanreview.mit.edu/article/developing-successful-strategic-partnerships-with-universities/.

[20] University, Meet Industry: 4 Ways Faculty Can Make and Keep Strong Industry Partnerships. (2018, October 25). Retrieved September 28, 2020, from https://venturewell.org/industry-partnerships/.

	Universities	Industry
Benefits Economic-related	• Source of revenue (both public and private) • Patents/IPRs/licensing income • Additional income or financial benefit to researchers • Create business opportunities • Contribution to local/regional economic development	• New products and/or processes • Improved products and/or processes • Patents, prototypes, generate IPRs, etc. • More cost-effective than similar research • in-house • Improved competitiveness • Access public grants • Promote economic growth/enhancement of wealth creation
Institutional-related	• Exposure of students and faculty to practical problems/new ideas and/or to state-of-the-art technology, with positive effects on the curriculum • Provide a "test bed" for feedback on research ideas, results/interpretations for the refinement of academic ideas/theories • Stimulate technological advancement and/or research activities in certain key areas • Acquisition of or access to up-to-date equipment • Training and employment opportunities for students • Build credibility and trust for the academic researcher among practitioners • Stimulate the development of spin-offs (or spin-off companies) • Provide opportunity for companies to influence and encourage the development of particular lines of university research • Joint publications with industry • Publication of papers by academics	• Improved innovative ability and capacity/ Keep up to date with major technological developments • Advance new technologies • Accelerates commercialization of technologies/Increases speed of innovation to market • No inter-firm conflicts of interest • Provide much needed legitimacy for industry products • Access to new knowledge and leading-edge technologies and/or a wide variety of multidisciplinary research expertise and research infrastructure • Influence university research directions and new programs for industry good • Access to specialized consultancy/Identify relevant problems/Solve specific technical problems • Product testing with independent credibility in testing • Training/continued professional Development • Opportunity to access a wider international network of expertise • Act as a catalyst that leads to other collaborative ventures • Joint publications • Hiring of talent graduates
Social-related	• Service to the community • Enhancement of university's reputation	• Enhance reputation by becoming more socially responsible business

Fig. 9.5 Outcomes of university-firm collations (Ankrah, S., & Omar, A. T. (2015). Universities-industry collaboration: A systematic review. *Scandinavian Journal of Management*, *31*(3), 387–408)

University bioengineering professor John Desjardins' initiative to bring together US biomedical companies and engineering students to develop innovations in medical devices. The main objective was to have a program that enabled bioengineering students to make improvements in medical devices to better meet the needs of patients around the globe.[21]

According to Desjardins, this partnership was beneficial for the students and the companies involved because it allowed students to develop field research and focus on the real needs of patients and clinics as opposed to what engineers think is needed. In doing so, students gained practical experience, obtaining valuable knowledge and receiving the opportunity to contribute to the innovation of the medical device industry. These skills and experience prove useful for students when seeking employment. For companies, this program allowed them to build relationships with clinics in countries like Tanzania, for which companies usually do not have the time or resources to develop a greater knowledge of the market and its needs. The project resulted in improvements in the technology and design of existing medical devices.

This program is one of many examples in which companies and universities collaborate to make the most out of each other's strengths. Companies have the resources to fund research and the experience to take innovations from an idea to an actual product being commercialized.

University of Cincinnati. Conversely, universities that sometimes lack funding for research, benefit from companies' ability to provide funding while they provide a cadre of students and researchers who have the capacity to develop innovations. For example, Procter and Gamble collaborated with the University of Cincinnati's Simulation Center to model and simulate capabilities for advancing product and process development. The University of Tennessee and Siemens teamed up for work on medical imaging technology, and Caltech and Boeing established an agreement to collaborate on a wide spectrum of aviation technologies, including those for the Boeing 787 "Dreamliner."[22] Perhaps most notable in recent times is the joint venture between AstraZeneca and the University of Oxford to develop a COVID-19 vaccine.

Overall, these partnerships between companies and universities are mutually beneficial and produce innovations that have the ability to solve customers' problems and better address their needs, foster economic growth and development, and increase the skillset of the workforce.

Another type of collaboration between universities and companies involves companies offering certificate programs for students to gain supplemental knowledge, and other companies are becoming actively engaged in modifying

[21] Industry and University Collaboration: How Partnership Drives Innovation. (2019, September 24). Retrieved September 28, 2020, from https://venturewell.org/industry-and-university-collaboration/.

[22] UIDP, *10 Case Studies of High-Value, High-Return University-Industry Collaborations*, Columbia, S.C.: UIDP, 2013.

the way institutions teach. One program, created in 2018, is the Collaborative Leaders in Academia and Business (Capital CoLAB) is a collaboration between universities and companies in the digital industry whose main objective is to ensure graduates develop digital skills and foster innovation.[23] This is important because employers are faced with a lack of confidence about new recruits being well prepared with the skills needed in today's fast-paced corporate world, such as using analytical reasoning for complex problem-solving. It is necessary for companies to focus on developing workforce skills at the undergraduate level, and this can be accomplished through partnerships with higher education institutions to guarantee that students are prepared for employment.

The way this collaboration works is through two main strategies. The first involves teaching students the skills that partner companies have established as the most useful and practical in the workplace. This will help develop a new generation of professionals who are better prepared for the working world and can become business leaders. The second approach involves showcasing the latest innovations and research coming from these companies. Some of the universities and companies involved in this type of collaboration include Georgetown University, American University, Johns Hopkins University, EY, JPMorgan Chase, and Capital One.[24]

MNC Collaborations with Labor

The inherently conflictive relationship between companies and organized labor has not diminished over the years. Their disparate interests and constituencies make it as such, across industries and across nations. Nevertheless, when adversarial parties embrace a Me To We approach, positive outcomes can occur. A notable example is the labor-management partnership formed by 11 major San Francisco hotels (the San Francisco Hotels Multiemployer Group) and the Hotel and Restaurant Employees Local 2.[25]

The United Auto Workers alliances with Ford and General Motors, the Kaiser Permanente Labor Management Partnership that helps workers enhance their job skills and advance their careers, and a number of

---

[23] See: https://greaterwashingtonpartnership.com/skills-and-talent/capital-colab/.

[24] Zimmerman, E. (2019, May 01). Major Companies Partner with Colleges for Education Opportunities in Emerging Tech. Retrieved September 28, 2020, from https://edtechmagazine.com/higher/article/2018/07/major-companies-partner-colleges-education-opportunities-emerging-tech.

[25] Stuart R. Korshak, "A Labor-Management Partnership," Korshak, Kracoff, Kong & Sugrano, L.L.P., April 2000.

labor-management partnerships in Chile to protect members from job losses and negotiate higher wages are also noteworthy.[26]

Without a doubt the German Works Council and European work councils, in general, are the industry standard for Me To We in the labor-management relations sphere. Works councils are a common form of ensuring, by law, a voice for the workforce in a company's deliberations in many European countries. In particular, in Germany and the Netherlands, works councils have rights to prior consultation (and, in some cases, agreement) over a wide range of employment issues. There are three main views about why works councils primarily exist: to reduce workplace conflict by improving and systematizing communication channels; to increase bargaining power of workers at the expense of owners by means of legislation; and to correct market failures by means of public policy. Germany, again, is a prime example of the works council advocating for employees and acting similar to unions. With mutual accountability and a strong sense of ownership among German workers, it is not surprising that Germany's productivity is high.[27] Outside Germany, there are European Works Councils—bodies representing the European employees of a company.[28] Through them, workers are informed and consulted by management on the progress of the business and any significant decision at European level that could affect their employment or working conditions.

Member states are to provide for the right to establish European Works Councils in companies or groups of companies with at least 1000 employees in the EU and the other countries of the European Economic Area (Norway, Iceland, and Liechtenstein), when there are at least 150 employees in each of two member states. A request by 100 employees from two countries or an initiative by the employer triggers the process of creating a new European Works Council. The composition and functioning of each European Works Council is adapted to the company's specific situation by a signed agreement between management and workers' representatives of the different countries involved. Subsidiary requirements are to apply only in the absence of this agreement.

---

[26] AFL-CIO, *Labor-Management Partnerships*, https://aflcio.org/what-unions-do/labor-management-partnerships; Indira Palacios-Valladares, "From Militancy to Clientelism: Labor Union Strategies and Membership Trajectories in Contemporary Chile," *Latin American Politics and Society*, (52), 2.

[27] "Germany Productivity1962-2020 Data | 2021-2022 Forecast," *Trading Economics*, https://tradingeconomics.com/germany/productivity.

[28] 27 Employment, Social Affairs and Inclusion, https://ec.europa.eu/social/main.jsp?catId=707&langId=en&intPageId=211.

MNCs and Apprenticeships

Another form of shared value in which bottom-up plays a role is *apprenticeships*. An apprenticeship is a system for training a new generation of practitioners of a trade or profession with on-the-job training and often some accompanying study (classroom work and reading). Apprenticeships can also enable practitioners to gain a license to practice in a regulated profession. Most of their training is done while working for an employer who helps the apprentices learn their trade or profession, in exchange for their continued labor for an agreed period after they have achieved measurable competencies.[29] Apprenticeship lengths vary significantly across sectors, professions, roles, and cultures. They can be anywhere from one to four years and can involve formal licensure offered by a trade union, professional association, or government. In terms of accountability and ownership, apprentices are responsible for mastering a technical body of trade skills, attending any required courses the employer specifies, adhering to health and safety standards, and following company processes. Apprenticeships foster a sense of ownership on the part of the apprentice since they work in partnership with regular employees of the firm and are considered "members of the team." This esprit de corps transmits a sense of ownership on the part of the apprentice. Walmart, Sears, Roche, Siemens, Virgin Media, Schneider Electric, and Volkswagen are but a few of the major companies that provide apprenticeship opportunities.

MNCs and Local Economic Development

Multinational firms play an indispensable role in regional economic development, particularly in terms of clusters. "Cluster" refers to the geographic concentration of interconnected businesses, suppliers, and associated institutions in a particular field. These agglomerations are considered to increase the productivity with which companies can compete, nationally and globally. The Silicon Valley, Route 128, India's Bangalore software cluster, and the textile cluster in Catalonia are some of the better-known clusters. While we commonly think of cluster development as top-down, in reality it can be bottom-up and also symbiotic. Example, the clustering of producers of rattan furniture in West Java resulted in a whole village being absorbed and created many

---

[29] International Labour Organization, *A Framework for Quality Apprenticeships*, Geneva: ILO, 2019. https://www.ilo.org/wcmsp5/groups/public/%2D%2D-ed_norm/%2D%2Drelconf/documents/meetingdocument/wcms_731155.pdf.

small-scaled satellite industries in nearby locations.[30] In the United States, the existence of Stanford and University of California at Berkeley on the West Coast and Harvard and MIT on the East Coast were the "bottom" that attracted the information technology, defense, and pharmaceutical industries to locate in those locales.

Mexico has numerous clusters, electronics being among the most prominent. The country is the sixth-largest producer of electronics worldwide and third largest of computers. Guadalajara, in the State of Jalisco, is known as "The Silicon Valley of Mexico," and its constellation of public and private universities in STEM and vocational-technical institutes provide a vital source of human capital for OEMs such as Samsung, LG, Toshiba, Foxconn, Flextronics, and Hewlett-Packard.[31] In 2019 foreign investment injected $312 million into the electronics industry, creating 5000 jobs. Jabil alone invested $20 million to manufacture GoPro cameras.[32] Parallel to investment projects in the cluster, Ciudad Creativa Digital is underway. This is an exciting new project that will create a hub for the digital media industry within Mexico. The goal of this project is to create a world-class hub of digital media development. CCD will span the creative industries, from TV, cinema, and advertising to videogames, digital animation, interactive multimedia, and e-learning.

While assets of human and physical infrastructure—the "bottom"—catalyze companies to move into a geographical space, coordinating bodies play a vital role in the mix, as well. In the case of Mexico, the Mexican Chamber of Electronics, Telecommunications and Information Technologies (CANIETI) has been an advocate for these industries in our country for more than 70 years, promoting their growth and development within a global setting through high-quality services. CANIETI is a self-governing, public interest institution, with legal status and capital of its own, different from that of its members.[33] As regard the State of Jalisco and its electronics cluster, its iCluster Jalisco Network serves as a mechanism for linking and coordinating the efforts of people and triple helix organizations interested, involved, and committed

---

[30] J. Schiller and B. Martin-Schiller (1997), "Market, culture and state in the emergence of an Indonesian export furniture industry," Journal of Asian Business, 13, 1:33–55.

[31] "Mexico: A New Hub for Electronics Manufacturing," I-Connect 007, September 25, 2018. https://smt.iconnect007.com/index.php/article/112848/mexico-a-new-hub-for-electronics-manufacturing/112851/?skin=smt#:~:text=Starting%20in%20the%20late%201980s,underwent%20a%20significant%20economic%20restructuring.&text=Today%2C%20electronics%20manufacturing%20overall%20is,%2443.3%20billion%20to%20%2474.9%20billion.

[32] "Electronics Industry in Jalisco Pushes Development," *LATAM-OUTSOURCE*, July 31, 2019. https://latam-outsource.com/2019/07/31/electronics-industry-in-jalisco-pushes-development/

[33] CANIETI, http://www.canieti.org/Inicio/English/englishcan/about.aspx

to the clustering processes and their impact on the competitiveness and innovation of the Jalisco economy.[34]

The prominence of ESG among multinational firms, accompanied by strategies and metrics in their reporting to shareholders and stakeholders, is ever-increasing. So too is its next iteration—shared value—as more and more industry leaders, across sectors, embrace the philosophy of mutual inclusiveness of ESG goals and objectives and financial performance (namely, the bottom line).

To illustrate, Kate Spade, a US-based retailer, partnered with Abahizi Dushyigikirane Ltd. to develop a business opportunity to empower marginalized women in Rwanda to produce a line of handbags for distribution through its specialty stores and online. In another case, Chevron funded the Niger Delta Partnership with an investment of $100 million. That group engaged Georgetown University's Business for Impact initiative and its partner, Frontier Design Group LLC, to produce an extensive case study report on program impact and lessons learned.

It is fair to say that AB InBev is the industry standard for ESG and shared value among multinational firms. A global company based in Leuven, Belgium, with a reported US$46.9 billion revenue in 2020. It produces more than 500 beer brands sold in 150 countries.

Two examples of AB InBev shared value are Smart Agriculture and Smart Drinking.

Smart Agriculture. In the first instance, a global brewer like AB-InBev is dependent upon high-quality agricultural crops to brew their beers. As such, they help support the livelihoods of farming communities worldwide, working with over 20,000 direct farmers across 13 countries and 5 continents to grow natural ingredients —including barley, corn, rice, hops, sorghum, and cassava—that allow them to brew what they and the consuming public believe to be truly excellent beers. By supporting their direct farmers to be skilled, connected, and financially empowered, AB InBev helps them improve productivity, profitability, and the efficient use of natural resources, such as soil and water.

When it comes to research and technology, the firm's SmartBarley initiative, launched eight years ago, leverages data, technology, and agronomist insights to help more than 5000 enrolled farmers improve their productivity and environmental performance. Today, SmartBarley is present in over 12 countries across five continents. In an effort to increase yields and improve resilience, AB InBev maintains an R&D center, based in the US, and a cadre

---

[34] I-Cluster Jalisco Network, https://icluster-jalisco.spribo.com/president-message.

of over 150 agronomists and researchers globally who develop high-quality seeds and share best practices with farmers.

In terms of sourcing, as beer is principally produced and consumed locally, local sourcing remains a critical part of AB InBev's business model in most of their key markets. The firm is intent on securing a resilient and high-quality supply of crops for the long term. For example, their businesses in Africa have pioneered the use of under-commercialized local crops to create new affordable beer brands, like Eagle Lager, made with local sorghum in Uganda, and Impala, made with local cassava in Mozambique. This strategy, which has been expanded to countries in Latin America, allows them to reach new consumers while increasing incomes for local smallholder farmers.

AB InBev's goal for Smart Agriculture is that by 2025, 100 percent of their direct farmers will be skilled, connected, and financially empowered.

Smart Drinking. In 2010, the World Health Organization (WHO) prioritized confronting harmful alcohol use as a global public health imperative, calling for action by governments, civil society organizations, academia, and the alcohol industry to reduce harmful drinking by 10 percent by 2025. Well before then, AB InBev began planning its Global Smart Drinking Goals (GSDGs) initiative. The centerpiece of the company's efforts was launched in 2015, when the company announced its intention to invest at least $1 billion by the end of 2025 to achieve four goals:

1. Change social norms around harmful drinking through social norms marketing campaigns.
2. Create guidance labels on all eligible product packaging to enable consumers to make more informed choice
3. Reduce the harmful use of alcohol by at least 10 percent in six cities by the end of 2020, and implement the best practices globally by the end of 2025.
4. Diversify the company's product offerings to include more no-alcohol beers and lower-alcohol beers (NABLAB).

To achieve the goals, AB InBev announced City Pilot locations for reducing the harmful use of alcohol and implementing best practices by 2025. The locations were Brasilia, Brazil; Columbus, United States; Jiangshan, China; Johannesburg, South Africa; Leuven, Belgium; and Zacatecas, Mexico.

For example, Carling Black Label launched a #NoExcuse campaign in South Africa. Carling Black Label is the biggest beer brand in South Africa, with a focus on male consumers who are among the heaviest drinkers on the continent. The brand's messaging focused on the changing meanings of masculinity, especially in light of the high rates of domestic abuse. The brand needed to address how to maintain its strong sales position with men while keeping South Africa's women safe.

In Brasilia, the focus was on road safety by targeting hotspots where accidents, including those related to drunk driving, occur most frequently. With increased police presence through "saturation patrols," the number of deaths decreased 35 percent in 2017 and 29 percent in 2018.27.

In Columbus, the City Pilot team launched a Safe Rides program in 2017. This program intended to reduce alcohol-related car crashes through free round-trip transportation when consuming alcohol. AB InBev funded this campaign, which had three elements: Lyft coupons, increased enforcement, and an associate media campaign.

Based on substantial academic research demonstrating that consumers respond best to actionable advice, AB InBev initiated a package labeling program that aims to place Smart Drinking labeling on 100 percent of its products, including in markets where it is not required by regulation. Ultimately, this labeling, which uses simple text and icons to advise consumers to always eat food while drinking, alternate non-alcoholic beverages, never operate a vehicle or heavy machinery when drinking, and similar messages, will appear on both primary and secondary packaging of all the company's products worldwide.

With its initial investment over the first five years of more than $335 million across the four goals, AB InBev is having a positive impact on harmful drinking. To illustrate, in the 2021 sustainability report by Jefferies, a multinational investment bank, highlighted AB InBev was as an exemplar of sustainable business practices. The report cited the firm as having the most comprehensive, technology-driven strategy on alcohol consumption, using data to drive policy on harmful drinking, as well as investment into start-ups and growing the no/low alcohol business.

The bottom line here is that AB InBev is clearly demonstrating how to create shared value for both business and society.

The multinational enterprise embodies Me To We—in practice in many instances and aspirationally in many others. Through its relationship with suppliers, workers, universities and vocational-technical institutions, and local economic development agencies, MNCs pursue and can achieve win-win outcomes effectively and sustainably. One can only suspect that these relationships will increase and expand in the foreseeable future.

10

Implementing M2W in the Firm

As discussed in previous chapters, the implementation of M2W strategy is fundamental for businesses to gain a broader competitiveness through the creation of social value. However, this process of social value creation must be executed correctly. Like any other business process, *how* it is implemented matters. Failure to implement the M2W strategy correctly may result in fewer business benefits and an undesired level of social impact.

The core requirements for successfully implementing the M2W strategy include having the right measurement mechanisms in place, involving the company's leadership in the process, and, finally, establishing the right communications around it. In this chapter we will take a look at the three of them. These principles are related to the notion of ownership and accountability as presented in our M2W approach. More specifically, the right measurement links with accountability, while leadership at all levels links to ownership. Communication is the required element to properly connect these ideas.

Measurement

The business maxim "what can't be measured cannot be improved" also applies to the M2W mindset. By measuring impact, companies can improve initiatives based on data-driven decisions, eliminate the skepticism that directors may have around its business value, and refine scalable solutions for multiple stakeholders' problems using impact as a decision-making criterion.

R. Ernst, J. Haar, *From Me to We*, https://doi.org/10.1007/978-3-030-87424-7_10

The Importance of Measuring Shared Value

Put succinctly, measuring shared value can provide business leaders with relevant information to make the right decisions, both in terms of business and social goals. This means that besides positioning companies as socially responsible, quantifying shared value helps investors convince themselves that addressing social issues can yield important economic results. On many occasions, leadership needs to be brought around to this way of thinking through evidence. Although this last point sounds to be lesser importance, having a company's leadership deeply involved in the M2W philosophy can help guarantee its success. When a company's leadership is not fully committed to M2W projects, it can result in failure of the implementation initiative. For example, Victoria's Secret parent company L Brands claims the company is committed to fighting against racism and social injustices; however, one of its top executives publicly made an insensitive comment about the LGBT community, claiming that the company would not hire members of the community for its fashion shows. This example shows a clear disconnect between the company's social objectives and the mindset of its leadership.[12]

Measuring shared value requires establishing the right connections between the creation of social and business (or economic) results. Companies have developed many ways to track business and economic results, such as revenues, profitability, market share, growth, and productivity. However, when it comes to measuring social impacts, the story is different. Unlike most traditional business metrics which are quantitative in nature, measuring social impact requires mostly qualitative metrics. These metrics are not only harder to keep track of, but also difficult to implement. Nonetheless, it is important to have a system that can gauge social metrics and relate them to business results.

Failing to understand or track the relationship between social and business results can result in important losses in terms of opportunities to innovate, grow, and impact at the right scale. Only by establishing the appropriate measurement framework will companies be able to optimize results and communicate better with the different stakeholders involved. To do so, they must establish the precise social impact measurement tools and possess the right measurement strategy.

---

[1] Retrieved from https://www.hollywoodreporter.com/news/victorias-secret-backlash-ed-razeks-comments-trans-size-models-spark-outrage-1160446.

[2] Retrieved from https://www.lb.com/responsibility.

Shared Value Measurement Strategies

A common mistake many companies make is thinking that there is a one-size-fits-all model. A shared value strategy is similar to any other business strategy, and as such it is unique for each company. Each shared value strategy will differ based on particular factors like the industry and location, but also on specific social elements. Thus, a company may not implement the same strategy in different countries without adapting it to specific social conditions. For example, Starbucks has focused its social practices on providing skills, training, and technological tools to 1000 young coffee farmers in Colombia's post-conflict zones, showing an adaptation of their strategies to the Colombian context.[3]

There are three different levels in which shared value occurs and every company should ideally consider them all. These levels are reconceiving products and markets, redefining productivity in the value chain, and enabling cluster development.[4] Companies can decide whether one of these or a combination suits them best for their shared value measurement strategy. By doing so, companies can ensure that the right metrics are implemented at the right level. Figure 10.1 summarizes the business and social results for each one of these levels.

The first level, reconceiving product and markets, targets unmet needs to increase revenue and profits. It can occur, thanks to increased efficiencies, the optimization of existing processes, or new and improved processes. From a business perspective, this usually means market growth and increased market share. For example, companies in the food and beverage industry in developing countries can focus on delivering products at reduced sizes that are affordable to a wider consumer base. The social impact of this level includes, but is not limited to, improved stakeholder experiences, improved consumer health and education, and reduced negative environmental impact. For example, creating products intended for the base of the pyramid, companies in the food industry rethink their products in terms of their nutritional value such that it can help consumers' overall health and nutrition.

Redefining productivity, the second level, seeks to address internal operations that occur across the different stakeholders of the value chain. This, in general terms, means increasing productivity and reducing risk, especially in what relates to third parties who provide products and services. Concrete

---

[3] Retrieved from https://stories.starbucks.com/stories/2017/starbucks-invests-in-next-generation-of-colombian-coffee-farmers/.

[4] Creating Shared Value. Retrieved from: https://hbr.org/2011/01/the-big-idea-creating-shared-value.

LEVELS OF SHARED VALUE	BUSINESS RESULTS	SOCIAL RESULTS
Reconceiving product and markets: How targeting unmet needs drives incremental revenue and profits	• Increased revenue • Increased market share • Increased market growth • Improved profitability	• Improved patient care • Reduced carbon footprint • Improved nutrition • Improved education
Redefining productivity in the value chain: How better management of internal operations increases productivity and reduces risks	• Improved productivity • Reduced logistical and operating costs • Secured supply • Improved quality • Improved profitability	• Reduced energy use • Reduced water use • Reduced raw materials • Improved job skills • Improved employee incomes
Enabling cluster development: How changing societal conditions outside the company unleashes new growth and productivity gains	• Reduced costs • Secured supply • Improved distribution infrastructure • Improved workforce access • Improved profitability	• Improved education • Increased job creation • Improved health • Improved incomes

Fig. 10.1 Business and social results by level of shared value. (Source: Porter, M., Hills G., Pfitzer, M., Patscheke, S., Hawkins E.: "How to Unlock Value by Linking Business and Social Results" (2012))

examples of this level include, but are not limited to, reduced logistical costs (as with CPG firms such as P&G and Unilever), efficient use of value chain resources, increased product and service quality, and improved employee and supplier capabilities.

The third and final level, enabling cluster development, is oriented toward the improvement of a company's external conditions, particularly in what refers to societal conditions. This tends to be locally focused, as it seeks to address opportunities related to specific locations where a company has interests or influence. For example, companies in Silicon Valley have partnered with universities in the area like Stanford University and University of California to tap into the pool of talent and foster innovation.[5] Furthermore, pharmaceutical company Novartis and Harvard University have formed numerous collaborations to advance research in the biomedical sciences.[6] The stakeholders involved might be local industries, government institutions, and even infrastructure. Societal benefits created here are usually measured at the local level.

---

[5] Retrieved from https://scet.berkeley.edu/global/global-partners/.

[6] Retrieved from https://www.novartis.com/news/media-releases/novartis-teams-harvard-develop-next-generation-biomaterial-systems-deliver-immunotherapies.

The Measurement Process

Like other business metrics, social impact needs to be constantly monitored so that a company's management knows what works and what does not from the M2W perspective. Only by doing so can a company's M2W-related initiatives be improved.

Gauging social impact through measurement tools requires a rigorous system, just as with business metrics. Most of the time they are measured together, not as two different things. A major challenge is that for many companies' social impact measurement tools are underdeveloped or are very hard to implement. FSG,[7] a social impact consultancy company, establishes four steps in this measurement process:

- *Systematically identify the social issue to target:* This first step should consider the three levels of shared value. There are many things that a company can focus on when it comes to measuring social impact, so prioritizing what needs to be specifically addressed and measured is the first before establishing any metric. For instance, manufacturing companies can aim at improving their environmental impact, assist the communities where they operate, and increase the well-being of their employees. However, many of these companies will prioritize one of these objectives since many are not in the position to target all issues given their limited resources and lack of expertise.
- *Make the business case including targets, activities, and costs involved:* Once potential social impacts have been identified at the three different levels, companies need to understand how the social impact will improve business performance. This should include establishing the costs and targets to decide later on if they are worth pursuing or not.
- *Track progress through inputs, outputs, and financial performance:* Social impact should be tracked like any other business variable. Similarly, it should be improved in the same way. This can be done by comparing revenues and costs against projected values.
- *Measure results to unlock new value:* This last step is where things add up. Here it is necessary to compare whether the expected social impact occurs or not. Depending on the outcome, a company can decide whether changes need to be implemented or if things are going in the right direction. Ultimately, this step validates if the link between business and social impact occurs as predicted.

---

[7] Measuring Shared Value. Retrieved from: https://www.fsg.org/publications/measuring-shared-value

As illustrated, the first two steps of FSG's process focus on the strategic part of measuring shared value. The last two are concerned with the actual measurement of shared value. This way, the steps ensure to cover everything that is needed to measure and improve the social impact of a company. Additionally, the process also considers that these four steps are not just something that need to be done once. Like many other business practices, they are an iterative process that must be measured, evaluated, and repeated in order to improve continuously.

Design and Measurement

Design plays a major role in almost any business process. Although this discipline is sometimes thought of as being related only to how things function, look, and feel, in fact design plays a major role in how organizations operate. In recent decades, design has been gaining importance as a systematic way to address problems by identifying them and then finding solutions. This has been accomplished mostly thanks to the influence of design thinking, a particular design approach that focuses on solving problems through the use of both rationality and intuition, and by focusing on human needs instead of abstract business processes. A good example is that of Monash Health, an integrated hospital and health care system in Australia, which had concerns about the frequency of patient relapses involving drug overdoses and suicide attempts. The organization had not reached a consensus on how to address this problem. Through a series of workshops with doctors, nurses, and clinicians, they came to the realization that the solution involved designing a new treatment process, centered on patients' needs rather than on perceived best practices. Its implementation was successful, with patient relapses falling by 60 percent.[8]

The field of strategic design, which uses design thinking, has been gaining traction, thanks to its usefulness in terms of helping businesses build their strategies in a rigorous and methodic way.

One of the main characteristics of design thinking is that it addresses problems through multiple iterations. It consists of a cycle made up of the following steps: empathizing, defining, ideation, prototyping, testing, and implementation. This means design thinking is an iterative process where a solution is not expected at once. Instead, a problem is addressed as something that needs to be worked upon continuously. For example, P&G uses design

---

[8] Retrieved from https://hbr.org/2018/09/why-design-thinking-works#.

thinking to address customers' needs and constantly reinvent their product portfolio. The company has continuously studied consumers' frustrations with cleaning chores and created multiple products to address these needs such as the "Swiffer Sweeper" and the "Mr. Magic Clean Eraser."[9] Just like the measurement of shared value, design thinking lies on the principles of continuous improvement. This approach is very convenient for companies that wish to improve their M2W strategy and process. The challenge, however, is that many companies are not willing to wait for results, and implementing ideas through design thinking might take time.

For companies that are willing to wait, using design thinking can produce powerful benefits, including those applied to social impact. Through iterations and continuous improvement, they can make sure that their measurement process is aligned with their business objectives.

Examples of Shared Value Measurement

An example of a successful implementation of FSG's measurement strategy is Coca-Cola's Coletivo initiative in Brazil. Through this project, The Coca-Cola Company was able to "increase the employability of low-income youth while strengthening the company's retail distribution channels and brand strength to increase local product sales."[10] Through youth training programs and by tracking their progress, Coca-Cola was able to enhance access to business opportunities and build employability skills for some of Brazil's most vulnerable youths. This not only helped retailers improve their operations but it also generated a stronger brand connection and increased their sales. Lastly, it also helped the company generate a tangible social impact.

The benefits of this type of programs are becoming clear to a wide range of businesses across different industries. Through them, companies can solve societal problems while at the same time fulfilling their business goals. But this is not as easy as it sounds. To achieve impactful results, companies need to have access to relevant data. Only by doing so will they be able to measure a program's impact and whether it really meets business expectations. When a program is not properly tracked, companies miss the opportunity to improve and decide on the right strategies. More often than not, this is the reality faced by companies, even those that embrace the M2W mindset. The main reason for this is that, even though the concept may be accepted by a company, the

---

[9] Retrieved from https://www.imd.org/research-knowledge/articles/beyond-the-beautiful/.

[10] How To Measure Shared Value, The Latest Business For Good Buzzword. Retrieved from: https://www.fastcompany.com/1680804/how-to-measure-shared-value-the-latest-business-for-good-buzzword.

tools to measure it are not properly developed. Thus, shared value measurement is an important challenge that companies must face.

Leadership

Given the collaborative nature of the M2W approach, leadership plays an essential role in its implementation. Top management is instrumental in starting the dialogue with stakeholders and creating long-term relationships with them, as well as sourcing critical resources, guiding decision-making to align with M2W principles and objectives, and fostering M2W mentality throughout the company.

Leadership Styles

Implementing M2W involves approaching economic and social issues strategically and simultaneously. Thus, effective implementation is a complex and dynamic process that requires efforts from multiple stakeholders and actors. These efforts will most likely start from the top management team. Why? First, because the top management team and company leaders have the power to drive organizational change and influence decision-making[11] so that it aligns with the objectives of the M2W mindset. Additionally, company leaders are able to foster initiatives by working with multiple stakeholders, including employees, suppliers, NGOs, universities, government, and local communities. Under the leadership of CEO Torgeir Kvidal, Yara—a global leader in fertilizer sales—brought together more than 60 organizations, including multinational companies and the Tanzanian government, in a partnership aimed at creating a fully developed agricultural corridor from the Indian Ocean to the country's western border.[12] Furthermore, company leaders' knowledge of company strategy and vision allows them to identify, prioritize, implement, adjust, and measure the impact of initiatives. Walmart CEO Doug McMillon worked with his counterparts in over 30 major consumer goods companies, such as PepsiCo and Unilever, to create the Closed Loop Fund, to provide zero interest loans to cities for investments in local recycling programs.[13] These capabilities make top management members critical in the

---

[11] Scagnelli, S. D., & Cisi, M. (2014). Approaches to shared value creation: CSR 2.0 or something more. *Insights and issues about the new sustainability perspective.*

[12] Retrieved from https://hbr.org/2016/10/the-ecosystem-of-shared-value.

[13] IBID.

implementation of the M2W strategy and the achievement of social and economic benefits.

While it seems that leadership is only from the top-down, shared responsibility as required by our M2W approach involves a leadership from the bottom-up as well. Leadership should include a shared responsibility component from each of the different stakeholders involved.

Based on this information, what types of leaders (at all levels and through all stakeholders) are best suited for successfully implementing the M2W strategy? The answer to this question is not straightforward because there is no concrete evidence of one specific type of leadership that is uniquely effective in developing the M2W mindset and successfully implementing the M2W initiatives. Some of the types of leaders and their advantages in the implementation of the M2W strategy are discussed.

Transformational leaders. These leaders are able to identify when change is needed and are able to effectively create a vision and communicate this vision in order to execute change.[14] They include Jeff Bezos of Amazon, Jack Welch of GE, and Reed Hastings of Netflix, who have helped their companies to successfully adapt and become leaders in their industries. This is especially important for M2W because transformational leaders are able to identify complex issues that can be solved through M2W initiatives and find innovative ways to implement these initiatives. Additionally, these types of leaders are well suited to engage with numerous stakeholders and influence them in the adoption of the M2W mindset. Transformational leaders are also able to guide and inspire stakeholders' "leaders" to commit to the execution of M2W initiatives, making them well-suited for M2W implementation.

Charismatic leaders. These types of leader are highly eloquent, being able to engage and persuade others through their communication abilities. They motivate others to better themselves and work for the greater good.[15] By using their charisma, these types of leaders can inspire and energize stakeholders such as employees and suppliers to implement initiatives that are aimed toward the M2W mindset. Because these types of leaders tend to be highly creative and like to "think outside the box,"[16] they are good at finding groundbreaking ways to increase profits while addressing social issues.

Participative leaders. Also known as democratic leadership, this style encourages all members of the organization to provide their input and make

---

[14] Bass, B. M., & Riggio, R. E. (2006). *Transformational leadership*. Psychology press.

[15] Conger, J. (2015). Charismatic leadership. *Wiley encyclopedia of management*, 1–2.

[16] Avolio, B. J., & Yammarino, F. J. (Eds.). (2013). *Transformational and charismatic leadership: The road ahead*. Emerald Group Publishing.

decisions together.[17] Examples include Indra Nooyi, the CEO of PepsiCo, and Richard Branson of the Virgin Group, who have often reinforced the importance they place on their employees for business success. While this can result in slower decision-making, it can have several advantages when it comes to the implementation of M2W approach. For instance, stakeholders will be more likely to accept and willingly engage in initiatives that were reached by a general consensus while accepting and recognizing leaders at different activities. Additionally, when stakeholders are given a voice, they will not only feel appreciated, but they will also tend to take a more active "leadership" role in the execution of such decisions as well as feel liable for the effective implementation of initiatives.

Ethical leaders. These leaders promote ethical or appropriate behavior by exemplifying such behavior, and emphasize the importance of values, honesty, moral actions, and fairness.[18] These characteristics make ethical leaders well-suited to promote and foster the M2W mentality by creating awareness and highlighting the importance of addressing social issues. For example, Ben & Jerry's founders Ben Cohen and Jerry Greenfield have been recognized for their reliance on ethical values since the company' inception. Starbucks' CEO Howard Schultz has also focused on ethical values and prioritizing the well-being of its employees and the communities where the company operates. Their leadership style fosters teamwork and an overall sense of community, which is essential in bringing stakeholders together to collaborate on M2W initiatives. Ethical leaders use their action to influence others to work toward greater goals that benefit the organization and society simultaneously. Moreover, ethical leaders can foster innovation among employees, which is useful in finding ways to address social issues without sacrificing economic benefits.

M2W Leaders' Skills and Competencies

Different leadership styles can be beneficial for M2W implementation since there is not one particular style that is ideal for the M2W strategy. However, there are several competencies and characteristics that are highly valuable when it comes to the effective implementation of the M2W mindset:

---

[17] Chen, Y. F., & Tjosvold, D. (2006). Participative leadership by American and Chinese managers in China: The role of relationships. *Journal of Management Studies, 43*(8), 1727–1752.
[18] Brown, M. E., & Treviño, L. K. (2006). Ethical leadership: A review and future directions. *The leadership quarterly, 17*(6), 595–616.

Social/Networking: M2W requires engaging and socializing with multiple stakeholders across sectors. For this reason, having a growing network is critical for leaders aiming to develop M2W initiatives. These relationships are essential for leaders to remain aware of critical issues, make informed decisions, and foster collaboration with different actors to have a greater impact.[19] Additionally, social relationships provide valuable information and insights that are necessary to identify opportunities for implementation. For instance, BD, a medical technology company based in New Jersey, was able to commercialize a product to address obstructed labor, thanks to the strong relationship Vice-Presidents Gary Cohen and Renuka Gadde had with the World Health Organization. Through this relationship, BD was able to pursue a business opportunity and address urgent global health needs.[20]

Communication. Beyond growing a network, M2W leaders must also build their communication skills. This is an essential competency for creating and building relationships with and between multiple stakeholders. Effective communication allows leaders to engage in information exchange, foster collaboration and understanding, stimulate ideas and initiatives, and drive consensus among multiple stakeholders with different perspectives.[21] Effectively communicating the M2W mindset to stakeholders allows for goal alignment; well-informed actors are more likely to have a clear vision that facilitates the achievement of M2W objectives. Recently, leaders have been taking advantage of social media to communicate their M2W efforts. For example, Uber's CEO Dara Khosrowshahi and Dell's CEO Michael Dell have been using social media to communicate the company's cultural norms and emphasize its efforts on diversity and accountability.[22]

Expanded perspective/Analytical view. M2W leaders have the ability to observe and analyze current and future trends.[23] This involves processing and integrating large amounts of information related to complex problems and envisioning actionable pathways to solve these problems. Leaders must

---

[19] FSG. (2015).Kyle Peterson. What Do Shared Value Leaders Have in Common? Retrieved from https://www.fsg.org/blog/what-do-shared-value-leaders-have-common.

[20] Retrieved from https://www.hbs.edu/faculty/Pages/item.aspx?num=53149.

[21] Chen, Y. R. R., Hung-Baesecke, C. J. F., Bowen, S. A., Zerfass, A., Stacks, D. W., & Boyd, B. (2020). The role of leadership in shared value creation from the public's perspective: A multi-continental study. *Public Relations Review, 46*(1), 101749.

[22] Retrieved from https://www.inc.com/john-eades/6-simple-reasons-all-leaders-should-be-actively-using-social-media.html.

[23] FSG. (2015).Kyle Peterson. What Do Shared Value Leaders Have in Common? Retrieved from https://www.fsg.org/blog/what-do-shared-value-leaders-have-common.

possess the ability to view issues through a holistic view that enables identifying and integrating information that is relevant to address these issues.[24]

Clear vision and purpose. Advocating and pushing for the M2W mindset across the organization can be a difficult task for leaders because they will usually encounter resistance from different stakeholders to change. In order to overcome these barriers, leaders must have a clear vision of where they see the company going under the M2W approach and a clear purpose of what the company wants to achieve through their M2W strategy. Having a clear picture of the organization through the M2W lens and effectively communicating it to stakeholders is essential for leaders to advocate and gain support for M2W initiatives.[25] For example, Katherine Pickus, the Divisional vice-president of Global Citizenship and Policy at Abbott, has shifted the company's business model and has put a wider range of stakeholder as a guiding principle of the company's vision and purpose. Under her leadership Abbott developed a program to strengthen the production capacity and capabilities of local dairy farmers in India, resulting in an increased production of high-quality milk that benefits both dairy farmers and Abbott, which uses milk in manufacturing nutritional products in India. She has focused on how to *"further apply the unique assets of our business—from our medical technology and nutrition expertise, to our understanding of consumers' health needs—to find new ways to improve lives."*[26]

In addition to these capabilities, an M2W leader must be able to transform the organizational culture so that the way in which members of the organization think and react aligns with the M2W mindset. This requires a collective effort from all the members of the organization to match the company's true purpose and decisions, which are reflection of this purpose. Figure 10.2 describes some of the most important tasks for leaders who are on the road to successfully adopt the M2W mindset.

M2W and Organizational Culture Transformation

Organizational culture includes the values, norms, and practices that inform the behavior of members of an organization. Simply put, organizational

---

[24] Metcalf, L., & Benn, S. (2013). Leadership for sustainability: An evolution of leadership ability. *Journal of business ethics, 112*(3), 369–384.

[25] Ibis (9).

[26] Retrieved from https://www.sharedvalue.org/different-perspectives-shared-vision-two-abbott-leaders-discuss-how-sustainable-business-can-improve-lives/.

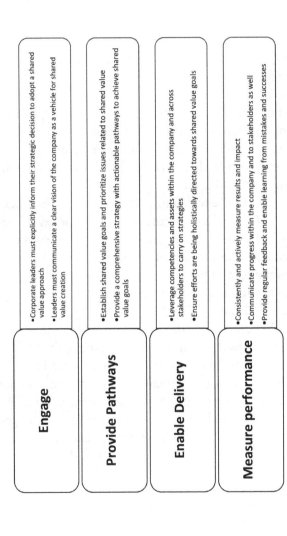

Fig. 10.2 Leaders' blueprint toward the adoption of the M2W mindset (FSG. (N.D.) The Building Blocks Of Creating Shared Value. Retrieved from https://www.fsg.org/publications/creating-shared-value-how-guide-new-corporate-revolution)

culture is defined as how companies "do things."[27] This culture defines how individuals within the organization react to stimuli and guide decision-making. When an organization is facing the need to change its approach toward the M2W strategy, the organizational culture must transform as well. As Lisa O'Keefe of Reddit notes: "The more leaders can share what a company values in its culture, the easier it's going to be for the culture to become a reality and not just these random words uttered without meaning or random quotes on a wall."[28]

However, changing the organizational culture is not an easy process, and most of these efforts tend to fail.[29] For example, Nokia's failure to adapt and remain competitive can be partly attributed to a failure to change its culture. The company had become embedded in a culture of "status quo" that contributed to a state of myopia that impeded Nokia's ability to innovate. The company's leadership had also become part of this culture, and this made it even more difficult for employees to change their mindset and successfully keep up with the dynamism of the industry.[30]

Driving action, competitiveness, and performance require leaders to lean on the values and culture of the organization. For the M2W mindset to become a cornerstone of the company, the organizational culture must support this mentality, and this mindset of creating social and economic value must resonate with the team. Once the values and mindset for the organization are clearly determined and defined, they should guide the way in which performance is measured and evaluated.

Additionally, having the correct incentive system in place is an important aspect for leadership to consider in the implementation of the M2W approach. Organizations establish reward and compensation systems in order to motivate and enable goal congruence of employees.[31] Thus, compensation systems must be set in place to motivate employees to devote time and effort to M2W activities and goals. For example, Nestlé considers creating job opportunities for youth as an important initiative of their strategy and has integrated this as part of managers' bonuses. Nestlé evaluates how well this initiative has been

---

[27] Watkins, M. (2013). What Is Organizational Culture? And Why Should We Care? Harvard Business Review. Retrieved from https://hbr.org/2013/05/what-is-organizational-culture.

[28] Lisa O'Keefe, Culture IQ Blog, September 2, 2020.

[29] Glesson, B. (2017). How Values-Based Leadership Transforms Organizational Cultures. Forbes. Retrieved from https://www.forbes.com/sites/brentgleeson/2017/03/10/how-values-based-leadership-transforms-organizational-cultures/?sh=287ca4a81fbd.

[30] Retrieved from https://medium.com/multiplier-magazine/why-did-nokia-fail-81110d981787.

[31] Malmi, T., & Brown, D. (2008). Management control systems as a package Opportunities, challenges and research directions. Management Accounting Research, 19(4), 287–300.

fulfilled and rewards managers who have met their targets.[32] In our approach, the compensation goes beyond the organization into all stakeholders involved in the ownership and accountability with the clear objective of attaining shared responsibility.

Essentially, implementing M2W requires leaders to guide the teams' efforts and evaluate their performance based on a broader conception of value creation. In addition to traditional metrics and milestones, performance measures and incentives systems must strive to determine/gauge social value creation. This requires for the organizational culture to be in tune with the ideals and purpose of the M2W strategy, such that the actions and behaviors of the members of the organization are guided by this philosophy. Figure 10.3 shows strategies and best practices that leaders can use to engage stakeholders and measure performance in accordance to the M2W mentality.

Leadership and M2W: The Example of HP[33]

HP provides a great example of the adoption of this mentality, starting with its leaders. The company has initiated an extensive process to embed this approach into the minds and actions of the company. Its leaders believe that for this approach to work they must be able to engage employees across the company in deep and sustained ways. Because of its larger size, HP operates with an organizational structure that provides a lot of autonomy for its managers (i.e., empowering ownership in the M2W fashion). Thus, the success of this process also requires managers to incorporate new goals into their planning, strategy formulation, and implementation. This means that the company actively involves leaders of different business units and functions to execute these goals.

For the M2W mentality to "stick," the company must first win the minds of those at the top. Why? Because corporate leaders are those who set the tone, and while it is also necessary to involve employees in the adoption of this approach, companies like HP find that it is most effective to work from the top-down. This involves a shift in the strategic direction of a company, and, ultimately, those responsible for establishing the strategic direction are at the top. In sum, if corporate leaders are not on board with the M2W approach, this mindset will not permeate to all members of the organization. Clearly, the bottom-up will follow.

---

[32] Albertsson, A., & Bertland, F. (2014). How Creating Shared Value integrates with Management Control Systems.
[33] IBID.

Good: Communicate clearly defined shared value strategies	Better: Communicate the financial value driven by shared value	Best: Communicate social and financial impact of shared value in quantitative and comparable terms
• Provide a clear explanation of how social and environmental strategies drive economic growth with concrete facts and figures	• Incorporate reporting on the financial value of shared value in standard investor communications	• Describe the causal link and relative contribution of shared value business models to key financial metrics
• **Enabling Factors:**	• Explain the strategic positioning of shared value models by referencing growth for specific business lines, societal trends and peer comparisons	• Use and communicate metrics that combine financial returns with social and environmental impact and are comparable across companies
• Integrate key functions across the company	• **Enabling Factors:**	• **Enabling factors:**
• Establish concrete and actionable plans for reaching the established goals	• Utilize rigorous and reliable methodologies that are disclosed to investors	• Ensure external verification of data and methodologies
		• Utilize common industry-wide standards

Fig. 10.3 Leadership best practices: communicating and measuring the M2W strategy (3BL Media. (2020). Shared Value Initiative. Hybrid Metrics: Connecting Shared Value to Shareholder Value. Retrieved from https://www.3blmedia.com/News/Hybrid-Metrics-Connecting-Shared-Value-Shareholder-Value)

HP has begun to engage senior management by conducting an "audit" across the firm to reflect on the intersection between social issues and strategy, assess the existing landscape, benchmark competitors, and gauge the engagement of its managers in regard to social issues. In order to increase involvement, the company has developed workshops and conducted individual interviews with over 150 senior managers across the company. These provide a stage for managers to discuss and obtain valuable information related to the creation and implementation of a new strategy. HP found that this initiative has created a ripple effect that has contributed to increased excitement and momentum for the implementation of its new strategy and the establishment of ambassadors within the firm.

Leading Across Boundaries—Organizational and Geographical

Leaders of larger organizations, many of which have a global presence, face additional challenges in the implementation of M2W approach. They must ensure that their commitment to social value creation is not isolated or confined to particular business units, functional areas, or geographic locations. Instead, leaders of these corporations must aim to integrate the M2W mentality into a wide range of functions, roles, and locations. It is important the upper management and even the board level show engagement with the M2W mindset and oversee their implementation across the organization and geographic boundaries. In some cases, larger multinationals may require a team fully dedicated to overseeing M2W initiatives. For example, Alcoa—one of the world's largest producers of aluminum—created the position of "Chief Sustainability Officer" to lead its social initiatives, assign responsibility of social goals to relevant business units, and report to the board of directors.[34] The involvement of different players in the overall stakeholder ecosystem evidently covers the geographic dimension.

Communication

Proper communication is the final requirement for implementing the M2W strategy successfully. Like measurement and leadership, communication is a decisive element at the moment of implementing the M2W strategy. Without

---

[34] FSG. (n.d.) Creating Shared Value: A How-to Guide for the New Corporate (R)evolution. Retrieved from file:///C:/Users/maria/Downloads/Shared_Value_Guide.pdf.

the proper communication, companies will most likely have a hard time speaking to the right audiences and getting their message across.

The Importance of Communicating the Strategy

When it comes to communicating the impact of M2W, companies often think that writing a report that sums up what they have done is enough. They tend to believe that everyone will read it, and that as a result their message will get through. In reality, this is rarely the case. No matter how good a social or business impact a report may have, it needs to have a clear and well thought-out communication strategy that considers different audiences.

A good way to think about the different audiences is to think of them as individual stakeholders. Each one has a unique relationship with the company, with special interests and desires that need to be addressed in a particular way. More often than not, the act of communicating a social campaign can backfire if the right message and audience are not properly defined. Like any other type of business strategy, M2W needs to be communicated in different ways according to the stakeholder group that is being addressed. It is not the same to communicate the impact of the M2W initiative with the board of directors than with a local community.

A famous recent example is the case of Pepsi and their ad that echoed the Black Lives Matter movement. Back in 2017, the company thought that it would be a great idea to build a campaign around the social movement with the participation of celebrity Kendall Jenner. As a company that likes to connect with consumers, they saw this as an opportunity to show their support for the movement through an ad. Contrary to what they expected, they ended up receiving harsh criticisms for trivializing the social movement and trying to make a profit out of it.[35] The result was that Pepsi had to apologize and take down the ad after a significant reputational hit. Poor communication decisions like this can be found everywhere throughout business literature, and yet the importance of communicating correctly seems to be ignored.

A company may be creating important social impact for different stakeholders, and this, in turn, may be creating business value for the company. However, if this is not communicated clearly and properly to the right audiences, the effects of the M2W strategy face the risk of going unrecognized, or, even worse, having a negative impact on the company. One of the main reasons why initiatives to communicate shared value often fail is because

---

[35] Retrieved from https://www.theguardian.com/fashion/2017/apr/04/kendall-jenner-pepsi-ad-protest-black-lives-matter.

companies tend to use one-size-fits-all communication strategies instead of tailor-made ones that consider specific stakeholder characteristics.

Strategies for Communicating the M2W Strategy

According to Harvard Business School lecturer and FSG managing director Mark Kramer,[36] to correctly communicate a strategy, it is necessary to first identify who the target audience is. Sometimes there might even be different audiences, and each one needs its own communication strategy. In other words, the message should be adapted based on the audience being addressed.

Kramer points out to four different audiences that companies need to address when discussing initiatives aimed at creating value for a wider range of stakeholders and their impact. Figure 10.4 summarizes these ideas:

- *Corporate Watchdogs*: These are organizations that monitor corporations, sometimes for very specific goals and metrics. This category considers NGOs, activists, civil society, and government agencies. Data are very important to them, and they are not easily impressed by good deeds or shiny reports. They usually try to disclose important information that is not shared with the public. For instance, DiversityInc lists top-rated companies for diversity and inclusion, based on human capital practices and outcomes.[37]

Audience Type	What they care about	What they want to hear
Corporate Watchdogs	Monitoring corporations	Actual data and relevant information
Employees	Meaning and purpose	Real social impact
Investors	Business value	Shareholder value creation
General Public and Customers	Responsible brands	Real and concrete actions to address social problems

Fig. 10.4 Crafting messages for different audiences

---

[36] The Right Way for Companies to Publicize their Social Responsibility Efforts. Harvard Business Review. Retrieved from https://hbr.org/2018/04/the-right-way-for-companies-to-publicize-their-social-responsibility-efforts.

[37] Retrieved from https://www.diversityinc.com/about-the-diversityinc-top.

- *Employees:* People who work for the company want to be proud of what they do for society, not only for the value they create for shareholders. Social impact is very meaningful for them. The concepts of meaning and purpose are particularly important for this group.
- *Investors:* Traditionally, this group has cared mostly about business value, but this has been changing in recent years. The idea of social and economic value as a competitive advantage has been gaining traction, becoming a more relevant topic in discussions by addressing social value as having a positive impact on business and investors. For example, Nestlé's annual reports include metrics on economic performance and social impact, which align with their conviction of being successful in the long term by creating value for shareholders and for society.[38]
- *General Public and Customers:* There is only so much impact that publicity and media campaigns can have on this segment. They understand that money can buy media campaigns. That is why concrete and impactful actions speak louder to them than superfluous promises and advertisements.

Each of these audiences requires a specific message that acknowledges their unique interests and other relevant characteristics. Understanding each of them in detail according to a company's business is essential to implement a proper M2W communication strategy. Although almost all companies handle the same audiences, it is important to understand how particular aspects may change from one industry to another.

By connecting with an audience through the right message, a company can potentially communicate its positive impact while reducing the chances of the message backfiring. On a business level, this helps stakeholders understand the importance of the M2W strategy, and, most importantly, it helps initiatives gain momentum and move forward. On an external or social level, this helps create positive brand awareness, generating a competitive advantage. When everyone can agree that the M2W mindset has a positive impact for society and business, M2W initiatives prosper.

Communicating M2W Strategy Through Storytelling

Audiences want powerful content that engages them; for messages to get through, aside from identifying a company's respective audiences and their interests, it is also necessary to build stories. Stories have the power to help

---

[38] Retrieved from https://www.nestle.com/csv/what-is-csv.

companies transform dull messages into exciting pieces of information to which audiences can connect. For example, the clothing brand H&M has developed their "Close the Loop" campaign which shows individuals of all races, cultures, and professions wearing the clothes that they want to wear regardless of social norms while also emphasizing that the only rule in fashion is "recycling your clothes." This message tells a story that can resonate with a wide range of consumers while also highlighting the company's efforts on using recycles materials to manufacture their clothing.

By communicating through storytelling, companies can tap into the emotional side of audiences. This does not mean that storytelling is equally effective for all audiences, but it does help the message get through when raw facts and data are not enough. Storytelling is by no way a means to replace accurate information; it is only a strategy to connect with audiences. Social media is the best example.

Stories are one of the most powerful ways in which ideas can be communicated, and the M2W strategy can benefit from using storytelling strategies. According to Contently, one of the top content agencies, there are four elements to great storytelling:

- *Relatability*: Audiences connect to real stories. The more they can identify themselves with a story, the better.
- *Novelty*: New things have the power to capture our attention. Instead of using worn-out stories, it is best to address new topics or old ones in ingenious ways.
- *Fluency:* There is a commonly held belief that the more complex a story, the better. Contrary to what most people believe, communicating an easy-to-follow story is best.
- *Tension:* Nobody likes a story where nothing occurs. Addressing the "what is" and "what could be" is a great way to capture attention.

To build a great story around the M2W strategy one needs to consider more than a business perspective. As a matter of fact, most of the time, audiences do not want to hear about anything that is directly related to business. Even investors who care about business data want to make sense of it by going beyond the purely business side of information. Using storytelling as a way to communicate M2W topics is a great way to engage audiences.

Digital Media and the M2W Strategy

Digital media tools have an important role to play in terms of the M2W strategy. Just like storytelling techniques can help companies engage with their audiences, so does digital media. By aligning business and social strategies with the use of digital media tools like Facebook and Twitter, companies can generate opportunities for audiences to connect with them. However, to do so, it is not enough to simply create an account or page.

As with any other communication strategy, connecting with users on digital media and communicating the message require companies to understand the needs of their audiences. By achieving unity of purpose and achieving audience participation, companies can raise brand awareness. Companies that can effectively communicate their initiatives on digital media will engage users, helping them differentiate from competitors and thus generate a competitive advantage.

In essence, a digital media campaign should consider the following questions to guarantee engagement[39]:

- What is the purpose of your brand?
- Is there a social issue that can be linked to your brand's purpose?
- How can your company use the web to engage your audience in addressing the social issue?
- How can your audience participate in your campaign?
- How can the business and social impact of digital media for your business be measured?

A company that is able to answer these questions will be in a better position to connect with its audience on digital media channels.

In summary, the effective implementation of the M2W strategy is critical for businesses as it can help increase their competitiveness and performance. However, this process is a complex one, and failure to implement the M2W strategy correctly may be detrimental for economic and social performance. Nespresso, the producer of coffee capsules to be used in specialized machines, recovers some of the capsules in its stores and collection points to deconstruct and recycle them. It uses the coffee residue as fertilizer in rice fields that donate food to food banks. However, this process is a resource-intensive one that involves the capsule to be constructed and then deconstructed at significant

---

[39] The Role of Digital Media in Shared Value Creation. Retrieved from https://www.business2community.com/marketing/the-role-of-digital-media-in-shared-value-creation-0156540.

expense, which ends up being paid by the consumer, as Nestlé does not lose money on this product. An alternative to this would be producing the capsules or pods with fully biodegradable materials as many of its competitors do, avoiding significant costs to society and the environment in general and to consumers in particular.[40] As we see in this example, if the M2W is implemented incorrectly, the potential results include additional costs for the company and its stakeholders.

Businesses wishing to develop and implement a shared value strategy successfully must make sure that they have adequate measurement mechanisms in place as a way to gauge performance. They must also have the correct leadership team as they are the ones who instill and permeate the M2W culture within the organization and across other stakeholders. Finally, businesses must have the right communications strategy to effectively spread the message of the M2W strategy to a diverse range of stakeholders. These three elements are like pieces of a puzzle; and if one of them is not executed correctly, implementation can become ineffective and can be harmful for business' performance, competitiveness, and social impact. M2W enlarges the previous ideas by explicitly making all stakeholders owners, while making them responsible and accountable of the resulting benefits.

---

[40] Retrieved from https://www.triplepundit.com/story/2016/when-creating-shared-value-causes-value-destruction-case-nespresso/26491.

11

Conclusion

The Me to We paradigm poses many challenging and difficult dilemmas, along with unprecedented advantages and opportunities for companies large and small and their shareholders. With the unprecedented growth of stakeholder communities, their visibility prominence and power have grown to a point where, no matter the industry, they cannot be ignored.

Looking to the future companies will be challenged to build sustainable business advantages in a world where great is no longer good enough. Social tension, economic nationalism, and technological revolution, coupled with unprecedented volatility, are transforming the business landscape worldwide. As Arindam Bhattacharya, Nikolaus Lang, and Jim Hemmerlin argue in their book *Beyond Great*, based on the study of hundreds of companies and interviews with dozens of business leaders, those firms that succeed in the new business environment will need to exhibit a new kind of openness and flexibility along with the capability to design and implement new strategies and adopt operational norms in a milieu in which stakeholders are gaining greater influence within the business ecosystem.[1]

At the same time, more and more companies, along with the society at large, are asking the following question: What is the purpose of the firm in this day and age? Interestingly, only 7 percent of Fortune 500 CEOs believe that companies should focus principally on profit-making and not be distracted by social goals.[2] In particular, issues such as income inequality, climate change, and racial and gender issues have come to the forefront of large companies. An increasing number of firms are seeing opportunities to contribute

---

[1] Arindam Bhattacharya, Nikolaus Lang, and Jim Hemmerlin, *Beyond Great*, New York: PublicAffairs, 2020.
[2] McKinsey, "Purpose: Shifting from why to how," *McKinsey Quarterly*, April 2020.

R. Ernst, J. Haar, *From Me to We*, https://doi.org/10.1007/978-3-030-87424-7_11

to the greater good beyond CSR. To illustrate, apparel giants such as H&M, Kering, Nike, and PVH have collaborated to form Global Fashion Agenda, a nonprofit that promotes sustainable fashion with an emphasis on the efficient and environmentally sound use of resources to ethical recycling.[3]

Some of the questions companies are grappling with now are as follows: What is our purpose as a company and how does it contribute toward making the world a better place? Who benefits from our success and what are our responsibilities? How should we best balance shareholder and stakeholder interests? How do our history, tradition, and corporate culture enable us to do greater for ourselves and for society?

Related to the purpose of the company is the concept, activity, and goal of *value creation*. In the public's mind, there is significant doubt that large companies truly create value. In an annual Gallup poll in the US, findings revealed that respondents with little or no confidence in big business increased from 27 percent in 1997 to 34 percent in 2019.[4] It should not be surprising then to see why large enterprises, including many multinational firms, seek to engage with a broader set of stakeholders—beyond shareholders and employees—as European enterprises have done for quite some time. In fact, in Europe, the Me to We concept is embedded in corporate governance structures.

As mentioned previously in our book, in responding to society's call for value creation within the non-enterprise domain, the US Business Roundtable issued a "Statement on the Purpose of the Corporation" in 2019. Signatories acknowledged their companies' responsibility to customers, employees, suppliers, and communities and declared: "We commit to deliver value to all of them for the future success of our companies, our communities, and our country."[5]

This notion, then, of stakeholder capitalism mandates that business leaders accept and resolve the contradiction of low trust and high expectations. The time for trade-offs has passed, especially given the growing strength and influence of consumers groups and their lobbyists along with public and union pension funds—all who seek to hold corporations' feet to the fire to ensure they do the right thing for society and its diverse panoply of stakeholders.

As mentioned in Chap. 9, more and more firms are adopting ESG—three central factors in measuring the sustainability and societal impact of an

---

[3] Ibid.

[4] Marc Goedhart and Tim Koller, "The value of value creation," *McKinsey Quarterly*, March 2000.

[5] Business Roundtable Redefines the Purpose of a Corporation to Promote "An Economy That Serves All Americans," https://www.businessroundtable.org/business-roundtable-redefines-the-purpose-of-a-corporation-to-promote-an-economy-that-serves-all-americans.

investment in a company or business. Although not synonymous with shared value or a Me to We approach to corporate strategy and operations, ESG nonetheless embodies good corporate citizenship in the broadest sense. According to one report, solid ESG practices resulted in better operational performance in 88 percent of companies; the stock price performance of 80 percent of companies was positively influenced by good sustainability practices and lowered the cost of capital of 90 percent of companies; and companies with strong sustainability scores showed better operational performance and were less of an investment risk.[6] While one study alone does not make a compelling case for ESG having a positive impact on financial performance, one study of *more than 2000 empirical studies* found this to be true in 90 percent of the cases studied.[7]

Four company examples—from Brazil, Germany, the UK, and Belgium—illustrate ESG excellence across industries. Brazil's Natura is the fourth-largest cosmetics group in the world. Founded in 1969, its brands include Aesop, Avon, Natura, and The Body Shop, and it has become a global corporate environmental leader. An early adopter of the "triple bottom line," publishing results on social and environmental metrics as well as financial ones, it has been carbon-neutral since 2007. In 2010, Natura introduced refill packaging made of sugarcane ethanol. In 2020, it pledged to reach net-zero carbon emissions by 2030. Customers have responded to its efforts, with revenues growing on average almost 12 percent a year, from 2009 to 2019.[8]

As for SAP, the world's third largest publicly traded software company, especially known for its ERP software, its commitment to ESG has been a long-standing one. In 2021 the firm announced its intention to become carbon-neutral in its own operations by the end of 2023—two years earlier than previously stated. Recently, the company reduced its greenhouse gas (GHG) emissions more than planned. As a result, SAP was able to overachieve by 43 percent on its target for reducing net carbon emissions in 2020, generating 135 kilotons (kt) instead of the anticipated 238 kt. In striving to become carbon-neutral, SAP takes into account all of its direct and indirect emissions, as well as selected emissions arising in the supply chain, including those linked to business flights, business travel in rental cars, and third-party data centers.

---

[6] "From the Stockholder to the Stakeholder: How Sustainability Can Drive Financial Outperformance," University of Oxford, Arabesque Partners, March 2015.

[7] Gunnar Friede, Timo Busch and Alexander Bassen, "ESG and financial performance: Aggregated evidence from more than 2000 empirical studies," *Journal of Sustainable Finance & Investment*, 5(4):210–233, 2015.

[8] Vivian Hunt, Bruce Simpson, and Yuito Yamada, "The case for stakeholder capitalism," *McKinsey Quarterly*, November 2020.

The company uses the approach of first avoiding, second reducing, and third compensating emissions.[9]

Unilever, the global consumer goods company, began developing its Sustainable Living Plan in 2010. A decade later it sources 100 percent of its agricultural raw materials sustainably. The company and its suppliers set standards not only on agriculture but on deforestation and human rights, by 2020. The Sustainable Agriculture Program (SAP) monitors 11 social, economic, and environmental indicators, including soil health, biodiversity, and human capital. SAP also sets minimum standards for its suppliers, such as those related to deforestation and human rights. In Brazil, Unilever is part of a collaboration with the Round Table on Responsible Soy (RTRS) and Aliança da Terra to boost sustainable soy cultivation by supporting growers to adopt better farming practices. Bayer Crop Science of Germany, Santander of Spain, and Yara of Norway are also collaborations in this initiative.[10]

Lastly, AB InBev, a multinational drink and brewing company based in Leuven, Belgium, that markets approximately 630 beer brands in 150 countries, has been a trendsetter in ESG with a broad and innovative portfolio of shareholder-oriented activities. Few firms are as closely aligned with the United Nations Sustainable Development Goals as AB InBev.[11] In viewing the life cycle of beer, for example, the firm has committed to spending at least $1 billion to influence social norms and individual behaviors to reduce the harmful consumption of alcohol, which includes drunk driving. The impact to date has been a reduction in road fatalities by as much as 90 percent on specific roads in China and a 26 percent decrease in in Atlanta, Georgia, alone. Other related initiatives include ensuring skilled, connected, and financially empowered farmers across local supply chains; promoting smart agriculture and improving farmer livelihoods through technology and sustainability farming practices; utilizing recycled and returning packaging; and improving water availability and quality and investing in partnerships for water stewardship.[12]

When discussing ESG, however, one caveat is in order. The current siloed approach in assessing societal impact is divorced from the analysis of

---

[9] SAP, *Sustainability, Healthy and Corporate Social Responsibility (CSR)*, https://www.sap.com/about/company/sustainability-csr.html.

[10] Vivian Hunt, Bruce Simpson, and Yuito Yamada, "The case for stakeholder capitalism," *McKinsey Quarterly*, November 2020; Unilever, *Sustainable and Regenerative Sourcing*, 2021, https://www.unilever.com/planet-and-society/protect-and-regenerate-nature/sustainable-and-regenerative-sourcing/.

[11] United Nations, *Transforming our world: the 2030 Agenda for Sustainable Development*, New York: United Nations, 2015.

[12] AB InBev, *Bringing People Together for a Better World*, AB InBev ESG Report 2020 HD Final.pdf (ab-inbev.com).

competitive strategy and growth and misses important sources of competitive advantage. This is why shared value and even stronger the Me to We approaches are more viable, sound, and impactful.[13]

Our extensive research, case analyses, and interviews with companies and independent organizations facilitated the development of the Me to We paradigm and led us to conclude the following.

The original concept of "shared value" must be broadened. Besides reconceiving products and markets, redefining productivity in the value chain, and enabling local cluster development, proponents of shared value must embrace a broader meaning competitiveness and elevate the role of governability. Embracing a broader meaning of competitiveness requires an ownership-oriented value chain where organizations are committed to results, understand the details and relevant information necessary for decision-making are disciplined, and are focused toward achieving improved results for the business and society. Elevating the role of governability means organizations and actors must be willing to accept responsibility, acknowledge the consequences of their actions, and, more importantly, not dwell in shame but actually take action. By adding ownership and accountability to the three original pillars of shared value masterfully conceived by Porter and Kramer, one arrives at a "quintet" of shared values that can guide the enterprise and its constituents.

Companies have traditionally focused on satisfying shareholders' interests and achieving profits; recently, companies have been moving away from this approach and focusing on satisfying a wider range of stakeholders. Our framework of "Me to We," inspired by shared value, requires shifting from a shareholder to a stakeholder primacy mindset. For this to happen, the sole focus of the organization should not be on short-term gains/profits but on long-term value creation by considering multiple stakeholders' interests.

The role of government may be limited but significant nonetheless. Although most of the time the government is not directly involved in the actual "business" of companies, it is a key player as it can provide the incentives for a better redistribution of benefits across all players in an ecosystem. The role of government runs the gamut from regulator, facilitator, partner, and adversary. Its actions impact shareholders and stakeholders alike. Private-public partnership is are an important tool that has the potential to achieve societal progress at a large scale and through innovative ways. Admittedly, successfully executing PPPs is not an easy task because it requires managing many of the multiple

---

[13] Michael E. Porter, George Serafeim, and Mark Kramer, "Where ESG Fails," *Institutional Investor*, October 16, 2019.

challenges and interests as well as building trust relationship and mitigating risks.

Shared value will become increasingly tied to competitiveness. Shared value can play a vital role in a firm's ability to compete effectively by enlarging companies' ecosystem and considering all members of the supply chain. Shared value increases the size of the pie by creating synergies; by taking a more socially conscious approach to business, firms can ultimately increase their economic profits and their competitiveness. Exploring societal needs will allow companies to determine opportunities to differentiate and reposition themselves in existing markets as well as potential opportunities in new markets. The focus on shared value creates opportunities for innovation and opportunities to create better products and services and, as a result, increase their competitiveness.

Globalization will increasingly impact "Me to We" within the international business domain. The challenges brought forth by globalization require managers to think about new strategies to effectively and proactively deal with market uncertainties and demand volatility. One way is to focus on managing supply chains in a more transparent and cost-efficient way. Companies must develop initiatives across multiple industries and actors to ensure more integrated and sustainable end-to-end supply chain, from component acquisition processes all the way to product launching; also, cluster development can help take advantage of complementarities and similarities of cluster members.

Fair Trade will grow in importance to both shareholders and stakeholders in global business. Fair Trade certification arises as a result of concerns over worker exploitation and environment and natural resources degradation. Stakeholders and shareholders have become more conscious about the need for investment and commerce, especially transnational transactions, to be transparent, fair, and safe. The ideas of Fair Trade are directly related to the idea of switching from shareholders to stakeholders. The collective conscience of consumers has played an important role in the advocacy for more transparent and fair production, packaging, and distribution of goods and services.

The bottom of the pyramid is the most fertile ground for shareholder-stakeholder convergence. Perhaps no dimension of the transformation of business from a purely shareholder to a stakeholder focus is more compelling and more vivid than that of the bottom of the pyramid (BOP). It is critical that shareholders of firms that do business with, or consider doing business with, emerging markets—with attention to the BOP segment—understand the fundamental differences between innovation activities in industrialized nations and developing ones. Companies know that affordability, flexibility, and functionality are essential in in the BOP market where the principal forms of innovation encompass product, process, service, and business model innovation.

Multinational firms will need to provide greater consideration of stakeholder concerns in their operations. The growth and expansion of MNCs has shed light on the lack of sustainability of their current economic and social model. In today's environment, it has become apparent that many MNCs have been profiting from lower standards in terms of their labor practices and environmental standards, especially in developing nations. MNCs should rethink their purpose and move away from a stakeholder primacy mentality by working on monitoring practices across their supply chain, establishing codes of conduct for suppliers, and creating partnerships with universities to foster innovation. In the long run, showing that the company's sole purpose is not focused only on profits can actually generate growth in sales by creating a sense of trust and loyalty from customers, reduce costs by improving efficiency in the use of resources, and help attract and retain better talent and boost employees' potential and motivation.

We assert that there are five main takeaways from our volume—conclusions which we believe will have far-reaching impact:

1. The "Me To We Mentality" requires firms to focus on a broader set of interests beyond those of shareholders to consider interests of multiple stakeholders. Firms must take accountability for their actions and embrace competitiveness as a broader concept, which involves focusing on economic and societal gains simultaneously. This requires firms to examine their currents practices across the supply chain and work toward more transparent, sustainable practices and ensure all actors are accountable.
2. Responsibility needs to be shared. The new ecosystems require a mutual responsibility for all players involved. The traditional view of up-down direction and domination requires a bottom-up involvement and embracement. It is only through a complete and honest transparency in the allocation of responsibilities that the sustainability and success of the enlarged pie is guaranteed.
3. Firms can create a more profound impact on societal issues by collaborating with other actors including government and universities and taking advantage of clusters. Such a collaborative relationship can enhance the likelihood that business and societal (ESG) goals and objectives will be met, with new ideas and new approaches benefiting all parties concerned.
4. Multinational corporations must ensure that transactions across borders are beneficial for all stakeholders. This requires monitoring their activities across the globe to ensure fairness and appropriate labor practices, and

sustainable processes across the value chain. Additionally, MNCs can and should focus on a broader range of consumers such as those from the BOP, which can help these organizations increase their profits while satisfying these consumers' needs and contribute to their well-being.

5. The implementation of the Me to We approach to stakeholder-shareholder relations requires appropriate leadership that can disseminate these principles across the organization and modify the existing corporate culture. Additionally, measurement is essential as a way to gauge progress and performance of the Me to We principles.

The nineteenth-century industrialist and father of Japanese capitalism, Shibusawa Eiichi, argued that business should pursue *sanpo-yoshi*—"three-way good"—for buyers, sellers, and society.[14] The nexus between shareholders and stakeholders will become increasingly closer and symbiotic in the future. As the Me to We concept takes hold in more and more companies, regardless of size, we can expect companies to embrace, measure, and monitor their performance in the pursuit of doing good while doing well.

---

[14] Patrick Fredenson and Kikkawa Takeo, eds., *Ethical Capitalism: Shibusawa Eiichi and Business Leadership in Global Perspective*, Toronto: University of Toronto Press, 2017.

Index[1]

---

[1] Note: Page numbers followed by 'n' refer to notes.